THE
SMOKE SCREEN
OF
JUTLAND

THE
SMOKE SCREEN
OF
JUTLAND

COMMANDER JOHN IRVING
R.N. Retd

DAVID McKAY COMPANY, Inc.
NEW YORK

First published in the United States of America in 1967 by
DAVID MCKAY COMPANY, INC.

MADE AND PRINTED IN GREAT BRITAIN BY PURNELL AND SONS, LTD.
PAULTON (SOMERSET) AND LONDON

CONTENTS

DIAGRAMS

LIST OF ILLUSTRATIONS

Unless otherwise stated all pictures are reproduced
by courtesy of the Imperial War Museum

PROLOGUE

Smoke Screen

THE first of June 1916: the morning sunlight filtering through his office windows could not dispel the worries of Admiral von Müller, chief of the Imperial German Admiralty's *Marinekabinette*. On the desk before him lay a telegram from Admiral Scheer reporting that on the previous evening his fleet had been engaged with superior British forces, and was now returning to Wilhelmshaven; he noted in his diary that the German losses 'make it appear very doubtful that we can call this a victory'.

But as he well knew, it was a victory that the Central Powers needed at this juncture, more than anything else, both as a stimulant for their civilian populations and as a reminder to the world's neutral nations of the undoubted prowess of German arms and of the certainty of ultimate German victory. When in September 1914 Germany's well-laid plans for a swift victory had been checked by Joffre's triumph on the Marne the ailing General von Moltke had warned the Emperor, Kaiser Wilhelm II: 'Your Majesty! We have lost the war!' Both General von Falkenhayn and Admiral von Holtzendorf had expressed the view that the collapse of Germany's original war plan had now exposed them to the perils of a war of exhaustion—with Britain exercising complete Command of the Sea: her fleet would use her historic weapon of 'sea-blockade' to strangle her enemies' economic life, while she herself used her great shipping and financial strength to keep herself and her allies supplied.

To be sure, the march of events after the Marne had cushioned Britain's enemies against realisation of their danger: Hindenburg's successes on the Eastern Front had distracted attention from German failure in the west, as had the news of Bulgaria's accession to the Central Powers, the British evacuation of the Gallipoli peninsula and the siege of General Townsend's force at Kut-el-Amara. Finally, towards the end of February 1916, the massive German attack on Verdun had opened and hope for a speedy decision in the west had been reborn, only to fade again as the vigour of the

7

early onslaught languished, until by May Verdun had become 'an open, wasting sore'.[1] Its power of distracting public attention from the hardships and privations within Germany had vanished.

Primarily as a result of the economic blockade established by the British Fleet, stocks of essential raw materials were low and seaborne imports had dwindled to the merest trickle. Conscription had curtailed home food production, and rural selfishness and the activities of 'black marketeers' had combined to distribute unequally what food stocks there were. The pathetic butter ration, the dark and unpalatable *Kriegsbrot* and the *ersatz* coffee and the exiguous meat ration after Easter 1916 caused widespread discontent, and there seemed little prospect that conditions would improve in the future. As the British Fleet and its 'blockade' were held generally responsible for this civilian suffering, it was over the British fleet that substantial victory would most stimulate the Germans now.

Not only the Germans: for it seemed possible that news of a German naval victory would encourage the northern neutrals to withdraw their shipping from British service on the one hand, while conviction of the ultimate success of German arms might persuade them on the other hand to tolerate a 'sharpening' of Germany's submarine offensive. Then, early that afternoon, Scheer gave Müller the 'estimated losses' of the British as being two to three in Germany's favour. He hesitated no longer. A bulletin on the battle was prepared and issued that night (1st June) for world dissemination. It was indeed a master stroke: the German despatch stole the stage a full twenty-four hours in advance of any official British report: it concealed the German losses, while exaggerating those of the British and inventing entirely fictitious damage sustained by British battleships in a gun duel with their German counterparts. If it did not exactly claim a German victory, it certainly implied a British defeat.

Germany went delirious: in an orgy of victory celebrations, the Reichstag voted a fresh £600 millions for the prosecution of the war. The news that British command of the sea was as good as broken was also the cause of some rejoicing in many neutral countries. On the German communiqué, a Danish newspaper commented that the silence from Britain could be interpreted as 'confirmation'; the Dutch pointed out 'the position at sea is of course now completely reversed' and even landlocked Switzerland—which had begun to feel the nip of the British blockade—observed, 'the losses sustained by the British fleet give Germany the right to speak of victory'. The

[1] General Ludendorff: *War Memories*.

British 'sea-tyrants' had been humbled at last. Hegel's dictum—
'it is not things as they are which matter, but the image which others
can be induced to make of them'—had been proved true.

Still before any British bulletin had been issued, the German
Kaiser decided to gild the lily by proclaiming a great German sea
victory, and the German wireless lost no time in following this lead.
In the United States the value of the pound was slashed and British
stocks declined. In Salonica, Rear-Admiral Keyes recorded, 'the
British Navy's shares went down to zero' at a highly inconvenient
stage in negotiations between the British and Greek governments.

In Britain, nothing was known by the public for some time. As
the first of June wore on, vague rumours of a naval battle did filter
inwards from the east coast ports; but the government was silent,
and the Admiralty—although well aware that some naval engagement had taken place in the North Sea—made no effort to ascertain
any details. Only when German wireless claimed 'a German
victory' did they wireless their Commander-in-Chief, Admiral Sir
John Jellicoe, for information that would permit a 'prompt contra-
diction of enemy claims'. By noon of the following day, appalled at
the neutral reactions, the Government pressed for an announcement,
and the Admiralty asked Jellicoe for more news as 'some information
must be given tonight'. Without waiting for his report, they rushed
their own communiqué to the press bureau that evening.

As an inept and utterly unsatisfying report this first official
announcement can have had few equals: it was admirably frank and
it laid no claim to victory; it gave British losses in uncomfortable
detail, while contenting itself with the assumption that 'the enemy's
losses were serious'. The disappointment of the British people was
consequently profound: brought up in the tradition that their fleet
was invincible, their most cherished illusions had been shattered
overnight, and they had been left with no hint that their ships still
in fact commanded the seas. The British press struggled nobly to
make the best of this unpalatable news, but the attitude of official
Britain that day was accurately summarised by Lord Hankey, who
recorded that to him the battle was the 'most bitter disappointment
of this terribly disappointing war. One's confidence—perhaps an
overweening confidence—in the powers of the Fleet is shaken'.
In the fleet itself—where men had given of their best, where their
comrades had died with *their* faith undiminished—the Admiralty's
communiqué aroused a wave of indignation which for a long time
was neither forgotten nor forgiven. When they heard that their
seamen going to hospital had been jeered at by the people ashore,

'it was almost too much'. Admiral Jellicoe himself telegraphed the Admiralty complaining that their communiqué gave a totally false impression of the battle.

Disturbed by this stern protest, the Admiralty issued a further despatch in which they claimed the sinking of no fewer than three German capital ships, but it was no longer enough to allay public dissatisfaction: the public in Britain also needed a victory. When they provided yet a third communiqué for the Press on Monday morning, 5th June, they included a 'narrative', an 'appreciation' and a 'summary' of the battle. The 'appreciation' was for some undisclosed reason by Mr. Winston Churchill, at the time an unpopular political figure; while the 'summary' was composed by an anonymous 'high-ranking naval officer' whose name has happily never been officially revealed, for he introduced an obviously inspired bias in favour of the efforts of Vice-Admiral Sir David Beatty's 'Battle-Cruiser Fleet' starting up the Jellicoe-versus-Beatty controversy which has bedevilled the battle's reputation ever since.

The British had lost 6,097 men in the action, while the Germans lost only 2,551: but of the British casualties 3,500 had been killed in the three battle-cruisers whose magazines had exploded—the *accidents* rather than the *incidents* of battle. Again, expressed as a percentage of the total modern tonnage in each fleet there was not half of one per cent to choose between the ship losses. But as Lord Hankey pointed out, 'victory is measured not by comparison of casualties and losses, but only by results'. On the morning after the battle, Admiral Sir John Jellicoe found himself in undisputed possession of the North Sea and, as Hankey added, 'to all intents and purposes this state of affairs continued'. An American newspaper commented that the Germans had assaulted their gaoler but were 'now back in gaol'.

If this gave heart to the British people, it was coupled with a widespread belief that the British Admiralty had put up a smoke-screen of words to conceal something—or to shield someone: there was a widespread resolve to get at the truth as soon as a return to peace lifted the veil of secrecy. But the Admiralty had no intention of revealing the vital part it had played in assisting the German fleet's escape and the public learned in due course the veracity of a cynical injunction attributed to Mr. McKenna, a former First Lord: 'Never fight a public department. You cannot win. It marshals facts which are incontestable.'[1]

When the war ended, the post-war First Sea Lord, Admiral Lord

[1] Admiral Lord Fisher, letter to *The Times*, 13th Sept. 1919.

Beatty, had no intention of opening to public criticism certain aspects of the battle: they might reflect less than favourably upon his personal image. It is only now that a final verdict can be pronounced, and it is the same as that reached by the Danish newspaper *Tidens Tegn* less than a fortnight after the battle: 'Even if the victory was not a complete one . . . it must be credited to Admiral Jellicoe.'[1]

(ii)

The German High Seas Fleet which had so quickly claimed 'victory' after Jutland emerged only on three more occasions during the rest of the war, cautious sorties out of sight and gunrange of the British battle fleet. The officers and men of the British Grand Fleet saw the enemy only once more—when the Germans passed in surrender through the silent lines of British battleships on their way to internment in Scapa Flow. That evening, the British Commander-in-Chief signalled: 'The German Flag is to be hauled down at sunset and is not to be re-hoisted without my permission. . . .'

That was the end of the Jutland story, but its beginning must also be considered. Christmas 1915 may be taken as the starting-point, in General von Falkenhayn's office, as he composed his Christmas memorandum to the German Emperor.[2] If the Central Powers' position seemed now almost unshakeable, its armies encamped almost everywhere on Allied territory, he knew that in reality they were beleaguered—shut out from intercourse with the outer world by the steel ring of Allied sea command, at the hub of which was the British battle fleet. How could England be driven out of the war? He would attack France and 'bleed her armies white', thereby striking off what he chose to regard as Britain's 'sword arm'. He hoped Britain would not accept the burden of holding the whole Western Front on her own, but as added 'persuasion' he envisaged ruthless submarine warfare against Britain's shipping. Thus, while preparations were made for an immense offensive against the ancient French fortress of Verdun, von Falkenhayn discussed his proposal for ruthless submarine warfare with Vice-Admiral Reinhard Scheer, newly chosen by the Kaiser for the Command of the German High Seas Fleet, in preference to Vice-Admiral Franz Hipper—the only other officer of sufficient seniority. Both Scheer and Hipper were courageous men, experts in ship-handling and able tacticians; both were of Prussian middle-class stock. Scheer had latterly commanded Germany's squadron of modern super-Dreadnoughts, the Third

---

[1] Newbolt, *Naval Operations*, Volume IV.
[2] General von Falkenhayn, *General Headquarters* 1914–16.

Squadron; Hipper had commanded the battle-cruisers of the First Scouting Group. But it was the harsh and forceful Scheer who had become identified with the group of naval officers pressing for relentless submarine warfare against the Allies.

Discussing ways of striking at the British blockade with von Falkenhayn, Scheer suggested the age-old method of decoying a part of the enemy into a trap, overwhelming it with superior force, and destroying it. He would have to create the opportunity and seize it when it offered. On 21st February 1916, the German assault on Verdun began with almost every augury of success, and the Kaiser visiting his fleet soon afterwards was constrained to grant Admiral Scheer's request for permission to try out his plan. Scheer made several sorties into the North Sea to ascertain how best to attain his object: he feinted towards the Thames estuary, and he made a sortie towards the Yorkshire coast, but none gave him the desired opportunity. At Easter 1916, his battle-cruisers bombarded Lowestoft and Yarmouth, and the First Lord of the Admiralty promised these towns' mayors that such raids would be made almost impossible in future by a redistribution of Britain's fleet which would enhance its chance of catching the raiders. Scheer welcomed this proposal.

By now, Admiral Jellicoe was also aware of Scheer's intentions. Jellicoe commanded the Grand Fleet of 28 modern battleships at Scapa Flow. He was a sea officer of great naval and administrative experience, and a gunnery expert who thoroughly knew and understood the weapons of battle. By his unceasing endeavour he had brought his fleet to a very high level of efficiency. He had warned the Admiral of his Battle-Cruiser Force, Sir David Beatty, months before that the enemy might try to decoy him.

Beatty was younger than Jellicoe and very different from him in many ways: Jellicoe was cautious, unruffled and self-effacing; Beatty was courageous to a fault and inclined to be impetuous, with a tendency to the flamboyant which showed itself in the well-known *three*-button monkey jacket and large-peaked cap pulled down raffishly over one eye. In the eyes of a gladiator-conscious public, he supplied the panâche they desperately required; he had no specialist experience in either gunnery, signals or torpedo and he had never commanded a fleet prior to his appointment. He was a protégé of Mr. Churchill during his period as First Lord of the Admiralty prior to the outbreak of war. How this singular appointment came to be made is best described in Mr. Churchill's own words:

> I had never met him before . . . He came of hard riding stock . . .
> was a very fine horseman, with what is called 'an eye for country' . . .

I was however advised about him at the Admiralty in a decisively adverse sense . . . His heart it was said was not wholly in the service. He had been offered an appointment in the Atlantic fleet suited to his rank. He had declined this appointment . . . and he should in consequence not be offered any further employment . . . My first meeting with the Admiral induced me immediately to disregard this unfortunate advice. He became at once my Naval Secretary . . . It became increasingly clear to me that he viewed questions of naval strategy in a different light to an average naval officer; he approached them . . . much more as a soldier would . . . His mind had been rendered quick and subtle by the situations of polo and the hunting field . . . I had no doubts whatever when the command of the Battle-Cruiser Squadron fell vacant in the spring of 1913 in appointing him over the heads of all to this incomparable command.

This was the ebullience of the youthful Churchill rather than the wisdom of the statesman of later years; like Pitt before him, he had an early phase when as an amateur strategist and dilettante naval tactician he made grievous mistakes—and a later phase, in the Second World War, in which profiting by the first he reached the pinnacles of this greatness. As for his reference to the 'incomparable' battle-cruiser command, he wrote in a later volume of his aptly-titled autobiographical *World Crisis* that he had in 1911 'recoiled from the battle-cruiser type' and had excluded the battle-cruisers projected for the programmes of 1912 to 1914.

The political success of the German bombardment of Lowestoft and Yarmouth was an incentive to further efforts. Admiral Scheer realised that for his decoying tactics to succeed they must be used further northward than East Anglia. A swift bombardment of some important coastal town nearer the Firth of Forth could not fail to bring out Beatty's battle-cruisers and he might also hope to cut off any British squadrons sent out of the Tyne or Humber. Scheer therefore planned to bombard Sunderland by Hipper's battle-cruisers while he himself remained some thirty miles offshore and out of sight. Hipper would lead any intercepting British forces onto the guns of his waiting battle fleet. To guard against the sudden appearance of Jellicoe with the main body of the British fleet Scheer proposed to rely upon Zeppelin reconnaissance supported by a line of watching U-boats, which would give him ample warning to withdraw to safety in time.

Should poor visibility prevent the all-important Zeppelin reconnaissance, Scheer had an alternative plan ready: he would advance with his whole fleet northward from the Bight, sending

Hipper fifty miles ahead, to show himself off the Naze of Norway before dark. Scheer was sure that the pro-British Norwegians would waste no time in reporting Hipper's presence and that the British Admiralty—sensitive to possible attack on the supply lines to Russia or on their 'blockade' cruiser squadron, or even a German breakout into the Altantic—would promptly act to intercept them. Scheer visualised Admiral Beatty hurrying across the North Sea, possibly with battleship support, to be caught in the nutcracker trap of Hipper and the German High Seas fleet. By early May his plans were ready in every detail.

He had planned to bombard Sunderland on 17th May, but was obliged to delay it by the necessity for repairs to the damaged battle-cruiser *Seydlitz*, which would be ready only on 29th May. His impatience grew with the delay, but when that date came the weather was unfavourable for Zeppelin reconnaissance. The mists had only partly thinned by the morning of the 30th, but he could delay his fleet movement no longer, as his patrolling submarines would have to return soon. He abandoned his Sunderland project and decided on the alternative plan.

Just before five o'clock on the afternoon of 30th May, he wirelessed executive operational orders in cipher to all units. Admiral Hipper was to leave the Jade anchorage at 2.30 a.m. and proceed northward up the Jutland and Danish coast, well offshore, to arrive off the Naze by 7.00 p.m. in ample time to be seen and reported to London. If British ships in superior force were encountered he was to lead them down towards Scheer who would be cruising with the re-mainder of the High Seas Fleet off the north-west coast of Denmark.

The night of 30th May came in clear and dark. At 2.00 a.m. Hipper's battle-cruisers, light cruisers and destroyer-flotillas slipped silently out of the fleet anchorage and proceeded in the first light of dawn through their swept channel. Half an hour later Admiral Scheer followed with 22 battleships in three squadrons. By 10.30 a.m. both forces had cleared the minefields, with Hipper hurrying on at 15 knots to their 7 p.m. rendezvous with Destiny off the Naze; the sea was clear and calm, the weather was brilliant.

Just after 2.00 p.m., the masthead lookout of *Elbing*, the light cruiser stationed at the western end of Hipper's cruiser screen sighted a small merchantman to the westward; the cruiser detached two destroyers to investigate the stranger. The destroyers closed in fast, hoisting the International Code signal 'Stop Instantly'. The small stranger, the Danish steamer *U. Fjord*, slowed at once and came to a stop, blowing off surplus steam in a white plume that showed up clearly against the sky.

1

Contact

FOR almost twenty-two months since the outbreak of war in August 1914 Britain's Grand Fleet, operating from its northern Scottish bases, had fulfilled a vital strategic role in Allied war plans. Its powerful battle-fleet of modern super dreadnoughts had been the 'core' of the most impressive Sea Command the world had ever known and had set steel bonds about the enemy powers; it had maintained in all weathers and conditions, although teased continuously by enemy mines and submarines, an unshakable grip upon the vital lines of sea communication of Britain and her Allies; it had kept unsleeping vigil upon the German High Seas Fleet, barring its egress into the Atlantic. Under its aegis ubiquitous patrols protected the stream of seaborne supplies essential to the existence of the British people at war and needed by their Allies in the field. Upon its strength rested the security of the lonely squadrons which were exercising the supreme offensive expression of Sea Command—a blockade which was slowly but surely eroding the economic life of the enemy peoples. Periodically this great Fleet swept through the length and breadth of the northern waters of the North Sea—a challenge to the German High Seas Fleet to break the confining bonds—but the gauntlet had never been picked up. More recently the British fleet had sought by deliberate enticing movements to draw the German Fleet out of harbour and into battle à outrance, but every attempt had failed.

Early in May 1916 the British Commander-in-Chief, quite undaunted by this non-success and back in Scapa Flow with his battle-fleet after the failure of one of these fleet movements, was already putting the finishing details to his next enticement-plan —'Operation M'—which he proposed to carry out on 1st June– June 2nd in the hope of decoying his shy enemy out into open water. It was very noticeable, however, that this time his plans were being made in a slightly changed atmosphere, for from various neutral

15

sources information had filtered through to London that something was afoot in the German naval bases: just what this 'something' might be, there was as yet no means of determining. There had, besides, been indications like these before, which had come to nothing. Very soon, however, the air began to clear, for on 18th May Jellicoe received a signal-telegram from the Admiralty informing him that the presence of an unusual number of U-boats had been detected in the North Sea, especially in its northern section.

There was nothing that could be read into this beyond the possibility that it could be the herald of a renewed submarine offensive against Allied shipping. Nevertheless, Jellicoe, who was—and had always been—particularly sensitive to the danger of submarine attacks upon our commerce, without hesitation put into operation the various plans long prepared to deal with such a situation.

He at once ordered intensive anti-submarine patrols, moved the patrol lines of the Tenth Cruiser Squadron—on its lonely 'blockade' watch between Scotland and Iceland—further to the westward, and directed his minesweepers to sweep continuously through the concentration area used by the Grand Fleet—an area to the eastward of the 'Long Forties' from 40 to 100 miles seaward of Aberdeen—in case some of the U-boats now reported to be at sea happened to be minelayers.

The Intelligence that a number of U-boats had suddenly concentrated in the northern section of the North Sea on 16th and 17th May had appeared, as it were, from 'out of the blue'; it leads us to consider the question of the amount of Intelligence available at the time. Of one thing we can be very certain in the light of post-war information: neither the German Admiralty, nor its Commander-in-Chief, Admiral Scheer, had any idea how deeply the British Intelligence service was able at that time to peer into their minds and intentions. Several normal sources were available to us, such as the neutral and British secret agents transmitting reports from the other side of the North Sea—usually rather belatedly owing to the difficulties of transmission. There were also the reports of the actual movements of enemy ships which could be derived from directional wireless; the direction-finding stations established at several points along the British coast[1] maintained a constant, unsleeping watch for any wireless traffic in the easily detectable 'singing' Telefunken note used by the Germans. Simultaneous cross-bearings from two, or

---

[1] At Ronaldshay (Orkneys), Peterhead, May Island (Firth of Forth), Bamborough, Flamborough Hd., etc. The Germans had similar D/F stations at Sylt, Borkum and near Cuxhaven; and a monitoring, decoding and repeating W/T station at Neumünster.

even three, directional (D/F) stations could at once reveal, within certain limits, the position of the ship or station originating the wireless message. In 1916, however, the art of direction-finding was still in its infancy, and a position so derived, when converted into geographical terms of latitude and longitude, was not always sufficiently reliable to be used for navigational purposes.[1] A possible error of two degrees was almost normal, and the cumulative effect of this upon bearings taken of a 'station' more than sixty miles distant militated against any reliability in the resultant 'Directional' fixes. D/F positions did, nevertheless, provide a good indication, if not of exact position, at least of enemy presence, and this could be invaluable.

Working side by side with this direction-finding, there was another service which kept a constant monitoring watch on *all wireless signals* made by German ships or stations. The signals intercepted were recorded and forwarded to a special department of the Admiralty's Intelligence Division, where if possible they were immediately decoded and passed to the Operations Division for necessary action.

Behind this latter feat lay one of the small but vital romances of the naval war. The extent to which we had been able to perfect the technique of decoding enemy messages was maintained as one of our most jealously guarded secrets, until long after hostilities had come to an end.

The romance began on 26th August 1914, only a very few weeks after the outbreak of war when the German light cruiser *Magdeburg*, on patrol in the Baltic, was sighted off the Gulf of Finland by two cruisers of Russia's Baltic fleet—*Pallada* and *Bogatir*. The two Russian ships promptly engaged her with gun-fire, set her on fire, and within minutes drove her ashore on the island of Odentsholm at the mouth of the Gulf. There she remained, ablaze, while the prisoners were removed: the successful Russian cruisers then withdrew. Some time afterwards, when the burnt-out hulk came to be examined by her captors, her safes were found to be intact and to contain, besides German secret naval codes and operating charts, the most secret coding and decoding *machines*, and also a copy of the Battle Orders issued to the German Fleet. All were removed and deposited with the Russian naval headquarters. Later that year, in October, when negotiations were afoot to arrange the despatch of

---

[1] The contemporary Admiralty *Manual of Navigation* specifically commented on the possibility of a $2°$ error and the unreliability for positional and navigational purposes of fixes sited over 100 miles from the Direction/Finding stations. Ship-to-ship direction-finding had not yet been developed.

British submarines to help the Russian Baltic fleet, the Russian Commander-in-Chief Admiral von Essen, decided on the advice of the Senior British Naval Officer, to despatch all these finds to London where the British Admiralty could perhaps make more effective use of them.

On the arrival of these code-books and coding equipment at the Admiralty, the Director of Naval Intelligence, Admiral Sir Henry Oliver[1], opened a cryptographic department, later to be known as Room 40, and engaged appropriate experts under Sir Alfred Ewing to unravel the details of the German system and exploit to the full this valuable capture.[2] Many months of hard work and experiment resulted in this Admiralty department eventually being able to decode and decipher an ever-increasing number of Germany's encoded wireless messages.

It is regrettably necessary to add at this point that it was not long before a strong element of friction entered into the relationship of the important and predominantly civilian staff of Room 40 and the service staff of the Admiralty's Operations Department to which the decoded enemy signals were passed: Rear-Admiral Thomas Jackson, as Director of Naval Operations (DNO), was in charge of this latter department. While freely admitting that the experts of Room 40 were indeed possessed of no mean intelligence, the Naval operations personnel would not concede that they were clever enough to add any naval interpretation to the signals they decoded. The operations staff seems, moreover, to have been unable—or unwilling—to take immediate action on decoded signals even in the temporary absence of the Director, as will be seen.

By the spring of 1916, almost the only German code which had not been cracked by this back-room department, despite the German Admiralty's having changed the code key weekly at first, and then daily, was the Commander-in-Chief's cypher.[3]

Of this remarkable achievement, the German Admiralty had no real knowledge, although they were beginning to entertain suspicions that the frequent appearance of British ships, in time to frustrate some intended operation of German warships which had been directed by wireless signal, could not always be entirely fortuitous. Indeed, by 1916, Scheer's chief of staff Captain von Trotha felt

---

[1] Who was later succeeded by Admiral Sir Reginald Hall.

[2] The room's full designation was Room 40 OB (i.e. the Admiralty's Old Building). The initial find of code equipment in *Magdeburg* was reinforced in December 1914 by a naval code-book trawled up by a British fishing vessel in the North Sea, and later also by diving searches of sunken wrecks of any German warship or Zeppelin found in shallow water.

[3] Cf. Moore and Wallace, *Cloak and Cypher*.

almost certain that we were able to break their naval codes. It was this ability to decipher German secret messages that now enabled the Admiralty to complete a picture of German U-boats massing in the North Sea: for some time past it had been noticed that German submarines, having successfully negotiated the hazardous swept channels through their protecting minefields and reached the safety of open water, made a routine coded wireless signal—'All's Well'— to their headquarters at Wilhelmshaven.

On 17th and 18th May several of these signals were heard by the wireless-monitoring stations along the British coast, and directional bearings gave the approximate location of their sources of origin. This information, passed to Admiralty Intelligence and decoded in Room 40, revealed the position of eight, ten and, later, twelve submarines. This was the first clear indication that something new was afoot. Five days later, on 22nd May, the position had clarified sufficiently for the Admiralty to advise its C-in-C. definitely of the presence in the northern North Sea of no fewer than eight U-boats: one of these was actually sighted on that day in the vicinity of the Grand Fleet's usual concentration area in mid-North Sea. She submerged before she could be sunk.

During the next few days the activities of our anti-submarine patrols made a serious impact on Admiral Scheer's plans. His U-boats in the North Sea were harried from pillar to post; their positions and formations were disturbed and whenever they appeared on the surface they were forced to dive. On the 26th *Columbella*— an armed merchant cruiser on her way to base—sighted a submarine to the north-west of the Shetlands. The submarine was the *U-75*; the cruiser fired eight rounds at her and forced her to submerge. Unfortunately, this submarine was able to continue her voyage later; on 29th May she laid the minefield to the west of the Orkneys in which Lord Kitchener and his staff were to perish a week later.[1]

On the next day, 27th May, the *U-74*, having laid a small minefield in the southern approaches to the Forth, was hurrying home on the surface—disguised with a mock sail as a fishing smack—when she encountered some armed British trawlers who sank her to the east of Peterhead after a short running fight. On the same day yet another submarine[2] was sighted, to the east of the Pentland Firth

[1] Lord Kitchener and his staff were en route for Russia in the cruiser *Hampshire* when, in a gale on 5th June, the cruiser struck one of these mines and was lost. There were only a dozen survivors. Lord Kitchener was not among them.
[2] Probably *U-66*, which by her orders should by this time have been on patrol off the Firth of Forth, some 150 miles to the south of the Pentland Firth.

itself, but the flotilla-leader *Broke* and a half-flotilla of destroyers sent out in chase sighted her and forced her down.

The efforts of Jellicoe's patrols at this time, by harrying the German U-boats and forcing them far out of position, greatly reduced their value as reconnaissance units.

These were indeed anxious days for all concerned—days in which although the final plans for Jellicoe's advance into the Skagerrak— 'Operation M'—were complete, the chances of it ever taking place seemed to diminish. They were days of growing uncertainty, for information received by the Admiralty's Intelligence division now confirmed earlier rumours of an unusual degree of activity in Germany's naval bases, and this was significant after the long quiescence of the High Seas Fleet. Nor was that all; it was known to our Intelligence Services that the German attack on Verdun was stagnating, although the casualties continued to mount; that there had been a bitter reaction in some German quarters to what was regarded as a shameful capitulation to America's demands over the sinking of the *Sussex*; and, especially, that the results of our 'blockade' measures were being felt more and more by the German and Austrian peoples. These and other factors were conspiring to induce among the enemy populations, for the first time, a 'sickness of spirit': not since the first disillusion on the banks of the Marne had victory appeared to be so far away. The exiguous meat ration enforced at Easter had only exacerbated their plight, for to the enemy peoples their armies seemed unable to break down the Allied defence and alleviate the situation. In their 'sickness', complaints even began to be heard of the inactivity of the German Fleet, for the creation of which people had ungrudgingly borne such a grievous financial burden: they were beginning to demand that it should do *something* to justify the pride and affection lavished upon it.

Everything combined to indicate the possibility of some German naval operation in the immediate future—an impression enhanced by the continued presence of the U-boats in the North Sea, which could be there as a submarine trap.

Quite what form any German naval move might take, however, remained a mystery. It could be some operation designed to break our 'blockade'; but this would necessitate a determined attack on the Tenth Cruiser ('blockade') Squadron, but this in its turn was protected by the might of the Grand Fleet. It seemed unlikely that the Grand Fleet would at this juncture be attacked deliberately for such a purpose. Again, the German operation might be designed to interrupt the steady flow of seaborne supplies now reaching our ally Russia. It was indeed appreciated by the German High Command that the tremendous effort we were making to re-equip the Russian armies by sea-routes via Norway, and by the summer routes direct to the White Sea, might eventually endanger their military security on the Eastern Front. The Germans might perhaps be contemplating a sudden raid on shipping in the Thames Estuary or awaiting 'examination' in the Downs; this was not very likely, but it might be in their mind, for if successful such a raid could intimidate neutral shipowners upon whose good offices we were placing growing reliance. On the other hand, it could be a German fleet advance designed merely to cover the emergence of more German surface commerce-raiders into the Atlantic. The recent safe return of the *Moewe* from such a commerce raid—unduly publicised in Germany, for the damage she had done to Allied shipping was less than half of one per cent—might give the enemy encouragement to repeat this form of attack. It had, indeed, been attempted once since *Moewe's* return—by the *Greif*, but she had been sunk before she was even out of sight of the Norwegian coast. There were nonetheless rumours that several raiders might be pushed out together onto the trade routes.

Lastly, with a shrewd tactician like Scheer, there was always the possibility that the German fleet might make some double move—that is to say the High Seas Fleet, or part of it, advancing northwards as a potential threat to the 'blockade' or to the Russian supply lines, while at the same time a second German force probed into the southern area of the North Sea for a possible raid on our coasts, or an attack on the shipping in the Downs. One of these movements could be a feint to draw our forces away from the other, or to induce us to disperse our forces and risk units being damaged and attacked in detail.

There were so many possibilities that the position was inevitably quite obscure, yet pregnant with danger.

(ii)

There is one source of Admiralty Intelligence which has not yet been mentioned—the 'diving patrols' which were continuously maintained at this time by British submarines in the Heligoland Bight, off the German minefields, and even close to the Jutland coast. Though hunted by Zeppelins and enemy surface craft by day and by night these submarines maintained their watch for any movement of enemy ships in or out of the swept channels through the minefields, or for the sound of enemy minesweepers making a final 'sweep' to ensure safe passage for German ships. In the absence of air patrols—for the Royal Navy possessed no dirigibles—these submarines fulfilled much the same rôle as had Nelson's inshore frigates in the past. They could give early *visual* warning of the actual movement of enemy ships, and thus supplement other Intelligence such as intercepted signals—which might have indicated some intended operation.

Unlike Blackwood's frigate, however, our submarines were confronted with the difficulty of getting their information back quickly to Admiral Jellicoe, and to the Admiralty in London. British submarines had to surface to communicate by wireless, and this in itself involved time loss, for they could not surface in the immediate vicinity of enemy patrols. Again, most of them were, unfortunately, equipped with a most inadequate wireless set, which had a range of only some 40 to 50 miles[1]—a shortcoming to which Admiral Jellicoe had frequently directed attention, but in vain.

Unless they were fortunate enough to be in contact with another submarine that was in touch with a shore station these patrol submarines had to close the British shores as best they could before they could pass on their news, which entailed a long delay—in an age of swift warship movement.

During these anxious days towards the end of May 1916, however, the diving patrols had nothing to report; they could do nothing to dispel the obscurity of the situation in the Bight. Then, quite suddenly, in the early morning of 30th May, the veil lifted at one corner. A coded wireless message, addressed by the German Commander-in-Chief to his U-boats in the North Sea, was intercepted by a British monitoring station and decoded in the Admiralty's Room 40. It contained orders to these U-boats to remain in their appointed stations as 'German forces may proceed to sea' on 31st May and 1st June.[2] A second signal sent by Scheer early on the 30th directing the German fleet to assemble in the Jade Roads by 7.30 p.m. was also intercepted, decoded and passed to the Operations Division.

At noon on the 30th, the Admiralty—which now had confirmatory evidence from other sources—telegraphed a provisional warning to Admiral Jellicoe at Scapa, to the effect that some sixteen U-boats were believed now to be at sea (mostly in the North Sea), adding

---

[1] Jellicoe, *Grand Fleet*. This defect was not remedied until 1917.

[2] Scheer's actual signal had said '*hostile* forces', meaning British forces, but a decoding error changed this into '*German* forces', the opposite meaning, before it was passed to the Operations Division for action; from our point of view this error made no difference.

that there were also indications that the German main fleet might put to sea early next morning. They could not as yet give their Commander-in-Chief any positive orders, for the motive and direction of the suspected enemy move were still obscure. They could however warn Jellicoe to be ready for any eventuality, and this they had now done.

Later that afternoon a report came in from the diving patrol off the German minefields: German mine-sweepers had been heard and seen clearing the northern swept channels through the minefields west of the Jutland coast. Although this report lacked the colour of the report of Captain Blackwood's inshore frigate off Cadiz two days before Trafalgar—that the ships of the combined French and Spanish fleets were 'hoisting their topsail-yards' in preparation for sailing—the diving patrol's report was redolent of the same urgency. There were new-swept channels and this in itself suggested that ship-movement through them was likely to take place in the immediate future. Just as Nelson's frigates had passed back their message to the little Admiral waiting fifty miles away and beyond the horizon, so that news was passed back from the submarines to the Admiralty, who relayed it promptly to their Admiral with his battlefleet leashed in Scapa Flow.

In Scapa Flow the Grand Fleet was lying quietly at anchor, stored, ammunitioned, fuelled and at four hours' notice for steam for eighteen knots. The Commander-in-Chief could look around the Flow and survey his fleet with justifiable pride, for under his hand this weapon had been tempered to a fine edge.

Its early shortcomings had been eradicated as far as was practicable. What had been a collection of warships had been welded into a homogeneous fleet—its officers and men made battle-worthy and weather-hardened by frequent 'sweeps' under all the conditions a grey and relentless North Sea could offer. They were united in purpose, and inspired by a personal affection for, and devotion to, their Commander-in-Chief such as few Admirals since Nelson have ever been able to earn unsought.

Like Nelson before him, Jellicoe had confided his general intentions to his subordinate admirals and his captains: his Battle Orders were concise and very complete. On the very eve of what might turn out to be a fleet action, however, the arrangements foreseen in these Orders had been modified by circumstance in two important details. Firstly, the powerful Fifth Battle Squadron, which by Jellicoe's Battle Orders had a special function as a free wing squadron to impart flexibility to the 'line of battle' should the need arise, would no longer be with the battlefleet—it had been transferred temporarily to Rosyth as support for Beatty's Battle-Cruiser Force while the Third Battle-Cruiser Squadron was at Scapa for gunnery exercises. The second detail, which occasioned the Commander-in-Chief even greater anxiety, was that his destroyer flotillas were in a process of reorganisation and flux.

At the outbreak of war, and for many months afterwards, the fleet had been woefully short of both destroyers and modern light cruisers—a consequence of pre-war Treasury parsimony, when a naval programme might carry destroyers *or* light cruisers—but not both. The return of Lord Fisher to the Admiralty in 1914 had resulted in an immediate building programme for such essential light forces, and the first of these new ships were beginning to join the fleet by the summer of 1915. At that time the Grand Fleet flotillas disposed of only 65 destroyers all told. From August 1915 until the spring of 1916 plan and counter-plan had been put forward by Admiralty and Commander-in-Chief for the readjustment of the Fleet's destroyer force. At one time the Admiralty was suggesting flotillas of 24 destroyers, which to Admiral Jellicoe were far too large to be handled efficiently; at others they altered the number of flotillas allocated to the Fleet: the whole purpose of this reorganisa-tion was where possible to free light cruisers for service, quite probably in the Mediterranean. After eight months of organisation and reorganisation, some sense of finality was ultimately achieved: the Grand Fleet destroyers were recreated into five flotillas (separate from those of the Battle-Cruiser Force) and a light cruiser, *Castor*, was allocated as 'flagship' of the Grand Fleet flotillas, with Commodore Hawksley as Commodore (F). By the end of May 1916, however, what with the addition of new destroyers to the fleet and the general ebb and flow of organisation and reorganisation, the new Commodore had had no opportunity whatsoever of exercis-ing his flotillas in combined manoeuvres, or in the functions which they would be called upon to perform. These were set out, generally, in Jellicoe's Battle Orders: they were required to make attacks on the enemy fleet and without orders if necessary. Just how important this lack of flotilla training was to prove became clear only at the height of the ensuing battle.

(iii)

At five o'clock on that evening, 30th May, an as yet undecipherable signal was intercepted by a British monitoring station and passed to the Admiralty: the signal made at 4.41 p.m., and addressed to all units of the German main fleet, was recognised by its character to be operational and obviously important.[1] Although it could not be deciphered wholly, the Admiralty felt that they could wait no longer and at 5.40 p.m. they telegraphed orders to Admiral Jellicoe to concentrate the Grand Fleet east of the 'Long Forties'. They added that there were now eight U-boats known to be in the North Sea, and again told Jellicoe to prepare for any eventualities.

Having thus initiated the movement of the British fleet, the Admiralty recalled all patrols on the East coast, and ordered the Harwich force[2] to return to port, refuel and be ready to sail if so ordered at daylight on the following day—the 31st. The Third Cruiser Squadron at the Nore was despatched to the mouth of the Thames estuary, and the Third Battle Squadron, also at the Nore, was warned to be ready to follow the cruisers. At the same time they issued orders to the three submarines, detailed in Jellicoe's own scheme, 'Operation M', to take up their prearranged positions west of the Vyl light-vessel (off the Jutland coast); unfortunately the Admiralty did not amend these orders so, as will appear, the submarines' journey there was fruitless. With the exception of this minor slip, however, the Admiralty's Intelligence and operational divisions were working very well this far.

At Scapa Flow, when the order from the Admiralty arrived, Jellicoe made the 'Prepare to leave Scapa' signal to his fleet, ordered steam for eighteen knots by nine o'clock, and indicated the order in which squadrons were to leave that anchorage. At the same time he telegraphed orders to Vice-Admiral Sir Martyn Jerram KCB, at Invergordon in the Cromarty Firth; Jerram had under his command a battle squadron and a cruiser squadron, and destroyers of the 11th Flotilla. This small force was enjoying—if one may use the term—its periodic phase of rest.

Jellicoe's orders to Jerram were as follows:

Leave as soon as ready.
Pass through latitude 58° 15' North, longitude 2° 00' East. Meet me 2.00 p.m. tomorrow 31st, latitude 57° 45' North, longitude 4° 15' East. Several submarines known to be in North Sea. (1930)

---

[1] The signal when eventually deciphered read: 'C.-in-C. [Scheer] to High Seas Fleet. The head of the Third Battle Squadron will pass Jade War lightship A at 2.30 a.m. Second Squadron will take part in the operation from the beginning and will join up astern of First Squadron. Wilhelmshaven Third Entrance will control W/T in German Bight.'—Cf. *Krieg zur See.*
[2] An Admiralty telegram at 5.55 p.m. informed the Commander-in-Chief that the Third Battle Squadron (at the Nore) and the Harwich Force would not be sent to join him until the obscure situation cleared.

Seven minutes later he made an operational signal to Vice-Admiral Sir David Beatty KCB, MVO, DSO, commanding the Grand Fleet's scouting force, the Battle-Cruiser Force[1] at Rosyth:

> Available vessels, Battle-Cruiser Fleet, Fifth Battle Squadron and destroyers, including Harwich destroyers, proceed to approximate position latitude 56° 40′ North, longitude 5° East. Desirable to economise destroyers' fuel. Presume that you will be there about 2.00 p.m. tomorrow, Wednesday, 31st May. I shall be in about 57° 45′ North, 4° 15′ East by 2.00 p.m. unless delayed by fog. Third Battle-Cruiser Squadron, *Chester* and *Canterbury*, will leave with me. I may send them on to your rendezvous. If no news by 2.00 p.m. stand towards me to get in visual communication. I will steer for Horns Reef from position latitude 57° 45′ North, longitude 4° 15′ East.

In itself, this was a normal operational signal; but two details deserve attention. The first is the mention of 'Harwich destroyers': there were eight of these—part of the 9th and 10th flotillas; they were temporarily based at Rosyth, were older than many of the others and had not the same turn of speed, but had to be taken along to swell the destroyer protection. The second point was the stress which Admiral Jellicoe laid upon the need for the Battle-Cruiser Force to stand towards him 'to *get in visual communication*'. The necessity for visual communication at sea was all-important, for so long as ships were in sight of each other it was possible to express information about any object or ship in sight in terms relative to themselves rather than in terms of latitude and longitude, which always introduced a considerable element of possible error.

A further point, which was the subject of some criticism afterwards, was the distance between the two-o'clock rendezvous positions assigned by Admiral Jellicoe to his own Fleet and to Beatty's Battle-Cruiser Force: he had calculated that at 2.00 p.m. on 31st May they would, if all went well, be about 69 miles apart. Beatty's force would be that much nearer to Heligoland: this has seemed, to some critics, an excessive distance for an advanced force to be detached from its main fleet. This distance was, however, entirely normal for such operations when the motives of the enemy were obscure and the initiative lay in German hands. Where the British were taking the initiative it was more usual—and had been since war had broken out—to reduce the distance to forty miles or even less. In this

---

[1] Presumably for political reasons, Beatty's force was known from February 1915 to the end of 1917 as 'Battle-Cruiser *Fleet*', a temporary and confusing designation which has been avoided above. Cf. Jellicoe, *Grand Fleet*.

particular case, where the Admiralty had no means of knowing what lay behind a possible movement of the German fleet, it was very necessary that the faster ships—the Battle-Cruiser Force—should be in a position well to the south of the Battle Fleet, so that if their presence were demanded urgently in southern waters they would be closer to them and could reach the scene more quickly. In the prevailing circumstances the 69-mile spacing was entirely unexceptionable.[1] It is particularly noteworthy in this connection that Admiral Jellicoe later stated:

> I felt no anxiety in regard to the advanced position of the force under Sir David Beatty, supported as it was by four ships of the Fifth Battle Squadron, as this force was far superior in gun-power to the First Scouting Group [commanded by Vice-Admiral Hipper] and the speed of the slowest ships was such as to enable it to keep out of range of superior enemy forces.[2]

In the three British naval bases, there now ensued that orderly bustle which the repetition of familiar movements seems to encourage: boats were hoisted, gangways and boat-booms brought inboard and stowed, and everything readied for putting to sea. In the Firth of Forth, off Rosyth, the Battle-Cruiser Force, having been ordered at 5.45 p.m. to raise steam for 22 knots, sailed from its anchorage at 9.00 p.m. It included the First and Second Battle-Cruiser Squadrons, with Admiral Beatty flying his flag in the battle-cruiser *Lion*; the Fifth Battle Squadron, with Rear-Admiral Evan-Thomas' flag in *Barham*; the First, Second and Third Light-Cruiser Squadrons, and two extra attached light cruisers and twenty-seven destroyers of the 1st, 9th, 10th and 13th flotillas. By 10.30 p.m. this compact force had cleared the harbour; an hour-and-a-half later it was off May Island, with the open North Sea ahead.

Further to the northward, at the head of Cromarty Firth, off Invergordon, lay the Second Battle Squadron of eight modern battleships under the command of Vice-Admiral Jerram flying his flag in *King George V*. At the same anchorage lay the First Cruiser Squadron of middle-aged armoured cruisers under Rear-Admiral Sir Robert Arbuthnot MVO, and part of the 11th flotilla of escort destroyers. This force had raised steam for 18 knots at 6.06 p.m. and sailed at 9.00 p.m., clearing the Inner Firth by ten-thirty and heading for its rendezvous with the Commander-in-Chief and the remainder of the Battle Fleet next morning.

[1] Beatty would have with him three light-cruiser squadrons—twelve light cruisers which, spread at a distance of five miles, would have been able to span seventy miles.

[2] Admiral Lord Jellicoe, *Despatch*. Cf. also Harper.

At Scapa Flow, in the anchorage sheltered by the heath-clad hills around, lay the First and Fourth Battle Squadrons, the Second Cruiser Squadron of elderly armoured cruisers and the Fourth Light-Cruiser Squadron of modern light cruisers: behind the hump-back of Fara island lay the destroyers of the 4th and 12th flotillas and part of the 11th; within the Flow itself was also the Third Battle-Cruiser Squadron, recently arrived from the Forth, together with its attendant light cruisers *Chester* and *Canterbury*. On the northern side of the Flow lay the Grand Fleet's seaplane carrier *Campania*.

In accordance with normal routine, the Grand Fleet destroyers sailed from their Fara anchorage at nine o'clock, just as dusk was settling over the hills, and moved out into the tideway of the Pentland Firth to await their battle squadrons; the first of these began to leave harbour at nine-thirty, the remainder followed in succession, until by ten o'clock all were clear; on board one of the battleships, *Collingwood*, was Britain's future King George VI, serving as a sub-lieutenant and second-in-command of her foremost turret. Left behind were the newly-completed battleship *Royal Sovereign* who, not having yet finished her working-up practices, was not ready to 'lie in the line of battle' and, in her usual lonely berth off the north shore of the Flow, the Fleet's seaplane carrier *Campania*. She had been ready to proceed at 9.30 p.m., but for some reason had not received a signal to sail with the fleet; she left Scapa, however, later but was ordered back in the early morning. Jellicoe, probably the most air-minded of contemporary naval officers, must have been very loath to do without her as she carried 10 seaplanes. As it happened, even had she been in company with the Battle Fleet, in the low cloud and bad visibility prevailing later that evening it is most unlikely that her seaplanes would have been any more effective than the one that went up from *Engadine*.

Clear of the Flow, the squadrons proceeded according to the routine organisation—silently and in darkness, even visual lamp-signalling being restricted to the minimum: a complete wireless silence was now in force.[1]

At the first light of dawn—about 2.30 a.m., for the summer daylight comes early in high latitudes—the several battle squadrons converged

---

[1] This was imposed by Jellicoe on leaving Scapa: 'C.-in-C. to all ships in company: Cease W/T [wireless] communication *except on sighting the enemy* or replying to the admiral (2200)'.

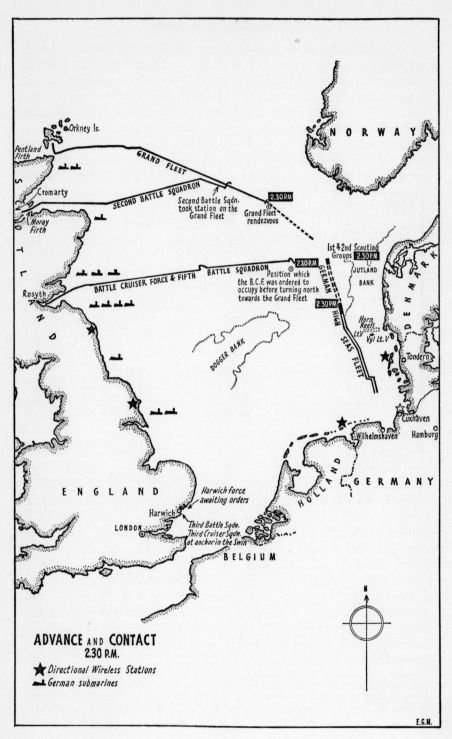

ADVANCE AND CONTACT
2.30 P.M.

★ Directional Wireless Stations

⊥ German submarines

29

on their Commander-in-Chief, who was leading the First Battle Squadron in his fleet flagship *Iron Duke*. They now assumed the war cruising formation ordered (1.15 a.m.)—organisation No. 5— of short parallel columns, each consisting of a division of four battleships, with the flagship leader ('guide') of each division disposed abeam of *Iron Duke*—the battleships in each column took their precise station, two-and-a-half cables (500 yards) apart from stem to stem, while the several columns were spaced at a manoeuvring distance of eight cables (1,600 yards) apart. The 'short' flanks

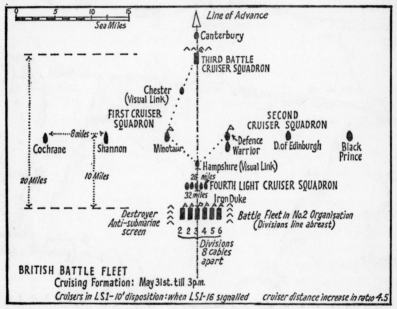

of this formation were screened by the destroyer flotillas; the cruisers were disposed ahead (in *LS 1–10* formation) on a broad lookout line perpendicular to the line of advance. The five modern light cruisers of the Fourth Light Cruiser Squadron were stationed four miles ahead of Jellicoe's flagship. The centre of the armoured cruiser screen was six miles further ahead; the Third Battle Squadron, flanked by its attached light cruisers *Chester* and *Canterbury* and screened by four destroyers of the Fourth Flotilla, was stationed four miles ahead of the centre of the cruiser line. The whole fleet was steaming at 16 knots[1] which left a couple of knots in hand for stationkeeping manoeuvres and similar emergencies.[2]

[1] After leaving Scapa the Fleet steamed at 17 knots until 9 a.m./31st commencing to zigzag 4 points (45°) on either side of its mean course at 2.35 a.m. At 9.0 a.m. fleet speed was reduced to 16 knots.

[2] The fleet had been ordered to raise steam for 18 knots before leaving Scapa Flow.

The particular formation chosen by Jellicoe, essentially a war formation, was the result of much thought and practical experiment; it complied with every tactical requirement—it was compact, it was protected from surprise and submarine attack and yet, by direct 'deployment', the twenty-four battleships could be formed into one continuous line of battle in some three and a half minutes.[1]

For the prior information upon which to base any 'wheeling' of his fleet that would be necessary to make such a deployment Jellicoe, like any other Commander-in-Chief, would rely upon the efficiency of his advanced scouting forces, and upon the accuracy and frequency with which they could pass in to him the relative position of the distant enemy.

It is interesting to note that with the dawn of 31st May the whole British fleet—both the Battle Fleet and the Battle-Cruiser Force—was clear of its bases and heading eastward for its rendezvous with destiny. It was actually *at sea* three and a half hours before the German High Seas Fleet had weighed anchor.

(iv)

At five o'clock in the morning, the Grand Fleet set its south-easterly[2] course for the appointed rendezvous; the weather was fine and clear, the sea sparkling. Soon after nine o'clock smoke was sighted out on the starboard beam: it was soon made out to be Jerram's Second Battle Squadron and the other ships from Invergordon; at 9.20 a.m. these turned on to a parallel course, the cruisers departing to take their place in the battle-fleet's cruiser screen. At eleven o'clock, Vice-Admiral Jerram turned his force to port and—neatly judging time and distance—cut directly across the line of the Grand Fleet's advance; with another eight point turn to port (1105) and a sixteen point (180°) turn to starboard later his squadron—in two divisions

---

This steaming speed was determined by experience as the most suitable for conserving the fuel supplies of the destroyers. It would be futile to drive 200 miles across the North Sea at an uneconomical speed, to be involved perhaps in lengthy operations off the German coast and then find that the destroyers were handicapped by shortage of fuel. The two knots in hand was often used to increase speed temporarily by ships turning in succession. With the fleet zigzagging four points on either side of its mean course, a steaming speed of 16 knots would be a *speed of advance* along the mean course of 15 knots.

[1] At a fleet speed of 17 knots.

[2] S50°E (Magnetic).

All courses and bearings throughout the text are expressed, unless specifically stated otherwise, as *Magnetic* courses and bearings: Magnetic variation (1916) 13¼° West.

All times, unless otherwise stated, are in Greenwich Mean Time: times of German events have been adjusted to GMT.

—dropped exactly into its proper station on the left-flank and thus nearest the enemy coast, the position reserved for the most powerful homogeneous squadron within the Fleet. It was characteristic that this should earn from Admiral Jellicoe, even in the midst of his preoccupation with other matters, the greatly appreciated signal: 'Manoeuvre well excuted!'—made by flags for all ships to see.

The battle fleet was now complete and concentrated in six columns each a mile long—eight cables apart. It had successfully passed—all unknowing—through the zone of Admiral Scheer's lurking U-boats and the movement of our battle-fleet out of Scapa had been quite undetected by the Germans. For this the vigour with which the anti-submarine patrols had persecuted the U-boats during the previous week was largely responsible. The movement of Jerram's Invergordon force, however, *had* been noted—unknown to the British Admiral—and reported to the German Commander-in-Chief. Just before seven o'clock that morning, the *U-66* which had been hunted remorselessly for four days and was in consequence very much out in her navigational reckoning, had surfaced to try to get an 'observed position'—only to find herself directly in the path of advancing heavy warships. To save herself, she just had time to dive deeply. She had, however, managed to obtain a quick glimpse of the oncoming enemy ships; three-quarters of an hour later, she surfaced and reported to Scheer what she had seen. The Invergordon force, as sighted, had been on the port leg of a four-point zigzag, and *U-66's* report, while correctly stating that 'eight battleships, cruisers and destroyers' had been sighted, gave their course as 'north-easterly', which was towards Norway.

To the southward the three principal units of the Battle-Cruiser Force—the 1st and 2nd Battle-Cruiser Squadrons and the 5th Battle Squadron—had passed May Island around midnight: they then headed eastward in line ahead with Vice-Admiral Beatty leading in his flagship *Lion*. They were steaming at nineteen knots directly for the appointed 2.00 p.m. position. At daylight the twelve light cruisers had taken up a lookout screening position perpendicular to the line of advance (*L-6* formation): the ships were five miles apart, with the centre of the lookout line eight miles ahead of *Lion* and with *Yarmouth* acting as 'link ship' midway between. *Engadine*— the Force's seaplane carrier—was stationed near the centre of the screen. The destroyers in company were disposed as submarine screens around the three main units.[1]

[1] The 2nd Battle-Cruiser Squadron was ordered to take station 3 miles on port beam of 1st Battle-Cruiser Squadron at 3.10 a.m.

The movement of this force had also been observed by Scheer's submarine watchers when it had reached a point some seventy miles out of the Forth. The light cruiser *Galatea* (Commodore Alexander Sinclair) in her station at the extreme south end of the lookout screen was attacked by a torpedo—which missed—at 3.50 a.m. It had been fired from *U-32* (Lieutenant Commander von und zu Peckelsheim), which had thereupon been obliged to dive swiftly and deep to avoid being rammed by the light cruiser *Phaeton* (Captain Cameron mvo) seen coming up fast on *Galatea's* port quarter. Discretion being the better part of valour, the U-boat commander decided to remain submerged until 5.30 a.m., when he surfaced to report what he *thought* he had seen—'two battleships, two cruisers and several destroyers steering south-south-east'. This was an even more inaccurate sighting report than that transmitted by the *U-66*: the Battle-Cruiser Force, when sighted in the early morning, had been on the starboard leg of its four-point zigzag which would have accounted in part for the error in the course; but this submarine's position as given was also very incorrect, yet another tribute to the hard work put in by our anti-submarine patrols.

When plotted on a chart the enemy courses reported by these two submarines gave Scheer the impression that these were two detached units of the British fleet, the one going north-eastwards towards the west coast of Norway, and the other southwards as if to pass on the British side of the Dogger Bank. There was apparently no connection between them and certainly no hint of any concentration—nothing to suggest that Admiral Jellicoe and the main portions of the Grand Fleet were otherwise than still snugly at anchor in Scapa Flow.

On the other hand, both reports implied the existence at sea of small detached units, which was very much what Scheer would have liked to encounter. The German post-war view was that these erroneous U-boat reports in no way affected the projected operation, but that on the contrary, they increased the hope that it would be possible to bring a part of the British fleet to action. Presumably this hope was centred on that part reported as heading towards Norway. In other words a situation appeared to be developing along lines which Scheer had tried to create, to gain the tactical advantage he needed for the furtherance of his long-range plans.

With Jellicoe's battle fleet now concentrated and steering for its rendezvous position, continually having to ease speed in order that the accompanying destroyers might examine passing craft and return to their station without excessive expenditure of fuel, the British Grand Fleet was in consequence beginning to fall behind its schedule.

The Battle-Cruiser Force was still speeding eastwards towards enemy waters: the light cruiser *Galatea* had reported the submarine attack at 3.55 a.m., and from then onwards an intensive lookout was maintained as the ships ploughed steadily through the calm, sparkling water. At 8.10 a.m., *Yarmouth*—the link cruiser 4 miles ahead of *Lion*—reported 'Submarine in sight to starboard'; immediately Beatty by signal (8.22) turned his whole force eight points (90°) to port, to remove it bodily from the danger of attack by torpedo. This new northerly course was pursued for some eighteen minutes while the Admiral ascertained further details of the incident: *Yarmouth* reporting that only a periscope had been sighted to starboard, and nothing had been seen since.[1] At 8.40 a.m. Beatty therefore turned his force back to the east, and then to south-east, ultimately resuming his original course-line around nine o'clock.

The deviation of course resulting from *Yarmouth's* submarine report, however, was to have some considerable influence on after events—for the wide detour, lasting some forty minutes in all, added nearly six miles to the distance the Battle-Cruiser Force had to steam to its appointed 2.00 p.m. rendezvous position, and made it certain that unless speed was increased—which was not done—the force would be behind time. There was more to this than a recoverable loss of time and distance: the Battle-Cruiser Force had already safely passed through the German submarine screen, and there is no record of any German submarine having been in the vicinity of these sighted positions; with ships moving at 19–20 knots through a calm, sunlit sea the spreading wake-ripples can suddenly curl and from some way ahead may be mistaken for the disappearing periscope trail of a U-boat: it is better to be mistaken than to be sunk. The real point at issue is that *Yarmouth* had 'sighted' a periscope to *starboard*—that is on the *starboard bow* of the advancing heavy units. The accepted practice in the fleet to meet this situation would have been to turn directly *towards* the submarine, thereby avoiding the danger of a torpedo if fired—for this would pass ahead or between the lines of the squadrons—and at the same time forcing the submarine to dive or be rammed—and thereafter to stay submerged, unable to see or to fire. To turn away, as Beatty did, and make a wide detour was certainly contrary to accepted fleet practice. It would only have been justifiable had the attack been made from a mass of submarines, and not from a single vessel.

The Battle-Cruiser Force resumed its course and held on until

---

[1] Some colour to *Yarmouth's* report had, in the meantime, been provided by destroyer *Turbulent* who reported sighting a U-boat steering south.

10.05 a.m. when, now more than half-way towards its appointed rendezvous, Beatty changed the look-out line of his advanced light-cruiser screen. He was fast approaching hostile waters, or at least the forecourt fronting the series of swept channels through the German minefields. Should an enemy be sighted from now on it would most likely appear from some direction to the east-south-east, or south-eastward—from the direction of Heligoland. Beatty now redisposed his screen by signal across his line of advance, diagonally from south-west to north-east; the light cruisers in the screen were, as before, to be six miles apart and work in pairs. This disposition clearly indicated an obvious appreciation that any danger must come from ahead or from his starboard bow.

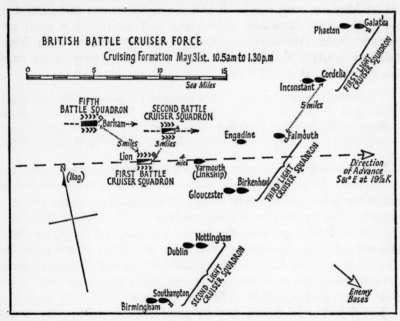

Five minutes after hoisting the redisposing signal to his screen, Beatty signalled a new disposition to the Fifth Battle Squadron: this powerful force was now ordered to take station five miles north-west of *Lion*—a rearrangement which placed his powerful but slower supporting Battle Squadron on the English side of the line of advance, and furthest from the direction from which the Admiral clearly expected any attack to develop. Were the enemy now to be sighted to the south-eastward and his faster battle-cruisers turn to chase at speed, the slower battleships would be left astern and out of the fight; nor, incidentally, was five miles the most convenient of distances for flag-signalling when in company.[1] This disposition was tactically unsound: Beatty had divided his Force and had, moreover, broken the cardinal rules governing the wartime cruising formation of a fleet—that it must be compact, and of a character which permits line of battle to be formed with the minimum of delay. His disposing signal at 10.10 a.m. complied with neither of these requirements. It placed his supporting squadron on the side furthest away from the most probable direction of enemy attack. Unfortunately such departures from rule in sea warfare tend to become the foundation for other, more grievous happenings later.

Whatever their merit, the new formations were promptly assumed and the Battle-Cruiser Force pressed on towards its rendezvous; the bright May sun rose overhead and the visibility was still perfect in every direction. Towards one o'clock that afternoon, a most important cypher message was received and passed to both Vice-Admiral Beatty and Admiral Jellicoe; it had been despatched from the Admiralty at 12.30 p.m.:

> No definite news of enemy. They made all preparations for sailing this morning. It was thought Fleet had sailed but directional wireless places flagship [*Friedrich der Grosse*] in Jade at 11.10 GMT. Apparently they have been unable to carry out air reconnaissance which has delayed them.

Here indeed was a message pregnant with consequence; the Admiralty's Intelligence division does not seem to have checked its reliability before passing it on; furthermore, it exemplifies the gulf that existed in the Admiralty at this time between the civilian de-coding experts of Room 40 and the naval personnel of the Operations Division. On the morning of 31st May one of the latter asked the civilian de-coding experts where their directional wireless placed the ship using DK as a wireless call-sign. He was at once told 'in the Jade River' and he asked no further question.

The decoders of Room 40 had previously given the Operations Division messages that our wireless monitoring service had intercepted, apparently to and from the German Commander-in-Chief, and all prefixed by the call-sign DK. Had the Director of Operations condescended to ask his civilian colleagues, as decoding experts, for an explanation of this they could have told him at once the DK was the wireless call-sign used by *Friedrich der Grosse*, Scheer's flagship, *when in port only*, and that when the flagship went to sea Scheer transferred this call-sign to the shore signal station 'Einfahrt 3'—in

---

[1] At 4.28 Beatty had ordered his rear battle-cruiser *Tiger* to repeat all signals to the Fifth Battle Squadron.

the Jade River—and used another call-sign. The result of this imperfection of human relationships emerged in the final signal despatched to our admirals at sea—with fateful results. The truth was that Admiral Scheer was already out at sea, over 120 miles from the Jade River, at the time the directional fix had been obtained on his 'flagship'; and by one o'clock as the Admiralty's signal was being digested in the two British flagships, Scheer's main fleet was less than 100 miles, and his advanced force under Hipper less than seventy miles, from Beatty's battle-cruisers. Action was considerably closer than the Admiralty thought.

(v)

The effect of the Admiralty's signal on both Jellicoe and Beatty was to remove any urgency for increasing speed[1] to compensate for the fact that both forces had fallen behind schedule. It could also encourage a false sense of security: the longer term consequences of this unfortunate Admiralty message were to be encountered again and again during the hours ahead.

Its first serious effect was upon the Battle-Cruiser Force where at 1.30 p.m. Beatty, aggravating its disadvantageous tactical disposition, re-disposed his Fifth Battle Squadron five miles north-north-west, and his Second Battle-Cruiser Squadron three miles east-north-east of his flagship *Lion*. In this he was clearly anticipating a turn to the northward in the near future to get into visual touch with Jellicoe as ordered. The stations now signalled to his squadrons would place the battleships on *Lion's* port bow on a northerly course, while the Second Battle-Cruiser Squadron would be on his starboard bow.

At the same time (1.30 a.m.), Beatty also re-disposed his cruiser screen so that its lookout line bore east-north-east and west-south-west, with its centre south-south-east from *Lion*. When the force turned northwards to meet Jellicoe, this screen would cover Beatty's flank and rear, with a lookout over the arc from which he obviously considered a possible attack would come. Taken in conjunction Beatty's two signals reveal a somewhat mixed appreciation of the situation: the cruisers' disposition was designed in the light of a danger zone to the east-south-east and southward; whereas the stationing of the powerful supporting battle squadron put them on the English instead of the German side of the Force. The Battle-Cruiser Force was, in consequence, as divided as before.

---

[1] Jellicoe had reduced the Battle Fleet's speed to 15 knots at noon—14 knots speed of advance.

Out of this re-disposition a still more awkward situation was created by the stationing signal itself for this was an order, definitely making the Fifth Battle Squadron an integral part of the Battle-Cruiser Force, and not an independent squadron; Admiral Evan-Thomas was given his 'station' from which he should not depart without specific orders to do so. Beatty's apologists make some play with his 'foresight' in stationing the Fifth Battle Squadron in such a way as to facilitate junction with the Grand Fleet later on. As that could not, however, occur for at least two or three hours at existing fleet speeds, there was ample time for such a preliminary disposition, if such it was, to have been made much later.

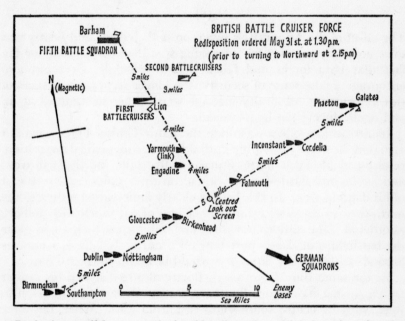

It is impossible to seek justification for this situation in the Admiralty's unfortunate 12.30 signal; this specifically stated that the 'flagship' of the High Seas Fleet was believed in the Jade River and did *not* refer to Admiral Hipper, or his battle-cruisers, or to any other ship.

The British Battle-Cruiser Force continued in its unsatisfactory formation towards its rendezvous; at noon *Lion* was estimated to be forty-one miles to the westward of this point. But this was incorrect: the noon position in her signal log was entered as 56° 44′ North, 3° 45′ East, whereas the mean of the observed positions of the rest of the ships in company placed *Lion* in 56° 46′ North, 3° 36½′ East—

six miles to the west of her own estimated position.[1] Whatever her position, she was bound to reach her allotted position late, and Beatty seems to have decided to hold on his present course until 2.15 p.m., before turning northward to get into visual communication with his Commander-in-Chief.

At two o'clock, therefore, when Beatty was in reality only ten miles from his reference position (although by his own estimate he was sixteen), and since he still had 'no news' of the enemy other than that contained in the Admiralty's message, he prepared to turn northwards: at this time he therefore signalled his Force his intention of altering course—leaders of squadrons together, the remainder in succession—to north-by-east at 2.15 p.m.

The executive signal to alter course was made at 2.15 p.m.: *Tiger*, the rear ship of the First Battle-Cruiser Squadron, acting as repeating ship, passed it to *Barham* for the Fifth Battle Squadron; the First and Second Battle Squadrons and their destroyer screens turned as the signal was hauled down and were round and steadied on the new northerly course soon after 2.17 p.m. at which time *Barham* led her battle squadron round to the same course, the two-minute delay arising from her effort to take up the proper station ordered in her 1.30 p.m. signal. As soon as the Battle Squadron was round on the new course, *Barham* was ordered by Beatty (2.15) to keep a good 'lookout [ahead] for the advanced cruisers of the Grand Fleet'. This was perhaps one way of getting into the 'visual communication' directed by the Commander-in-Chief; but a more effective way would have been to have arranged previously to detach one of his three light-cruiser squadrons forming the screen—where ships were working in pairs—and to have stationed it well ahead of the main force where it could act as a normal lookout screen ahead with visual links direct to Beatty in *Lion*.

The light cruiser screen was now well astern of the main battlecruisers; some of them, especially those of the First Light Cruiser Squadron—and *Engadine* the seaplane-carrier out on the eastern flank—had not yet been able to get into station, nor, owing to the distances involved, had they received the turning signal in time: *Inconstant* was $8\frac{1}{2}$ miles from the link ship *Yarmouth*, and *Galatea* seven miles beyond *Inconstant* again. These, therefore, were steering to the south-eastward to assume their proper stations in the screen before turning in compliance with the general move to the north. The light cruiser *Galatea*—flagship of the First Light Cruiser Squadron—with her consort *Phaeton* close astern, was at the extreme

---

[1] Cf. *Naval Operations.*

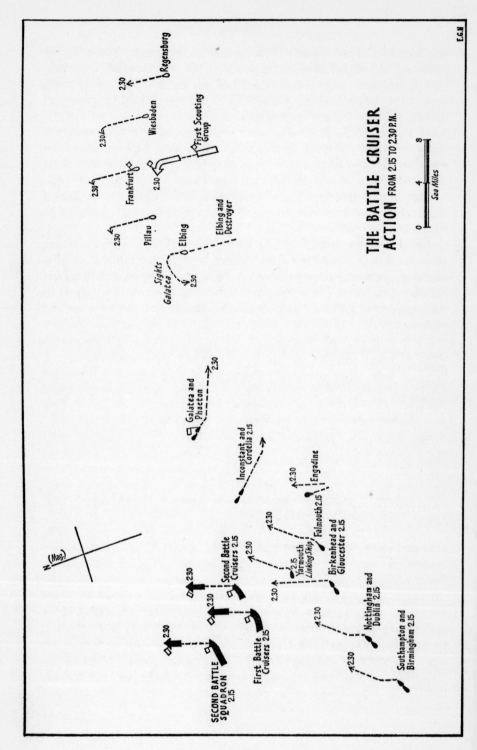

THE BATTLE CRUISER
ACTION FROM 2.15 TO 2.30 P.M.

0   4   8
Sea Miles

E.G.M

40

eastern end of the lookout line, nearest to the enemy coast. *Galatea* was holding on her course when at 2.08 p.m. her lookout reported a small merchant ship in sight some ten or twelve miles distant off the port bow.

Although Commodore Sinclair had been preparing to turn, he decided to hold on in company with *Phaeton* a little longer and investigate. Within less than a minute, however, it was noticed that the distant merchant ship was stopped, and that she was not alone: other craft seemed to be either in company or molesting her, and a plume of vapour from her exhaust pipe was showing clear and white against the eastern sky. A searchlight signal was at once flashed for *Yarmouth* to pass on to *Lion*: 'Two-funnelled ship has stopped steamer bearing ESE 8 miles. Am closing (1410).' At 2.17 p.m., Commodore Sinclair's persistence was rewarded: the strange vessel resolved suddenly into two vessels which seemed to be dropping clear of the stopped merchant ship; as one of them drew into sight, the stump foremast and tall aftermast revealed her clearly as a German destroyer.

'Action Stations' was immediately sounded off in *Galatea* and full speed ahead—28 knots—ordered; with *Phaeton* holding her station astern, the two light cruisers headed towards the enemy. Into *Galatea's* wireless room went the report:

> Enemy in sight. One destroyer.

But before this could be despatched, a second enemy destroyer had been sighted from the bridge, and the message was altered. In the confusion, the ships were reclassed as 'cruisers'. Hoisting the age-old signal: 'Enemy in Sight', at the yardarm, *Galatea* broke wireless silence at 2.20 p.m. with a signal to the Commander-in-Chief and to the Senior Officer of the Battle-Cruiser Force:

> Enemy in sight, two cruisers bearing east-south-east. Course unknown (1420[1])

Within very few minutes the signal was in the hands of both Admiral Jellicoe and Admiral Beatty. Contact had been made.

---

[1] The time in brackets and in 24-hour clock notation is a signal's 'Time of Origin'. It will be despatched almost at once. There is always, however, an appreciable time lag between making a signal and that signal being written and shown to its addressee. With signals in code or cypher this time lag is inevitably longer as the message will need decoding, etc.

2

Chase and Pursuit

HER 'Enemy Report' made, *Galatea* pressed on directly towards the enemy, closely followed by her squadron-mate *Phaeton*; the speed of the two cruisers was increasing momentarily as evidenced by their growing bow waves. On their foc'sles guns were being cleared away, at the mastheads battle-ensigns were streaming out. The enemy destroyers could soon be seen clearly: they were leaving the neutral ship's side and endeavouring to make off to the north-eastward, in which direction the visibility seemed to be deteriorating.

That the dramatic 2.20 p.m. signal had described the enemy as 'cruisers' instead of destroyers was, as it happened, immaterial, for five minutes later a German light cruiser could also be seen from *Galatea's* upper bridge. She was ten or eleven miles away, broad on the port bow, and was approaching at high speed with the obvious intention of covering the withdrawal of the destroyers. The newcomer was *Elbing*, the westernmost light cruiser of the screen covering the advance of Hipper's battle-cruisers of the German First Scouting Group which had by this time reached the latitude of Bovbjerg on the Danish coast.

Elbing promptly reported the presence of *Galatea* and *Phaeton* to Hipper at 2.25 p.m.: 'individual enemy light forces in sight'. At the same time she began to haul round steadily to the southward to provide protection for her destroyers. *Elbing's* signal was received by Hipper, who held to his course; it was also picked up by the German Commander-in-Chief, Admiral Scheer, some 50 miles away to the southward.

As *Elbing* came clearly into sight, *Galatea* challenged her by search-light, making the secret letters current for the day: not unexpectedly she received no reply. It is, however, a comment on German efficiency that the nature of our secret challenge was immediately reported back to Admiral Hipper for his general information.

Unfortunately, the simple coded message containing this report suffered mutilation, either in transmission or in reception, for as decoded in Hipper's flagship *Lützow* it read 'twenty-four to twenty-six battleships' instead of 'individual enemy light forces'. Until the signal was checked and verified this error, for a while, influenced Hipper's movements, as will be seen.

At 2.27 p.m. *Galatea* reported that she was pursuing the enemy in sight, and as the German destroyers were now comfortably within the extreme range of her foremost 6-inch guns, she opened fire on them at a range of 12,000 yards. The first shots had been fired in the battle.[1]

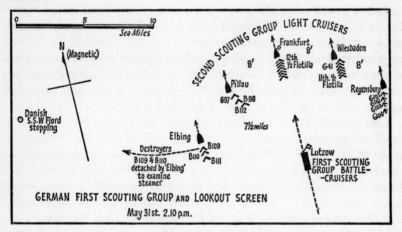

The sound of this gunfire had significant reactions in many quarters: as it reached Admiral Hipper and his German battle cruisers one and a half minutes later, he led his squadron round to the westward to bring heavy support to *Elbing* in case it were needed; at the same time the light cruisers in the German screen (with the exception of *Regensburg* and the flotillas) also turned and steered towards the south-westward with increasing speed. Meanwhile *Elbing*, seeing that her consort *Pillau* was now coming up astern of her fast, turned still more to the south, presenting her broadside to the two British cruisers in readiness to offer covering fire for the destroyers.

The same sound of gunfire reached the other light cruisers of the British battle-cruiser screen at about 2.30 p.m. and without any orders they turned simultaneously to the sound of the guns to support *Galatea*, working up to full speed as they turned.

[1] The maximum effective range of the 6-inch guns mounted in *Galatea* and *Phaeton* would have been about 14,000 yards.

Some 65 miles to the northward of the Battle-Cruiser Force—beyond the sound of the opening guns—Jellicoe, who was already half an hour late on his schedule, read *Galatea's* early signals. Taken at their face value they indicated little more than a brush between light forces, especially if read in the light of the Admiralty's report that the German High Seas Fleet flagship had still been in the Jade River three hours before. But Jellicoe was too shrewd to prejudge a situation on such slender evidence: wise in the ways of sea warfare, his impression was that the light cruisers might well have heavier cruisers somewhere near in case support were needed. He felt sure that Beatty's Battle-Cruiser Force with the Fifth Battle Squadron included could more than cope with any enemy light forces even if German battle-cruisers should appear on the scene. He therefore made no signalled comment on *Galatea's* reports, carefully preserving his wireless silence and retaining thereby the advantages of surprise and secrecy of movement. Nevertheless, in order to be ready for any eventuality at 2.35 p.m. he ordered his battle fleet, their attendant squadrons and flotillas to raise steam for full speed.

Less than fifty miles to the southward of *Galatea*, and also out of reach of the sound of her gunfire, Admiral Scheer, following in the wake of his battle-cruisers, had intercepted *Elbing's* signals and his wireless room could hear British wireless working close at hand. The German Commander-in-Chief, however, considered the British forces now reported would most probably be units of a detached force of light cruisers such as we frequently sent on 'nuisance raids' into the Skagerrak or Kattegat.

It was upon Admiral Beatty and the heavy squadrons of his Battle-Cruiser Force, some twenty-two miles to the westward of *Galatea*, that the sound of her gunfire had the most remarkable effect for it triggered a chain of tactical reactions, unfortunately fraught with disastrous consequences. At 2.15 p.m. Beatty's two battle-cruiser squadrons had turned on to a north-by-east course to get into touch with Jellicoe's battle fleet; two minutes later Evan-Thomas in *Barham*, then a little less than five miles distant from *Lion*, had also turned to the same course. All three squadrons, together with their destroyer screens, were therefore round on the new course and settling down on it when the first reports came in from *Galatea*.

It seems certain that at this stage Admiral Beatty did not consider that there was sufficient justification in these reports to override his orders to steer towards his Commander-in-Chief. When, however, at about 2.22 (or maybe a little later) *Galatea's* 2.20 p.m. report of 'two cruisers, probably hostile' in sight, was read in *Lion* the situation altered dramatically. Enemy light forces were in the vicinity and Beatty realised the desirability of cutting this enemy's escape route to the southward. At 2.25 p.m. he signalled to his destroyers to take up their positions for an anti-submarine screen on a course south-south-east. At the same time he signalled all ships in company to raise steam for full speed. *Barham* heading her Fifth Battle Squadron had received *Galatea's* report of two cruisers in sight and had also received the orders to the destroyers.

During the next five minutes the three squadrons continued on their northerly course *opening* their distance from the enemy by another mile and three quarters. Then came a further report (2.34 p.m.) from *Galatea* that she was chasing the enemy in sight. This crystallised Beatty's decision: in the past, more than once when in pursuit of enemy light forces and battle-cruisers, his quarry had managed to evade destruction by withdrawing before he could cut their escape route. This time he was resolved that this should not happen again; he would make sure of barring their road by cutting them off from their base as soon as possible. At 2.30 p.m. he accordingly made a 'preparative' signal to his force indicating his intention of altering course to south-south-east in the immediate future. Although this signal was normal procedure in the Battle-Cruiser Force it seems certain that as the Fifth Battle Squadron had only joined Beatty's force at Rosyth on the previous day Admiral Evan-Thomas was entirely unaware of this; for that matter he had not received any fighting instructions other than the general Battle-Cruiser Instructions from the battle-cruiser commander before sailing. When therefore this 'preparative signal'[1] was passed to *Barham* by searchlight, the Battle Squadron's admiral was put on the horns of an awkward dilemma. Was this signal merely for his information, or was it to be regarded as governing his future movements? A further complication, reinforcing if anything the impression that this signal was for information only, lay in Beatty's recent orders to the Fifth Battle Squadron to keep a good look out ahead (i.e. to the northward) for the Grand Fleet's cruiser screen.

By Beatty's 1.30 p.m. disposing signal, the Fifth Battle Squadron had received a definite station relative to *Lion*; the 2.15 p.m. signal to turn north-by-east in no way affected this. The Fifth Battle Squadron, having reached its station and turned to the course

[1] This searchlight signal was for some reason omitted from the compilation of signals published by the Admiralty (Command 1068) as a companion to *Battle of Jutland—Official Despatches with Appendices.* It was however officially referred to in answer to a Question in the House of Commons on 14th March 1927.

ordered had now no right to depart from this station unless specific-ally ordered to do so, or unless circumstances arose which prevented its Admiral from communicating a new order, or if the Rear-Admiral in *Barham* were suddenly to receive any information of which his Force Commander was unaware.[1] None of these circum-stances had arisen as far as Rear-Admiral Evan-Thomas was aware: he had received no specific orders addressed to his squadron; he was in possession of all the information available at the time to Vice-Admiral Sir David Beatty; and *Tiger* was still, as far as he knew, repeating all necessary signals to him.[2] It must be admitted in fairness that Evan-Thomas was aware of Beatty's 2.25 p.m. signal (which had been repeated to him by *Tiger*) that the destroyers were to assume a screening position for a south-south-easterly course, but nothing in this signal was directed to the Fifth Battle Squadron itself.

At 2.30 p.m. having therefore received no specific orders for his battle squadron, Evan-Thomas assumed that Beatty must have some other plan for it, and would later signal a separate course 'possibly to get the enemy light cruisers between the battle squadron and the battle-cruisers'.[3] This was a very reasonable assumption for the commander of a squadron whose function in the Grand Fleet was that of a fast free-wing squadron to be used for just such a purpose as he now expected. Evan-Thomas resolved to continue to the north until otherwise ordered, and he commenced soon after 2.30 p.m. to turn to north-by-west, the first (port) leg of a normal routine zigzag. Just as he was settling down on this manoeuvre, between 2.31 and 2.32 p.m., the distant sound of *Galatea's* opening salvoes, fired down to leeward, reached *Lion* and *Barham*.

At once there was a clear sense of urgency: Beatty decided to turn, and at 2.32 p.m., hoisted a general flag signal to the squadrons of his Battle-Cruiser Force to alter course to south-south-east—leaders of squadrons together, ships in column in succession. Almost at once, and with this general signal still flying—i.e. *not made executive by being hauled down*—*Lion's* helm was put over and she began to turn to star-board to the new course increasing speed to 22 knots at the same time. Rear-Admiral Pakenham, commanding the Second Battle-Cruiser Squadron in *New Zealand* three miles distant on *Lion's* bow,

[1] Cf. Bacon, *The Jutland Scandal* (Second Edition), page 177.
[2] *Tiger* had been 'repeating ship' for the Fifth Battle Squadron since 4.28 that morning. She reported to *Lion* at 3.05 p.m. that she had not been able to pass the 2.32 signal or any since then to *Barham*.
[3] Rear-Admiral Evan-Thomas, letter to the Editor of *The Times*, published 13th February 1927.

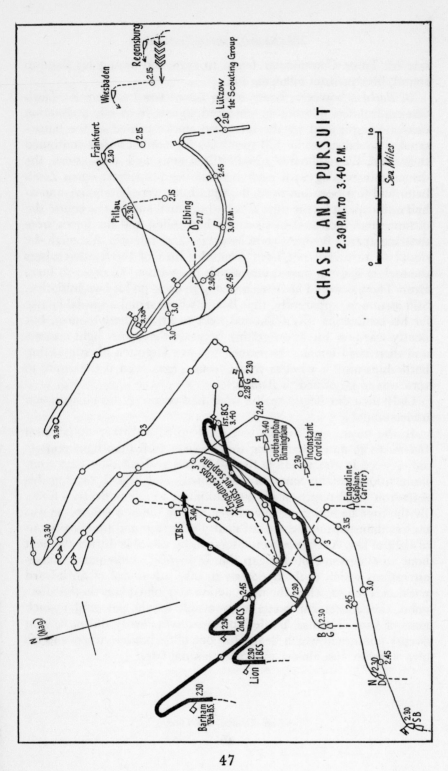

CHASE AND PURSUIT
2.30 P.M. TO 3.40 P.M.

Sea Miles

Regensburg
Wiesbaden 2.15
2.15

Lützow 2.15
1st Scouting Group

Frankfurt 2.15
2.30
2.45

Pillau 2.15
2.30
Elbing 2.17
3.0 P.M.
2.45
2.30
3.0
3.0
3.30

3.30

3

3.30

3.30

N (Mag)

1st.B.C.S. 3.40
2.28 G 2.30
P
2.45

Southampton 3.40
Birmingham ⊟ Inconstant
2.30 Cordelia

Engadine
(Seaplane Carrier)
3.15
3.15
3

3

V B S 3.40
Engadine stops out seaplane
X hoists out seaplane
2nd B.C.S. 2.45
2.30
B 2.30
G

2.30
Lion 1 B.C.S.
2.30
Barham Vth B.S. 2.30

N D 2.30
2.45
2.45
3.0
2.30
S B

saw his Force Commander begin to turn and swung his flagship round, his squadron following him.

In *Barham*, however, Beatty's flag signal was not seen, for *Lion's* fore-control top notoriously obscured signals from aft, a situation further complicated by the increased smoke caused as the battle-cruisers raised steam for full speed As the battle-cruisers continued their turn, Evan-Thomas' squadron fell more and more astern, the distance increasing with each beat of the propellers: when *Lion's* helm had first been put over, the squadrons were barely five-and-a-half miles apart; by the time *Lion* had steadied on her new course the distance had increased to six-and-a-half miles, and the forces were drawing apart a further two miles every three minutes. Although the signal to turn had not been seen, the turn of the battle-cruisers themselves had not passed unnoticed; but without an order to turn, Evan-Thomas would have been wrong to do so on his own initiative. Still assuming, apparently, that Beatty would signal a special course for his battleships, Evan-Thomas held to his northerly course; but Beatty was now intent on getting between the enemy light cruisers and their road home. He seemed to have forgotten his supporting battleships until a wireless signal from *Tiger* asked if the signal to turn was to be passed to *Barham*.[1]

Only then did Beatty realise what had occurred; his chagrin was understandable.

In the meantime, *Barham* had intercepted a further signal from *Galatea* (2.35 p.m.) suggesting that heavier craft than light cruisers alone were in the vicinity. Evan-Thomas realised now that communications might have broken down, and risked turning his squadron (2.38 p.m.) on his own initiative to follow Beatty's force. By the time he had done so and steadied on the new course, he was no less than ten miles astern of Beatty's flagship and practically out of sight of her. As chance would have it, he was able during the next hour to close some of this gap thanks to *Lion's* subsequent course-alterations which enabled *Barham* to take advantage of an inward position; even so, when the main action was joined later in the afternoon, this sinister gap made it impossible for the powerful 15-inch guns of Evan-Thomas' battleships to support Beatty during a vital twenty minutes in which Beatty lost one of his battle-cruisers and his own flagship *Lion* almost suffered the same fate.

[1] Evan-Thomas, *The Times*.

(ii)

Not unnaturally in the light of subsequent happenings, considerable attention has been centred upon this episode and a closer examination is desirable. The origins of this chain of misadventure clearly lay in Beatty's tactical blunder in disposing the Fifth Battle Squadron —his supporting squadron—in a station opposite to that from which by the disposition of his screen he obviously assumed the enemy might be anticipated, and at a distance too great for convenient signalling by flags. If suddenly—as had now happened—the enemy were sighted by his screen between east and south-east, and he had to chase at high speed or engage, Beatty would have had his slower heavy support force five miles astern from the very outset; it is an obvious axiom of warfare to enter battle with as much concentrated strength as possible, irrespective of the enemy's numerical inferiority.

The force which Beatty had concentrated was clearly not sufficient for the purpose, for when he encountered the Germans later on with his battle cruisers he outnumbered them six to five, but within half an hour he had only *four* against their five. As to the 'concentration without delay', in this particular instance *Galatea's* (2.20 p.m.) reports had reached Beatty at about 2.22 p.m. yet eight minutes elapsed before he made his preparative signal to turn, and at least ten minutes before he actually executed the turn at 2.32 p.m. Except for the distant rumble of a few 6-inch guns, there was no material information during that time that he did not have to begin with. During those ten minutes, while Beatty's force was increasing the distance between the reported enemy and his battle cruisers, there would surely have been time for any one of several well-known manoeuvres to have been executed to secure a compact and concentrated force: he could have adopted the familiar 'swing towards, and turn away' manoeuvre, while at the same time ordering *Barham* to close *Lion* at best speed, utilising the few minutes involved in the previous manoeuvre in working up to full speed; alternatively he could have closed *Barham* direct for a few minutes while *Barham* was simultaneously ordered to close *Lion*. The simplest and most obvious method would have been to have signalled Evan-Thomas by searchlight the order to close, either at 2.25 p.m. when ordering the destroyers to take up new screening positions, or, at the latest, by adding 'close' to the 2.30 p.m. preparative signal passed direct to *Barham* by searchlight. The former would have automatically reduced the gap to three-and-a-half miles and the latter to four-and-a-half.

Why no such simple manoeuvre was essayed was inexplicable: that no attempt was made by the commanding Admiral laid the coping stone to the errors of the previous disposing signals at 10.10 a.m. and 1.30 p.m., and was to produce a disastrous situation later on. The attempt in some quarters to attribute the blame for the gap to Admiral Evan-Thomas was less than just to this gallant officer, and could not be justified. Most of the criticism relied on such vague claims as that the senior officer of the force would naturally anticipate that his supporting squadron would close without further orders; or that the senior officer had every right to suppose that his supporting squadron would conform to his movements.[1] Neither of these excuses stands up to close examination, for anticipation does not absolve the senior officer of a force from not having ordered the 'close', indeed the failure to close up the Fifth Battle Squadron and concentrate his force sufficiently to meet any eventuality must be attributed squarely to Admiral Beatty as commander of the Battle-Cruiser Force.

This is not to deny that the signals staff of his flagship aggravated this failure; the signal to turn issued at 2.32 p.m. could have been passed by searchlight direct to *Barham*, just as the 2.30 p.m. preparative signal had been, but this method was not employed: flags—notoriously difficult to see—were hoisted in the flagship and made harder to see by wind and smoke-laden air. There were three distinct failures of recognised signals procedure, two on *Lion's* signal-bridge and one on *Tiger's*: when the 2.32 p.m. turning signal was made in *Lion*, *Tiger* also endeavoured to pass it on to *Barham*, but seeing neither ships' signals Admiral Evans-Thomas did not hoist an Answering Pendant[2] or acknowledge in any way, and this information should have been passed to Beatty who would then presumably have ordered other means of communication. It was moreover 3.05 p.m. before *Tiger* reported to her flagship that she had been unable to pass the 2.32 p.m. and later signals to *Barham*;

[1] Cf. *Narrative of the Battle of Jutland*, and Keyes, *Naval Memoirs*.
[2] When an Admiral made a flag signal it indicated his intention of carrying out the purport of that signal, and was a warning to ships addressed by the signal to be ready to comply with its purport; ships addressed were to show an answering pendant to acknowledge that the Admiral's signal had been seen and its purport understood. Should a ship fail either to see or to make out or to understand the purport of a flag signal, no answering pendant was hoisted, in which case the Admiral would learn that his signal had not reached its destination; he would then order some other means of communication—searchlight, lamp, wireless, etc.—to be used to ensure that the signal got through. Only when all ships addressed had 'answered' the signal would it be hauled down, the hauling down being the Executive Order for the order to be carried out forthwith. Where, with a distant squadron, a ship in close company with the Admiral was detailed to act as a repeating ship, the same procedure was in principle followed, the repeating ship informing the Admiral of any difficulty encountered.

she had in the meantime used her low-power wireless to ask Beatty if the turning signal was to be passed on to the Fifth Battle Squadron.

This digression from the narrative is necessary because of an injustice later done to Admiral Evan-Thomas when the blame was laid upon him for failing to close up his squadron.

(iii)

While Admiral Beatty had been preparing to turn his three heavy squadrons, *Galatea* and *Phaeton* had held on their course, firing rapidly upon the retreating German destroyers as these made for the shelter of the approaching German cruisers *Elbing* and *Pillau*. At 2.30 p.m. *Galatea*, deciding to push her reconnaissance ahead at high speed, led her consort round to port a little in order to bring the oncoming *Elbing* directly ahead; two minutes later she turned further to north-eastward as *Elbing*, passing some 14,000 yards distant, just outside the extreme effective range of *Galatea's* 6-inch guns, opened fire on the two British cruisers with her superior 5.9-inch armament. The German cruiser's shooting was admirable and she quickly drew out of *Galatea's* effective range while still maintaining an accurate fire. She quickly secured the first hit, the first in the action: the shell hit *Galatea* just below her fore-bridge, causing only local structural damage, for it failed to explode. The missile did some personal damage, however: a passing seaman, slightly curious, touched the shining object only to withdraw his hand instantly upon the discovery that it was indeed very hot after its long, fast passage through the air.[1]

At 2.38 p.m., hopelessly outranged by *Elbing*, and with *Pillau* coming down fast from the north-eastward now joining in the cannonade, *Galatea* and her consort turned abruptly to a north-west course. *Elbing* quickly followed but the two British cruisers, using their speed, drew just out of range.

Their plucky reconnaissance under fire had been very successful indeed, for at 2.35 p.m., from *Galatea's* bridge a large cloud of smoke was sighted on the eastern horizon; this the Commodore immediately reported by wireless to both Beatty and Jellicoe:

Have sighted large amount of smoke as though from a fleet bearing east-north-east (1435).

Though of course still not fully appreciated in the British ships, this smoke was from the German battle-cruisers of the First Scouting

[1] *Fighting at Jutland.*

Group,[1] which Admiral Hipper, in his flagship *Lützow*, had led round in succession on to a westerly course as soon as he heard the sound of the cruisers' gunfire.

Commodore Sinclair's courageous drive eastward had been more than successful: it had uncovered the possible presence of 'a fleet' fifteen miles still further east. Turning to the north-west with the remainder of his squadron—*Inconstant* and *Cordelia* conforming to his movements five miles on his port beam—he set out deliberately to entice the enemy light cruisers to follow him and if possible draw any other German ships in support of them in a direction which would enable Beatty to cut in behind them all. He now reported to his Admiral that he was leading the enemy north-westward, adding later, 'they appear to be following'—a rider that is said to have caused some amusement in the 'big ships'.

At 2.45 p.m., *Galatea's* Commodore was able to make another important signal:

Smoke seems to be of seven vessels besides cruisers and destroyers. They have turned northward.

What the Commodore could see, some $14\frac{1}{2}$ miles distant, was the smoke of Hipper's five battle-cruisers with *Elbing* and *Pillau* ahead of them, and *Frankfurt*, *Regensburg* and the destroyer flotillas bringing up the rear.

Galatea's 2.45 p.m. signal must have dispelled any doubts that remained in Beatty's mind: the signal ten minutes earlier had been of 'smoke as of a fleet'; now the smoke was identifiable as most probably coming from the ships of his old antagonist Hipper, together with attendant light craft.

Clearly his first task now would be to investigate this report and —if they *were* the German battle cruisers—to deal effectively with them. Reconnaissance was, after all, one of the purposes for which Admiral Fisher had fathered the production of battle-cruisers— to push home a reconnaissance where perhaps lighter craft could not. Furthermore, Jellicoe's general instructions for battle-cruisers entirely covered the situation now emerging: these laid down clearly that in principle the battle-cruisers' function was the destruction of enemy battle-cruisers; after their destruction, or in their absence, they might attack the van of the enemy battle fleet, relying on their own speed to keep out of difficulty. Prior to action, their function was to provide detailed information of the course, speed, composition and disposition of the units of the enemy's battle fleet, and to keep

---

[1] Or possibly from the destroyers ahead of them.

the Commander-in-Chief informed to enable him to dispose his battle fleet to the best advantage: at the same time they had the parallel function of denying to the enemy any knowledge of the British fleet's dispositions—by driving in their lighter scouting ships.

Admiral Beatty had been given a free hand by Jellicoe to carry out these general orders.[1]

All that had yet been reported, of course, was still only smoke; but *something* was there to create the smoke, and at 2.43 p.m. Jellicoe negatived zig-zagging in the battle-fleet and returned to his normal south-easterly course, increasing speed to 17 knots. At about the same time, realising from the sequence of *Galatea's* signals that the enemy light cruisers at least might attempt to escape by running for Kiel around Skagerrak and Kattegat, he ordered Rear-Admiral Hood—who with the Third Battle Squadron, and *Chester*, *Canterbury* and destroyers was some twenty miles ahead of the *Iron Duke*—to proceed towards the Skagerrak and be ready to cut this escape route also.

This was a shrewd move, but Hood, who had intercepted *Galatea's* signals himself and whose wireless room could now hear German wireless working fairly close nearby, had anticipated the possibility of this, and was already moving in the direction ordered.[2]

Twelve minutes later, at 2.55 p.m., having now read *Galatea's* further report that the smoke was from 'seven ships', Jellicoe increased the battle fleet's speed to 18 knots, and ordered steam to be raised for full speed. Five minutes afterwards, from *Iron Duke's* mast the electrifying general signal 'BJ–1' was flying—'Readiness for action stations in all respects'—and the British battle fleet cleared for action.

Admiral Scheer appears to have been quite undismayed by the reports sent in by his light forces: he continued his northward Odyssey at fifteen knots as before, still firmly believing that Jellicoe and, for all he knew to the contrary, Beatty's battle-cruisers also, were far from the scene.[3]

Scheer has since sought to cover this erroneous appreciation of the situation by expressing gratitude that the neutral steamer had brought about the initial contact between the opposing light forces:

It was thanks to that steamer that the action took place [Scheer wrote]. Had the destroyer not proceeded to the steamer and thus sighted the smoke of the enemy to the west, our course might have carried us past the English cruisers.[4]

[1] Jellicoe, *Grand Fleet*.   [2] *Fighting at Jutland*.
[3] Jellicoe, *Grand Fleet*.   [4] Scheer, *High Seas Fleet*.

Such incursions into the cloud-cuckoo land of 'what might have been' serve little useful purpose, for at the time of sighting the neutral steamer, at 2.10 p.m., the neighbouring wing-tips of Hipper's and Beatty's cruiser squadrons were less than twenty miles apart, and the visibility was then a good twelve to fourteen miles in any direction. Both fleets, moreover, were steering slightly converging courses: but for sighting the steam-plume of the stopped steamer *Galatea* and her consort would soon have turned to conform to the general north-by-east course of the Battle-Cruiser Force. It would not have been long in any case, therefore, before the two screens, or even the larger forces were aware of each other's presence.

Of greater importance was the fact that with each passing minute Hipper and his scouting group would be drawing, and would have continued to draw, further away from the support of their own High Seas Fleet. Had Hipper managed to slip unseen past Beatty's screen, he could not fail to have been sighted by Jellicoe's screen further to the northward, by which time Hipper would have been too far ahead to fall back on Scheer without being cut off by Beatty.

Any contact between the screens later than actually occurred must thus have been less favourable to Hipper, and Scheer would surely have been wiser to have expressed his gratitude to the steamer for precipitating the contact and thereby virtually saving him from the trap Jellicoe was setting for him further to the northward. It was, indeed, not a greatly dissimilar situation from that which had arisen in March 1803, when a fortuitous meeting with a Sicilian xebec enabled Villeneuve, emerging with the French fleet from Toulon, to evade the trap which Nelson had set for him just beyond the horizon.

(iv)

The cruisers of the Battle-Cruiser Force continued to endeavour to draw the enemy north-westwards without direction from their commanding admiral. By three o'clock, the rest of the First and Third Light-Cruiser Squadrons were all converging towards *Galatea* and generally conforming to her decoying tactics: twelve minutes later, *Elbing* was reporting their presence to Hipper and Scheer as 'eight *Calliopes*'.

To *Galatea's* dismay, just before three o'clock, it was noticed that the quarry—the German light cruisers—now appeared to be steering a much more northerly course and she had promptly reported this. Beatty, realising that this gave him a greater opportunity for cutting the escape route, at 3 o'clock altered the course of his battle-cruiser squadrons directly to east—a course which, had he known it, was heading directly for Hipper's battle-cruisers twenty-five miles away.

Hipper was then steering almost due west, but at 3.10 p.m., he at last began to haul round gradually to the north-westward in support of his light cruisers. *Galatea's* ruse was succeeding not only in drawing the light cruisers but also the heavier metal.

These eastward alterations of course had left Beatty's front unscreened by light cruisers and with no advance scouts to aid his final disposition for battle when in sight of his enemy.

It would have been of considerable advantage if—after the initial contact had been made by *Galatea*—the commander of the Battle-Cruiser Force had assumed control of at least one of his light-cruiser squadrons; as it was he was steaming continuously at 25 knots and it was out of the question for the older 'Town' class of light cruisers of which the Second Light-Cruiser Squadron was composed to get well ahead of him even if their Commodore were gifted with the ability to read the future.

It must be admitted that for Admiral Beatty the position was still anything but clear: since *Galatea's* report of smoke from seven ships, reported (erroneously) as steering north, Beatty had hauled his force round to the eastward to investigate and yet still be in a position to cut off the enemy's retreat to the Bight. Nor was his problem of probing the enemy's position made any easier by the vagaries of visibility, for mists were beginning to move up into low lying cloud and on the surface swirling mistbanks here and there were tending to pile up to leeward—the eastward—reducing the visibility in the direction of the enemy appreciably; Beatty, himself, was left to windward to show up clear against the skyline. He hoped soon, however, to be able to pierce this uneven veil, for at 2.46 p.m. he had signalled to his fleet seaplane-carrier *Engadine*, then about four and a half miles on *Lion's* port bow, to fly off a seaplane reconnaissance to the NNE-ward. The carrier had promptly turned east-by-north, while a seaplane was being prepared for hoisting out, and at 3.07 p.m. stopped for that purpose; one minute later, Flight-Lieutenant Rutland and Assistant-Paymaster Trewin as pilot and wireless operator took off from the relatively smooth sea surface in a Short two-seater seaplane, No. 8359, powered with a 250-horsepower Sunbeam engine. Heading northwards, the pilot found he had to fly low with a cloud ceiling of 1,000 feet, and even then the visibility beneath was only about one to four miles. After some ten minutes he managed to come up with the German light cruisers and identify them—by closing to within one and a half miles—as *Frankfurt*, *Pillau* and *Elbing*.

What with the poor visibility and the necessity for low flying, he found difficulty in keeping British and enemy ships in sight at the same time. He was, however, able to follow the movements of the enemy cruisers closely though he failed entirely to detect the presence of Hipper's battle-cruisers and provide the information which, in default of an advance screen of light cruisers, Admiral Beatty must now go without.

Rutland's seaplane remained in the air in close contact with the enemy until 3.40 p.m., long enough to note and signal that they were turning 16 points, altering course to the south. Then the seaplane returned to *Engadine's* side with a faulty fuel lead, and was hoisted in.[1]

Three of his reports reached *Engadine*, despite the deliberate wireless jamming set up by the four German cruisers. There is no record, however, of these reports ever reaching *Lion*.

Before the return of the seaplane, the situation had already begun to clear for at 3.15 p.m. watchers in *New Zealand* were able to make out five sparse columns of smoke on the horizon—the smoke of Hipper's battle-cruisers. Almost at the same time, Hipper caught a fleeting glimpse of the masts and funnels of the British battle-cruisers, hull down on the clearer western horizon some 17 miles from him.

Beatty now realised that the course he was steering was much too northerly, and that unless he held more to the eastward he might easily fail to cut the enemy off from their home ports. Accordingly, at 3.15 p.m., he turned his battle-cruiser squadrons onto a north-east course, and in consequence the two forces were now closing rapidly.

As far as Hipper was concerned, the glimpse he had gained could give him little idea of either the course or the composition of the British squadrons for they were almost end-on to him. Nevertheless, the sight was a shock to him. Until that moment, he had had no idea that the British Battle-Cruiser Force was near, so successful had the 'follow me' tactics of the cruisers of the First and Third Light-Cruisers squadrons been in preventing any reconnoitring by Hipper's light cruisers.

Within five minutes the British battle-cruiser squadrons could be seen quite clearly by Hipper. But he was still unable to see the Fifth Battle Squadron beyond them, although by a tremendous effort they had closed the distance separating them from Beatty to barely six

[1] This was the first recorded use of aircraft in a fleet action.

miles. At 3.29 p.m. Beatty changed the course of his battle-cruisers to east, which brought the Fifth Battle Squadron directly astern again so that in the next six minutes the hard-won decrease in the gap had expanded once more by over a mile. On this closing course, the enemy battle cruisers could soon be seen from *Lion's* bridge, a little over ten miles away on the port bow. Almost at the same time, reports of smoke from *Galatea* and *Falmouth* confirmed the position of the enemy battle-cruiser squadron.

Time was running out fast, for the enemy were now on the limits of the extreme gun-range of Beatty's 13.5-inch batteries. At 3.34 p.m., as the enemy now appeared to be turning, Beatty decided that the moment had come to form his line of battle; he ordered the Second Battle-Cruiser Squadron to take station astern of his own First Battle-Cruiser Squadron, thus bringing his battle-cruisers into one single line behind him. At the same time he ordered the 13th flotilla of destroyers to take up an attacking station two points on *Lion's* starboard bow, and the destroyers of the 9th flotilla to get ahead of the battle-cruisers—a far from easy task, for they were not the fastest destroyers in the fleet and the battle-cruisers were now making 25 knots.

At half past three, Hipper reported to his Commander-in-Chief: 'enemy heavy forces sighted, strength six ships'. He must have realised about this time, moreover, that if he continued to the north-ward Beatty's battle-cruisers would be able to cut his escape route to the Bight. Already, however, this resolute German admiral had decided upon his further moves for it seemed to him that Scheer's well-planned operation had reached its first stage even if by accident. A detached British force had appeared, far from its home base, and the situation which the German Commander-in-Chief had long hoped to create had developed earlier than had been anticipated. If he, Hipper, now turned to the southward, as if intending to make his escape to his own minefields and home ports, he felt certain that Beatty would follow him.

Hipper would then be able to lead Beatty straight on to the guns of the waiting High Seas Fleet, and the road would be open for Scheer's battlefleet to destroy the British squadrons and gain that tactical advantage he had long desired.

With this in mind, at 3.32 p.m. he ordered *Elbing* and her light-cruiser consorts of the Fourth Scouting Group to rejoin him at once and they swiftly turned 16 points to starboard: Hipper, waiting only to see that they had turned, at once led his battle-cruisers round in a 16-point turn to the south-eastward, reducing speed to 18 knots as he did so, to give his light cruisers a chance of rejoining him quickly. By 3.36 p.m., Hipper was round on the new course without incident and heading southwards towards the support of his Commander-in-Chief, with his light cruisers closing in behind him. He had still, however, not seen the Fifth Battle Squadron.

Fifty miles away, Scheer had begun to grasp the general situation, and when Hipper reported at 3.45 p.m. that he was steering southwards it ended some of his illusions. He had been steadily steering northward at 15 knots ever since Hipper had first reported Beatty's presence in the vicinity at 3.30 p.m.: he now elected to await further information before taking steps to assist his battle-cruiser admiral.

Far to the north, his presence still entirely unsuspected by both Hipper and Scheer, Jellicoe's battle fleet was now heading for Horns Reef. At 3.10 p.m. he had also ordered his armoured-cruiser screen to move out to a distance sixteen miles from the *Iron Duke*; the maximum steaming capacity of these elderly ships was only some $21\frac{1}{2}$ knots, however, and this rendered practically impossible any chance of their taking up this station, for at 3.25 p.m. the speed of the Battle Fleet itself was increased to 19 knots.

Two minutes later, at 3.27 p.m., Admiral Jellicoe at last broke wireless silence, to inform Beatty briefly of the battle fleet's position, course and speed. Fortunately the German wireless monitoring system totally failed to intercept this, so Scheer was left in ignorance of Jellicoe's approach.

Admiral Jellicoe now directed his flag officers to inform all officers and men under their command of what was afoot. He could do nothing but wait on events to the southward, trusting in the presence of the Fifth Battle Squadron supporting Beatty's battle-cruisers to settle the nuisance of Hipper's battle-cruisers swiftly, once and for all.

Aboard the British battle-cruisers, all hands had for some time been at 'action stations', and all was ready.

3

'An Unpalatable Result'

B Y twenty minutes to four, the opposing battle-cruiser forces
were closing each other rapidly, and Beatty could see that if he
held on as he was going there was a possibility that Hipper
might endeavour to 'cross his T'. Beatty was now steaming at 25
knots and might reasonably expect Hipper's ships to be doing the
same: as it happened the German battle-cruisers were only making
18 knots, to enable their light cruisers to rejoin them.

The classic tactical manoeuvre of crossing the enemy's T consisted
in so shaping one's course, more or less at right angles across that
of the enemy's battle line, that one's own line formed the short stroke
of the letter T, the long downward stroke being the enemy's fleet.
This was a much sought-after situation which gave the tactical
advantage to the fleet which had crossed the T: for a time it could
bring all its broadside guns, probably ten per ship, to bear with an
unrestricted field of fire upon the advancing column of the enemy,
which conversely could make use only of the ahead guns, probably
four, of its leading ships; the manoeuvre gives one fleet an enormous
gun power advantage over the enemy for a short time, during which
it can wreak considerable damage on the enemy's van—and even
crumple it—while suffering little itself. This manoeuvre had been
employed successfully by the Japanese admiral Togo at Tsu-Shima
in 1905: it was to be achieved later this day by both Jellicoe and
Beatty.

At 3.45 p.m., Beatty altered course two points to starboard,
coming round to east-south-east, and signalled his six battle-cruisers
to form line of battle in echelon bearing north-west of his flagship. By
this manoeuvre he would be able to bring more guns to bear ahead
and on the bow, it would also clear mutual smoke interference: by
hauling round further to the southward he was able also to preserve
the position from which he could cut the enemy's escape route via
Horns Reef. Ten minutes earlier he had already informed Jellicoe by

wireless that the five enemy battle-cruisers were in sight; now, at 3.45 p.m., he signalled their course (S 55° E) and his own position.

What is inexplicable is why Beatty had not *already* opened fire. Taking 21,000 to 20,000 yards as the maximum effective range of Beatty's 13.5-inch guns, and 18,000 yards as the range of his two rear 12-inch gun ships,[1] Hipper's force had been within effective range of the 13.5-inch gun ships (*Lion, Princess Royal, Queen Mary, Tiger*) since 3.40 p.m. While it would be unwise to close the enemy to within 15,000 yards, because of the torpedo danger from them, there was every reason to make the maximum use of the heavier gun power and longer range of the British battle-cruisers while they were still out of range of the German guns. It must also be remembered that the British battle-cruisers were more lightly armoured than the Germans: in previous engagements with these ships we had learned that their gunnery was very good, that they very quickly established hits although their accuracy tended to fall off under enemy gunfire. To have opened fire early would have created a big advantage, while offsetting the disadvantages of the lightly armoured British ships.

Hipper and his officers fully expected that Beatty would open fire well outside their own extreme gun range and were unable to understand why he did not do so. They withheld their own fire for obvious reasons; as the vital seconds passed, the gap separating the opposing battle-cruiser fleets fell from 20,000 yards to 18,000 yards, and then to 17,000 yards, yet still the guns were silent. The prevailing visibility cannot be emphasised too much, either at this or at any stage of this day's fighting, for in it lies a clue to so much that otherwise cannot be explained. As the two battle-cruiser forces rushed headlong towards each other the German gunners could see their British targets clearly against the western horizon, standing sharply out against the fading sunlight and blue sky; with their better optical instruments, range-taking presented less difficulty for them.

From the British line, however, the light grey hulls of the German battle-cruisers were only dim and hazy shapes almost merging into the mist-laden grey eastern sky; the less adequate British rangefinders seem to have been quite unable to get any accurate 'cut' on these distant, hazy, shapes, or at best, to provide a big over-estimation of the range. But if ranging was the problem, there was no reason why Beatty should not have solved it minutes earlier, by firing single periodic ranging guns as he had at the Dogger Bank

[1] German 12-inch could range just over 20,000 and their 11-inch between 18,000 and 18,500 yards maximum.

action the previous year and as Sturdee had done at the Falkland Islands Battle. Instead, he held on until the limit of the extreme German gun-range was passed, and the German officers were able to heave a sigh of relief: the most dangerous moment for them was past.

The range was still falling, even within the limits of his 11-inch guns, and Hipper realised he had no need to wait any longer; at 3.48 p.m. he ordered 'Open Fire!' His ships fired a ripple salvo from front to rear, *Lützow* commencing with a range on sights *averaging* 16,500 yards.[1] The guns of Beatty's main armament had been 'loaded and at the ready' for some minutes; seconds after the orange flash of German gunfire was seen to snake down the distant hazy line of ships, Beatty also signalled 'Open Fire!' and his battle-cruisers roared their reply.

The range had been grievously over-estimated, due largely to poor visibility, however, for they had fired with an average of 18,500 yards on sights, whereas the 'target' ships had been barely 15,500 yards distant and closing fast. In less than thirty seconds the splashes from the first German salvo began to spring up around and just beyond the British line: the British shots had fallen a good mile over their targets, but with the hazy background and the inadequate optical instruments available, the detection of these errors presented great difficulties. The closing rate was also very great, and seems to have been underestimated in most of the British ships,[2] an error which aggravated the range-finding problems; they still had not 'found' their targets when at 3.51 p.m. Beatty's flagship *Lion* was hit twice. The Germans had already got our range and a minute later *Derfflinger*—the second in the German line—was straddling *Tiger*, with a salvo containing one 'short', one 'over' and two hits which knocked out for the time being both Q and X turrets.

The range was now only 13,000 yards.

For a couple of minutes Beatty had been altering around to starboard, to the south-eastward—slowly, in order not to disturb the fire-control of his ships. By 3.54 p.m. he was steering almost south with his squadrons in line ahead, each ship tending to steer a slightly snake-like zig-zag course to disturb the enemy's fire-control as much as possible. At this short range, however, the German was now firing not only with main 12-inch and 11-inch main armament, but with their secondary 5.9-inch guns as well, the splashes of the latter falling 'short' and providing a curtain of spray which hampered the

---

[1] Von Hase, *Kiel and Jutland*.
[2] At 3.50 p.m., two minutes after opening fire, Beatty reported by wireless to his C.-in-C. 'Am engaging enemy' and gave his position.

British gunners considerably. One minute later, *Queen Mary* shooting well and fast hit *Seydlitz*, the third in the German line, distinguishable by the red patch on her funnel, once and then again. Had *Seydlitz* not enjoyed the formidable armour of these German warships, the hits would have caused a disaster of the first magnitude.

The Germans had, it seemed, now got our range to a nicety. Despite the individual yawing of our ships, the enemy battle-cruisers were shooting accurately and very rapidly, and a salvo from either their main or secondary armament was arriving in the British line about every fifteen to twenty seconds. The British gunnery, on the other hand, seemed to be having very little effect; this was no doubt partly because of the poor visibility to the eastward, but also due to the hampering effects of the splashing of enemy short shots, and the annoyance of smoke. Before Beatty had turned to a course parallel to that of the enemy, the 9th destroyer flotilla—the older destroyers from Harwich, and slower ships—had managed to claw their way to the head of the line, en route for an attacking station. As he had turned southward, however, this flotilla had been brought back on to his beam and try how they might they could not again get ahead and the smoke from their funnels in their effort to do so was drifting right down the line.

Nor was the unfavourable visibility alone to blame for the meagre results being achieved by our guns: an even graver cause had arisen from an important signal error. At 3.46 p.m., while still on the approach course, Beatty had signalled (by flags) a normal 'distribution of fire' signal to his squadron. Such a signal is particularly necessary when there are more ships on one side than on the other, for it is a cardinal maxim of battle that no enemy unit must be left unmolested. Beatty's signal directed *Lion* and the *Princess Royal* to concentrate their fire on Hipper's flagship *Lützow*, trusting in that way to disable the enemy van; the remaining ships in the battle line were each to select as target their opposite number in the German line, counting from the rear of that line.

This particular signal was not taken in by *Tiger* or by *New Zealand*, and presumably not by *Queen Mary* either. In consequence, while *Lion* and *Princess Royal* at the head of the British line properly took *Lützow* on as their target—and scored hits on her—and *Indefatigable* at the tail of the British line engaged the rear German ship *Von der Tann*, *Tiger* and *New Zealand* both fired on the second German ship from the rear, *Moltke*, while *Queen Mary* engaged the third ship *Seydlitz*. The result of this incorrect distribution of fire was that the *Derfflinger* was left entirely unmolested! Her gunnery

THE TURRET TRAP
The Path of the Shells upwards: the Path of the Flash down

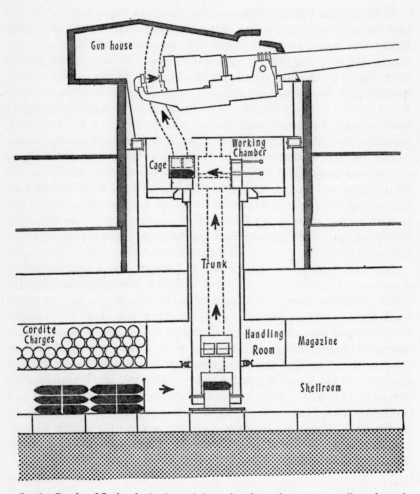

In the Battle of Jutland, the loss of three battle-cruisers was attributed to the absence of adequate anti-flash screening between magazine and handling-room. A shell bursting in the gunhouse could ignite a chain of charges all the way down to the handling-room and magazine. The Germans had already learned by bitter experience the need for this, and lost no ships to this cause.

officer found himself in a special paradise, in which he could engage *his* targets undisturbed by shot or shell.

This signalling failure was a further serious blunder which certainly reflected unfavourably on the signals training of the squadron's signals staffs.[1]

With salvoes falling thick and fast on both sides, the battle was quickly approaching a crisis point and at the range, which had been closed still more, it was obvious that something would have to be done. At 3.56 p.m., Hipper hauled out to open the range, turning his ships together into line ahead: there was, after all, no reason why he should risk a salvo disabling one of his own ships before he could fulfil his task of delivering Beatty safely to the guns of Admiral Scheer's battle fleet. A minute later Beatty also hauled out to starboard, opening the range still more, his battle line following him round.

For the next two minutes the German gunnery was distinctly in the ascendancy: their salvoes fell regularly and accurately in the British line and with a noticeably small 'spread'. Both Beatty and Hipper signalled their respective fleets to increase the rate of fire almost at the same time; Beatty also signalled (3.55) to the 13th destroyer flotilla off his bow that the moment seemed opportune to initiate a destroyer attack with torpedoes on the enemy line.

A minute later a shell struck *Lion's* Q turret, penetrated the turret armour, and burst in the gunhouse, killing or wounding the majority of the personnel there. The shock of the burst caused a charge to fall back from the open breach of an elevated gun, and this caught fire, dropped into the working chamber below and flashed off yet another charge, killing everybody in that compartment. Realising the imminent peril of the fire spreading downwards to the tons of explosive in the ship's magazine, Major Harvey, the Royal Marine officer of the turret, dragged himself dying to the voice pipe and ordered the magazine's flash doors to be shut, and the magazine to be flooded. There is no doubt that his action—for which he was posthumously awarded the Victoria Cross—saved *Lion* from imminent destruction.

(ii)

Queen Mary, two ships astern of *Lion*, now discovering the error in the fire distribution, opened fire on *Derfflinger*. The German gunnery

[1] One possible explanation is that when the distribution signal was made by flags in *Lion*, two other sets of flag signals were hoisted within the minute. It is interesting to note, however, that the Admiralty *Narrative of the Battle of Jutland* (HMSO, 1924) made no mention of this blunder in fire-distribution.

officer's paradise came to an abrupt end, for *Queen Mary's* first salvo straddled and her second secured a hit on the German cruiser. At the tail of the British line, *Indefatigable* continued the steady and mounting gun duel which she had maintained with *Von der Tann* from the outset. The change of course to the southward had left the range very short, and at her end of the line there was a tendency for it to be even shorter. The spirited duel persisted, however, with her opponent; straddled by the German ship, the *Indefatigable* returned the blow successfully straddling the German with her 12-inch guns. About one minute past four o'clock, however, a German salvo hit *Indefatigable* at deck level aft near the mainmast. It seemed to those watching as if her steering had been damaged, for she suddenly broke out of line to starboard, settling by the stern. As she hauled clear she was hit again by *Von der Tann* with two 11-inch shells, one striking her hull forward and the other her foredeck—both appearing to burst on impact. Thirty seconds later a sheet of flame enveloped the British battle-cruiser, followed by a sudden uprush of dense, dark smoke. The ship had blown up completely, leaving only a mass of falling débris to mark the passing of fifty-seven officers and nine hundred men.

The sternest part of the action thus far was now over, for as the range opened with the two squadrons on diverging courses, Hipper's guns fell silent, but not before they had secured another hit on *Lion* causing a fire amidships. Hipper was already beginning to turn his ships together slowly to close the range once more; but there was a lull in the firing for a few minutes, and this will be a convenient juncture in which to review the fighting thus far.

In the fifteen minutes or so since the commencement of the battle, the opposing forces had been made numerically even. Each side disposed of five battle-cruisers, but Hipper having succeeded in damaging four of the British gun turrets tipped the balance in the German favour. If one is to seek causes they could lie in the British over-estimation of the opening range, the delay in opening fire outside the range-limits of the German guns, and, unfortunately, the inaccurate shooting of the British ships, for in this period the German gunners secured four hits on the British line to every British hit on theirs. Reference can also be made on this point to the Dogger Bank action, where the same superiority of German gunfire over our battle-cruisers was very well concealed officially with exaggerated accounts of the damage we had been inflicting, whereas in fact the retreating German battle fleet had scored fourteen hits on *Lion* and *Tiger*, disabling the former, to only three hits scored on them in return.[1] The Germans have also said that very little damage was done to their ships in these early minutes of the fighting at Jutland, and have commented on the relative inaccuracy of the British shooting.

Before Hipper could reopen fire, the situation had taken a completely new turn: at 4.05 p.m., Admiral Evan-Thomas, with his four 15-inch-gun battleships of the Fifth Battle Squadron had finally been able to get a first glimpse of the rear enemy battle-cruisers. To him they were dim shapes merging into the misty grey background; but they were enough. Five minutes earlier he had sighted other dim shapes ahead—the enemy's light cruisers as they made for their station on the disengaged quarter of Hipper's battle-cruisers. At a range of 19,000 yards—nine and a half sea miles—*Barham* had opened fire and quickly forced these light cruisers, with a few well directed salvoes, to scuttle off to the eastward at high speed out of his range, dropping smoke-floats to cover their retreat. Only then had Evan-Thomas seen Hipper's rear battle-cruisers and also noticed for the first time—for he had received no signals of any sort since 3.55 p.m.—that Beatty had turned to the southward. Evan-Thomas, in spite of his efforts and his 24 knots speed, had managed to get no nearer than seven-and-a-half miles from Beatty; now seeing the direction of the battle-cruisers' movement, he promptly hauled his squadron round to conform, his director-gunner and gun-turrets keeping trained on the dim and distant enemy battle-cruisers. At 4.08 p.m. his two leading ships opened fire at over 19,000 yards, straddling *Von der Tann* almost at once and thereafter maintaining an increasing grip on the rear of the enemy battle-cruiser line although the gunlayers could seldom see, in the bad prevailing visibility, more than two or three of them at a time.

After two minutes *Barham* shifted her target to the second ship from the rear—*Moltke*—while other ships astern of *Barham* continued to harass *Von der Tann*. In the prevailing conditions of visibility at long range, and bearing mind that the director-gunners of the 15-inch battleships were for the most part laying and training on the flashes from the German squadron, the accuracy of their fire was commendable; the Germans expressed their amazement and admiration for the Battle Squadron's gunnery, commenting that only the poor quality of the bursting charges in our 15-inch projectiles saved the German battle-cruisers from disaster when hit.[2]

---

[1] Roskill, *Strategy of Sea Power*.
[2] Not the bursting charges but the fuses were at fault; they allowed the shell to break up on impact rather than penetrate heavy armour and then burst inside it.

When at 4.10 p.m. Hipper reopened fire on Beatty's battle-cruisers, there were greater opportunities for *Barham* and *Valiant* and *Warspite's* director-gunners' to select their target, and their firing became even more effective—even at the great range at which the ships were. Admiral Beatty said of this period, in his Despatch, 'the enemy's fire now seemed to slacken'.[1]

Admiral Hipper himself has since commented on the innacurate shooting of our battle-cruisers at this time, comparing it unfavourably with that of the Fifth Battle-Squadron's battleships.[2] One may reasonably ask what might not have happened in these early minutes had Beatty kept these battleships really close and in his line of battle against superior numbers, and as an integral part of his force, instead of failing to concentrate them and later virtually ignoring their existence except for a single signal at 3.36 p.m.[3]

With Hipper almost lost in the mist, but now beginning to close the range, Beatty also turned his battle-cruisers inwards intent upon bringing pressure if possible to bear upon Hipper's van. Although the range was still great, fire was reopened on both sides. There had been a considerable improvement in the situation as far as British gunners were concerned, for (4.11) the 9th flotilla had been told to clear the range so that their smoke would no longer be a nuisance.

Several different movements were in progress at about this time. The Second Light-Cruiser Squadron which had since early in the afternoon struggled to get up with the leading ships of the British cruiser line had at last been successful although it had become separated into two parts earlier in the afternoon; *Nottingham* and *Dublin* were now passing down the engaged side of *Lion* while *Southampton* (the flagship) and *Birmingham* on the disengaged side were drawing ahead. At about 4.20 p.m., the four light cruisers were reunited as a squadron and at last took their station about one and three-quarter miles ahead of the battle-cruisers as a lookout screen to the south. At the same time, while these cruisers were rejoining each other, the 13th destroyer flotilla had been moving across the line of the battle-cruisers' advance, in readiness to launch a torpedo attack on the enemy, and if possible force its head away to the eastward to enable Beatty to cut in more easily across its line of escape. The flotilla was now in three columns led by *Champion* (Captain Farie) the flotilla leader. As the flotilla advanced across *Lion's* bows, it unfortunately became separated by *Nottingham* and

---

[1] *Battle of Jutland: Official Despatches.*　　　　[2] *Fighting Forces*, January 1927.
[3] One can agree with the mild reproof administered by Mr. Churchill: 'It would no doubt have been better if the original cruising formation of the battle-cruisers and the Fifth Battle Squadron had been more compact.'—*World Crisis.*

Dublin with the result that the columns started across the space between the opposing battle cruisers separately. It had taken some time at the speed of the fleets for these destroyers to get far enough ahead, but at 4.15 p.m. *Champion* signalled his flotilla to move out to the attack, and nine destroyers turned towards the enemy lines.

Almost at the same time German destroyer flotillas emerged from the disengaged bow of the enemy battle-cruisers and led by their flotilla leader, the light cruiser *Regensburg*, began to develop an attack on the British line. The German attack had been decided by Commodore Heinrich, their flotilla commodore, as a means of relieving the developing pressure of the Fifth Battle Squadron's gunnery which was clearly establishing itself upon Hipper's rear ships.[1] There were thus two torpedo attacks developing simultaneously, and the rival flotillas raced at full speed across the no-man's-land between the rival battle-cruisers.

For five minutes and more after 4.20 p.m. the centre of this patch of sea was an inferno of gunfire, with destroyers steaming at full speed, their funnels belching smoke and their guns firing, half hidden by endless fountains of shell-splashes as both British and German battle-cruisers used their secondary armaments to keep their attackers at a safe distance. The rival flotillas raced past each other at a relative speed of well over sixty miles an hour, but the superior gun-power of the British destroyers dominated the mêlée. The German attack was launched, but it quickly lost impetus and resolution. The German destroyers fired their torpedoes—twelve in all—mostly aimed at the Fifth Battle Squadron, which merely turned away by sub-divisions—the accepted manoeuvre—for some minutes; the Squadron *saw*[2] two of the torpedoes, suffered no damage, and continued to fire on Hipper's ships.

Having fired their torpedoes, the enemy's destroyers raced back to their own line at utmost speed, splitting up to pass round Hipper's van and rear. They were pursued almost up to the guns of their battle-cruisers by the triumphant British destroyers—who then turned to make their own attack. Dashing on until they were only 7,000 yards from the enemy, *Nestor* and *Nicator* fired two torpedoes each: they met, however, with no success. They then turned round, closing *Lützow* to within 3,500 yards and although enveloped in splashes from the 5.9-inch battery of the enemy, fired again but still had no luck.

---

[1] Scheer, *The High Seas Fleet.*
[2] *Barham*'s after-battle report mentions a torpedo passing ahead of *Valiant* and another astern of her: *Official Despatches.*

The time was now 4.43 p.m.: from *Lion's* yardarm the 'Destroyers Recall' signal was seen to be flying so they turned back for their own fleet.

In the grim mêlée between the rival battle-cruiser fleets, two German destroyers *V-27* and *V-29* had been disabled, and were lying stopped and sinking fast: further to the westward two British destroyers, *Nomad* and *Nestor* had also been brought to a standstill, disabled.

Petard—one of the destroyers which had become temporarily separated from the rest at the outset—now decided to make one last attack: she had already torpedoed the *V-27*. Turning, and closing the leading German battle-cruisers to within 3,000 yards at high speed, she and *Nicator* fired three torpedoes and as they turned for home, belatedly answering the 'Recall', had the satisfaction of knowing that one at least might have hit. It was learned after the war that *Petard's* last shot had struck the battle-cruiser *Seydlitz* forward, tearing a hole some 500 square feet in extent, and permanently putting her foremost 5.9-inch gun out of action. Despite this considerable damage, and the fact that she soon shipped a thousand tons of water, so well had she been constructed that she continued throughout the early part of the action in the line of battle manoeuvring at high speed.

On the way back to the safety of her own line, *Petard* stopped near the disabled *Nestor* and asked if he could give her a tow. Commander Bingham refused to allow him to risk his ship, and sent him somewhat sadly on his way. The tide of battle then passed by the two crippled British destroyers left in the middle of what had been a shot-torn stretch of water—disabled, forlorn, stopped.

It is possible to make some assessment of these two destroyer attacks: the Germans had lost two destroyers, and two of ours had been left behind; the Germans had fired their torpedoes to no purpose, for the Fifth Battle Squadron had turned away and evaded them; the British destroyers had pressed home their attack and in all twenty-one torpedoes had been fired: they had hit *Seydlitz* (although at the time that was unknown) and had sunk the destroyer *V-27*. The determination with which the British had set about their task had thwarted the German attack so that it had not been pressed home; the British attack on the other hand *had* been pressed home with all the verve and élan that could be expected of our destroyer service. It had had the effect upon Hipper of forcing him to turn right away from the attack as soon as it began to develop, and to turn away again and yet again before he could be certain that his ships were out of torpedo danger. Each turn had opened the range and relieved the British battle-cruisers for a while from the acute pressure of the German gunnery.

In the meantime, while the destroyer attacks had been developing and interest had centred on the spectacle being enacted between the battle-cruiser lines, tragedy had struck again at Beatty's force. Once the immediate danger from torpedo had passed, Hipper had again closed the range, and, as Beatty was also doing the same, 'hot' firing was quickly resumed. Beatty's flagship was on fire amidships, but she was still shooting well. The fire was not yet under control and the smoke from it enveloped her and for a brief while she was concealed from the enemy. For some minutes, indeed, the German officers had the impression that she had gone down—leaving *Princess Royal* clearly visible to them, apparently leading the British line. In consequence at 4.21 p.m., *Derfflinger*—who had been engaging *Princess Royal*—shifted fire to *Queen Mary*, her next astern, thinking she was now the second ship and therefore his target. *Queen Mary*, however, was already under a steady fire from *Seydlitz*—and had been almost from the commencement of the action.

For five minutes *Queen Mary* stood up gallantly to the double onslaught at ranges of 15,000 yards, giving back as good as she was receiving—and better. Her salvoes were pitching accurately and very rapidly.[1] Twice in succession she successfully straddled *Derfflinger* and her last two salvoes both registered hits.

At 4.26 p.m. the end came with appalling suddenness when two salvoes from her antagonists struck her in quick succession. The first shells hit and burst on her port side abreast Q turret; the second salvo[2] of two more shells struck downwards through her foredeck:

> There was a dull red glow amidships, and then the ship seemed to open out like a puffball . . . There was another dull red glow somewhere forward and the whole ship seemed to collapse inwards.[3]

A tremendous explosion followed, accompanied almost instantaneously by a great column of black smoke mounting skywards one thousand feet and more. Her next astern, *Tiger*, only five hundred yards away had to swing hard to port, passing the scene of disaster through a dense smoke pall some thirty seconds later; there was

[1] Von Hase, *Kiel and Jutland*.
[2] Probably fired from *Derfflinger*, the other by *Seydlitz*.
[3] Description from *Tiger*, following next astern: *The Fighting at Jutland*.

a heavy rain of débris on her decks. Astern of *Tiger*, *New Zealand* had to haul out to starboard. By the time these two ships had passed the spot, the smoke pall was blowing clear. The after part of a ship could be seen with propellers slowly revolving in the air, masses of paper were blowing out of a hatchway and on the stern, an officer aloft could read the name—*Queen Mary*—then that, too, slid down under the water. Before *New Zealand* had completely passed on her way the last pitiful fragments had vanished, together with fifty-seven officers and twelve hundred and nine men. There were only nineteen survivors: of these, seventeen were picked up out of the water by the destroyers *Petard* and *Laurel*; two, an officer and a man, were rescued by German destroyers and taken as prisoners of war.

Two proud ships were now gone: Beatty's battle-cruiser strength was down to four against Hipper's five. There was perhaps some satisfaction in seeing that *Seydlitz* appeared to have been set on fire by one of *Queen Mary's* last salvoes. Almost at once, however, *Princess Royal*—the second in the line—was straddled, a salvo hitting her Q turret. For a moment she was shrouded by smoke from the shell burst, and on *Lion's* bridge, ahead of her, a signalman reported laconically: 'Please, sir, *Princess Royal* has gone.'[1]

Happily the signalman's report was wrong, for in a matter of seconds the *Princess Royal* was seen emerging from the smoke firing as steadily as ever. Beatty on his upper bridge had just turned to his Flag Captain, to remark grimly: 'What's the matter with our bloody ships today, Chatfield?'

Admiral Hipper had turned away as soon as he saw the British destroyers fire their torpedoes, spurred by the additional desire to draw clear of the fire of the Fifth Battle Squadron's battleships. But when the range had closed again, the battleships once more brought his rear ships under fire, and seemed likely to do considerable damage. The German rear was replying as best it could, however, and *Barham* was hit at 4.23 p.m. by *Von der Tann*, but little harm was done. The German battle-cruisers had indeed achieved more than Hipper could possibly have expected; with his southward movement to lead Beatty on to the guns of Scheer's battle fleet now showing such promise, it would have been foolish to jeopardise its success by allowing any of his ships to be disabled and having to drop out of the line. The Fifth Battle Squadron had again got the Germans' measure to a nicety, and on a converging course had reduced the range to a dangerous 14,000 yards. They were scoring a considerable number of superficial hits and it again became necessary for Hipper

[1] Keyes, *Naval Memoirs*.

to draw out of the reach of Evan-Thomas' guns before they disabled one of his ships. At 4.30, he turned to port, and as, at the same time, Beatty turned a little to starboard, the range rapidly opened from 14,700 yards to 18,000 yards within a few minutes. Firing between the battle cruisers temporarily died down, although Evan-Thomas' battleships continued to pound the enemy as long as they could see them.

Beatty's turn to starboard had brought *Southampton*, Commodore Goodenough's flagship, and the other three cruisers of the Second Light-Cruiser Squadron right ahead, distant about one and three-quarter miles. Just as Beatty turned, a lookout aloft in *Southampton* reported sighting a ship far off on the misty horizon four points on the port bow. *Southampton* at once signalled by wireless to the Commander-in-Chief and to Beatty,

> Urgent. One enemy cruiser. Bearing south-east, steering north-east.[1]

Turning directly towards this ship, Goodenough pressed on with his squadron to investigate. Two minutes later the sight that met the Commodore's eyes was something no British officer had seen since the outbreak of war: there, along the south-eastern horizon right ahead of them, was the whole German High Seas Battle Fleet, a seemingly interminable line of grey battleships steering northwards and already deployed in line of battle.

At 4.33 p.m. *Southampton* signalled to Beatty by searchlight:

> Battleships bearing south-east.

Then, as a good scouting admiral should, Goodenough pushed on unhesitatingly straight towards the enemy, to find out those details of the enemy's formation, course, speed, and numbers that the Commander-in-Chief would require when deploying his fleet later to deal with them. In five minutes *Southampton* was able to make a decisive report (4.38) to both Jellicoe and Beatty by wireless:

> Urgent. Priority. Have sighted enemy battle fleet, bearing approximately south-east, course of enemy north.

The German fleet appeared to be steering straight for Beatty's force. Almost simultaneously, the 13th flotilla's cruiser, *Champion*, also

---

[1] He also gave *Southampton's* position by dead reckoning. This estimated position of reporting ships is always included in enemy-sighting reports.

reported by wireless the course of the enemy battle fleet, adding that it was in line ahead and that 'Dreadnoughts' were in the van.

Here at last was a confrontation that Beatty must very rightly check for himself, and he swung his battle-cruisers round until they too were heading direct for the newly reported enemy. At 4.42 p.m., Beatty on his bridge could see the distant ships of the enemy battle fleet for himself.

His duty was now clear.

While the Battle Orders laid down that he could engage battle-cruisers when no superior force was present, he was clearly directed to reconnoitre when in the presence of superior force and to report their movements direct to his Commander-in-Chief. His personal feelings in that moment must have been bitter indeed: there had been the unfortunate Admiralty message at 12.30 p.m. 'locating' Scheer's flagship and, to some extent, the German fleet, in the Jade River; yet here they were four hours later 180 miles away from there! What degree of reliance could be placed upon Admiralty reports after that? Then too, there must have been chagrin that Hipper in the full knowledge of his Commander-in-Chief's approach had been leading Beatty's force right to his Chief like so many lambs to the slaughter.

There was no alternative now but to withdraw and at 4.40 p.m. in *Lion* the general flag signal for the whole Battle-Cruiser Force to alter course (leaders of squadrons together remainder in succession) sixteen points to starboard was hoisted. Beatty could not report what he had seen direct to Admiral Jellicoe for his own wireless had been destroyed during the previous half-hour; he therefore directed *Princess Royal* to pass the message by wireless for him.

A minute later, with the signal flags to turn still flying, *Lion's* helm was over and she began to swing round to starboard followed by *Princess Royal*, *Tiger* and *New Zealand*—all that now remained of the two battle-cruiser squadrons. As *Lion* turned to her northerly course, the 'Recall' signal was hoisted for the destroyers: this was the signal which *Nestor*, *Petard*, and the others had seen. Five minutes later, all the British battle-cruisers were round on the new course and in station astern of *Lion* as she headed north-west. Beatty's task now was to lead his ships in safety from the German battle fleet that was closing them fast from astern while exercising his new primary function as a scouting admiral.

Eleven-and-a-half miles away, at the limit of their gun range, the German battle fleet had turned by squadrons slightly towards him, and were now 'in chase'. Eight and a quarter miles off on his star-

73

board beam, in the mists, only dimly seen against the background, Hipper's five battle-cruisers—still apparently intact—were resuming line ahead to the southward after their last turn away from the torpedo attack. The tactical withdrawal which these torpedo attacks had imposed upon Hipper had, by forcing him to open the range, also given Beatty the opportunity to turn his battle-cruisers in succession without any interference.

The range was still opening, and to keep in touch with the German battle-cruisers, as was now Beatty's duty, he at once altered course four points towards them, steering northward, parallel to the course of his enemy. Firing soon broke out again, at a range of 17,500 yards, with *Lion* firing at *Von der Tann*, the enemy's rear ship, until unexpectedly the enemy line was suddenly obscured by smoke. Admiral Hipper was at that moment turning his own battle-cruisers sixteen points to starboard in succession to take station between five and six miles ahead of the leading battleship of his battle fleet which he had sighted three minutes earlier.

In the poor visibility now prevailing to the eastward, Beatty actually lost sight of the enemy battle-cruisers in the smoke and confusion of their turn, and for the next six minutes our battle cruisers' guns were silent. To the northward of *Lion*, however, Evan-Thomas' four battleships were still hammering at the enemy battle-cruisers whenever they were visible at ranges between 18,000 and 19,000 yards. When *Lion's* flag signal to turn was hoisted, *Barham* had been in full chase of the enemy and although he had intercepted *Southampton's* wireless signal reporting the enemy battle fleet in sight to the southward, and had also seen Beatty's battle-cruisers turn, he considered it his duty to continue his southward course and pound the German battle-cruisers while he could and until directed otherwise. He had not, of course, seen the actual flag signal to turn, for he had been eight-and-a-half miles away when it had been hoisted; nor, once again, had the signal been made to him by any other means. So he held on his way, the Fifth Battle Squadron and the battle-cruisers fast approaching each other on approximately opposite courses. At 4.52 p.m., when he was about a mile and a half off *Lion's* port bow, Beatty signalled *Barham* direct to turn sixteen points to the northward. Soon afterwards the two flagships passed, port side to port side, at almost a mile a minute—the battleships firing over the mastheads of the battle-cruisers as they went by. *Barham* had now seen *Lion's* signal to turn and repeated it to his squadron; when it had been acknowledged by his ships, he turned as directed sixteen points to starboard *in succession* at 4.55 p.m. and was round on his new course just before five o'clock. Beatty had had plenty of time in hand to turn his battle-cruisers in succession but, on account of the delay, the turn was fraught with danger for the battleships. *Barham* had reached a point some 4 miles astern of Beatty's ships: to the south-east, moreover, the van of the German battle fleet was coming up fast on a north-westerly course. They, too, were now at 20,000 to 21,000 yards but closing fast; they began at once to concentrate their fire on the battleship's turning point.

Although no British battleship was hit during the critical minutes of this turn, *Barham*, the flagship, was continuously deluged with splashes as the enemy corrected their range to get her; *Valiant*, her next in line, also got round without a scratch, but turned short to make certain. *Warspite*, astern of *Valiant*, also passed the critical turning point safely. The danger to the last ship to turn—*Malaya*— was the greatest, for by that time the German gunners had the range of the turning point to a nicety and their salvoes were churning the water into fountains every ten seconds. For a while *Malaya* was invisible amid the columns of jutting spray, but her captain had taken an outside course and she emerged unscathed to take her place in station in the line. As *Malaya* straightened up to the new course, *Barham* received savage hits, destroying her wireless and causing many casualties. With this exception the squadron had been lucky, for it would have been so easy for one or more hits to have disabled one of them, perhaps in her steering gear or machinery, forcing her to drop out of the line disabled, to become a target for the whole High Seas Fleet as it passed.

The Fifth Battle Squadron now found itself covering the rear of the battle-cruisers in their northward movement and it lost no time in engaging the enemies in sight: *Barham* and *Valiant* promptly re-opened fire on Hipper's battle-cruisers, while the two rear battleships *Warspite* and *Malaya* engaged the van of Scheer's distant battle fleet.

As the battle-cruisers held on northward, the second Light-Cruiser Squadron was pushing its reconnaissance straight on towards the enemy battle-fleet. The light cruisers were then in line ahead and end on to the German ships, who could not quite make out who these strangers were, and so withheld their fire. When, however, Commodore Goodenough had reconnoitred to within 13,000 yards of his mighty foe, he turned his squadron (by signal) together to the westward to seek the security of his own heavier forces.

He had obtained the information which he knew Jellicoe would need and signalled it (4.46 p.m.):

> Course of enemy's battle fleet north: single line ahead; composition of van 'Kaiser' class: bearing of centre east: destroyers on both wings and ahead: enemy's battlecruisers joining battle fleet from northward. My position, etc . . .

—the perfect 'enemy report'.

As *Southampton* turned, the familiar four funnels of a British 'Town' class light cruiser were clearly revealed to Scheer, who immediately opened fire with his rear and centre battleships. Twisting and turning amongst the splashes, Commodore Goodenough and his ships seemed to bear charmed lives as they hurried northwards to take up a convenient position off the disengaged quarter of the Fifth Battle Squadron. From that point of vantage the Commodore would be able to maintain a close surveillance on every move that Scheer's fleet made. This admirable example of light-cruiser scouting was to be repeated by Commodore Goodenough again and again before the day's fighting was over.

Ahead of our battle-cruisers, the eight light cruisers of the First and Third Light-Cruiser Squadrons, having noticed Beatty's turn to the north, were now converging to form a lookout screen ahead of his advance. These light cruisers had again acted instinctively, for no orders had been signalled to them since three o'clock.

A summary of the battle-cruiser force's achievements thus far cannot fail to be, as Admiral Jellicoe stated later in his *Despatch*[1] 'unpalatable': in greater numerical strength, and—on paper at least —with superior fighting power ship for ship, the British force had encountered a weaker force, but after three quarters of an hour of hot fighting had emerged with the loss of two ships. Of Beatty's four remaining ships, moreover, German gunnery had rendered five out of their sixteen gun-turrets unworkable, thereby for the time being reducing the fighting capacity of Beatty's force by over 30 per cent. In addition, his ships had suffered damage to their upperworks, their communications, wireless, searchlights and the like.

Per contra, the German battle-cruisers were still all in the line of battle, although a direct hit had started a fire in the flagship *Lützow*. *Seydlitz* also had suffered from a serious fire due to a hit and *Queen Mary*'s salvo had penetrated a turret putting it out of action and killing all the turret's crew, *Von der Tann* was virtually out

---

[1] *Official Despatches.*

of the fight with all her turrets out of action for the time being. Both *Moltke* and *Derfflinger* had been hit and *Seydlitz*, although Scheer refused to admit it afterwards[1], *had* been torpedoed by the intrepid *Petard*. This physical comparison, however, cannot remove the laurels from the German battle-cruisers for their superior gunnery on this occasion, nor can it explain how it was that they scored four times as many hits on the British battle-cruisers as they received in return. Beatty had commanded these battle-cruisers, the 'incomparable command' as Mr. Churchill had called it, for over three years. There had surely been time for him and his captains to have worked up to a higher standard than that displayed during this phase of the battle; his apologists have suggested that the battle-cruiser force had no facilities for target practice handy to their base in the Firth of Forth. That was so, but periodically squadrons visited Scapa for training, where there were such facilities; it was in their Commander-in-Chief's interest to make sure that more opportunities for practice were made available for his ships. Or was the scurrilous gun-room gossip true? Did the Battle-Cruiser Force really 'do its target practice on the enemy'?

Unquestionably the light and visibility had greatly aided the German gunners; while the German ships' light grey melted into a deepening hazy grey background, the British ships thus far had stood out clear-cut against the western horizon. Even at extreme ranges of visibility, the Germans with their better optical instruments had the superior vision, and were able to get quicker and more accurate range-finder readings. Again, the British gunners had been hampered in the early stages of the engagement by disadvantages of smoke and the splashes of enemy 'shorts'. British gunnery, however, had only knocked out five of the German battle-cruisers' twenty-two turrets, so that Hipper's force still retained 77 per cent of its fighting capacity. The Germans had also suffered damage to their upper-works, to their masts and wireless; *Seydlitz* had been torpedoed and had shipped a lot of water—but was still in her place in the line. Considering the damage done to Hipper's battle-cruisers at this stage, the Admiralty narrative of the Battle of Jutland stated:

> The damage done . . . was considerable, but German information on the point is not conclusive.

This, however, is not so: Admiral Hipper has since commented on the inaccurate shooting of our battle-cruisers, comparing it

[1] Scheer: *High Seas Fleet.*

unfavourably with the excellent shooting of the battleships of the Fifth Battle Squadron[1]. It is indeed doubtful whether the battle-cruisers did any serious damage during this time except that done to *Seydlitz* and *Derfflinger* by the ill-fated *Queen Mary*; *Von der Tann* and *Moltke* received most of their hits from the Fifth Battle Squadron. The Admiralty *Narrative* states that at 4.33 p.m.[2] 'the fire of *Lion* and *Princess Royal* forced the *Lützow* to turn away'. There is no evidence whatsoever to support this statement; the *Narrative* omits to mention that the British destroyer attack was the primary reason for Hipper's turn away.

There remains the delay of the Fifth Battle Squadron turning north after the High Seas Fleet had been sighted; it was a delay for which that squadron might well have had to pay a grievous price. The general signal made in *Lion* for the turn northwards was not hauled down; she turned with the flags still flying, and her consorts followed her round. The signal had not been repeated to *Barham* eight miles away and the battleship squadron was left to find out what was happening for itself. Still in chase of the enemy *Barham* passed *Lion* on opposite courses, and the same signal was then passed direct to her—to alter course sixteen points *in succession* to starboard; it was answered and was repeated by *Barham* to her Fifth Battle Squadron. It was, however, already too late for such a turn to be made in safety: the High Seas Fleet was now too close, and there was no time left. The signal should surely have been a 'Blue-pendant Turn'—a turn of ships *together* and not in succession, sixteen points to starboard. It could have been hauled down as soon as acknowledged, and the four battleships would have turned simultaneously. This would have reversed the order of the squadron, but the simultaneous turning manoeuvre would have ended with the Fifth Battle Squadron, close astern of its battle-cruisers and out of the immediate gun-range of the German battle fleet. It would have saved some damage to these great ships, and it would have saved many lives.

It would be unjust to Admiral Beatty to say that he *should* have signalled this form of turn; it would certainly have been better, however, had he done so. It would not be unjust, however, to say that had Evan-Thomas been cast in Nelson's mould his blind eye would have 'failed to see' Beatty's unthinking order to turn *in succession*—and his instinct would have made him turn his ships *together*.

[1] *Fighting Forces:* January 1927.   [2] *R.U.S.I. Journal: No. 485.*

4

The Scouting Admiral

T HE sudden appearance of the German battle fleet—barely twelve miles distant from our advanced forces—had completely changed the position. How unexpected this was must be emphasized, particularly in view of the Admiralty's message locating Scheer's flagship in the Jade River. The apparition must have been as great a surprise on the bridge of *Lion* as it was in the control-top of *Southampton*. There, on first sighting it, the seamen had thought the distant ships must be Jellicoe's Grand Fleet battleships: they were quickly disillusioned when an officer pointed out that the fleet in sight was coming from the direction of *Heligoland*, and not Scapa Flow.[1]

From the first moment that the High Seas Fleet came in sight Beatty's rôle was transformed immediately into that of a 'scouting admiral'—the eyes of his Commander-in-Chief. As he had not destroyed the enemy battle-cruisers he was precluded by Battle Orders from attacking the van of the High Seas Fleet, although he was allowed a great measure of discretion in his interpretation of these Orders.

Beatty having led his force round to the northward had encouraged both Hipper and Scheer to follow him. Admiral Scheer's movements up to this time are therefore of some interest. Having received *Elbing's* report some two hours earlier, to the effect that 'individual light enemy forces' had been sighted, and being then some fifty miles away, Scheer, satisfied that any light forces in Hipper's

[1] *The Fighting at Jutland*. It is interesting to note that Rear-Admiral Pakenham commanding the Third Battle-Cruiser Squadron in *New Zealand* says in his post battle report: 'In the Battle-Cruiser Fleet it had been constantly assumed that German battle-cruisers would never be found far from adequate support, and thus no surprise was felt when the battle fleet was sighted.' Perhaps *no surprise* is too strong a term; for example, Commander Bingham, left on his crippled destroyer *Nestor* said afterwards of sighting this fleet: 'This was more than I had ever bargained for . . . I was dumbfounded to see what it was, the main body of the German High Seas Fleet.' Or again, a report from an officer in the *Tiger*: 'The generality of officers and men were certainly unaware that anything was likely to happen' on this particular day.

vicinity could be dealt with adequately, continued his northerly advance with the battleships. His fleet was still disposed as it had been since leaving the mined area: his squadrons in line ahead, in the order of Third, First and Second squadrons,[1] extending over some five and a quarter miles as they advanced at a stately fourteen knots. Subsequent reports that the British 'light forces' had withdrawn to the northward and westward and were being pursued by his light scouting groups gave Scheer no reason to alter his view, or the course or speed of his fleet.

At 3.36 p.m. however, Scheer received a signal from Hipper that enemy 'heavy forces'—our battle-cruisers only—were in sight. This was unexpected, but, to Scheer, excellent news for here apparently was the detached enemy force he had been hoping to encounter. Scheer promptly closed up his battle line and signalled his ships to clear for action. Nine minutes later, he received a further encouraging signal from Hipper—that the latter was now engaging six British battle-cruisers on a south-easterly course, and was leading them therefore straight down to his Commander-in-Chief's fleet as had been planned in advance.

To Scheer the signal must have indicated the sort of situation he had hoped to create and one that could give him the tactical advantage—in part at least—which he had been seeking. He later confessed to some anxiety for his five battle-cruisers as they faced Beatty's six and he considered that his immediate task was to relieve the pressure on Hipper's materially weaker force.[2] By 4.05 he presumably felt it would be wise to anticipate events so he altered the course of his fleet by divisions in succession to the north-westward, increasing speed to 15 knots, in order to be in a better position to cut off any premature retreat which Beatty's force might be compelled to consider. A quarter of an hour later, with the general position still somewhat obscure, Scheer decided to move his whole fleet bodily westward so that when Hipper finally brought Beatty into sight the British force would be between two fires—between the German battle cruisers and the German Battle Fleet: the end should then come quickly. Scheer, therefore, signalled to his fleet to alter course by divisions to the westward.

This movement had just begun when he received, from Rear Admiral Boedicker of the Second Scouting Group, an urgent signal, reporting the hitherto unknown presence of the Fifth Battle

---

[1] The German fleet organisation *Keil-Linie* 3–1–2 meant squadrons in line ahead in the order of squadrons named.
[2] Scheer's *Despatch*, in *Battle of Jutland: Official Despatches*.

ADMIRAL SIR JOHN JELLICOE, GCB, KCVO
Jellicoe commanded Britain's Grand Fleet from 4th August 1914 to 28th November
1916.

VICE-ADMIRAL REINHARD SCHEER
commanded the German High Seas Fleet: a determined advocate of 'sink-at-sight' U-boat warfare, he used the outcome of the Battle of Jutland to support his case.

VICE-ADMIRAL FRANZ HIPPER
who commanded the German battle-cruisers at Jutland. A courageous and resolute leader who eschewed politics, he was Germany's greatest sea commander in World War I.

Squadron on the scene of the engagement. It will be recalled that *Barham* had fired on these light cruisers from four o'clock onwards and had driven them off to the eastward; then at 4.08 p.m. he had opened fire on Hipper's rear ships. The signal now in front of Scheer, moreover, reported in error that there were five 'Queen Elizabeths' present, whereas there were only four; this error, oddly enough, was perpetuated in German records throughout the battle.[1]

This report completely changed Scheer's plans, for to the German admiral—still completely ignorant of the loss of *Indefatigable* and *Queen Mary*—it at once seemed that Hipper with five battle-cruisers against six British battle-cruisers supported by 'five' powerful battleships must indeed be in a critical position. The German admiral, therefore, promptly negatived his fleet's turn to the west, almost as soon as it had commenced, and swung his squadrons back on to their former north course. He now felt that everything depended upon an efficient and speedy junction between himself and Hipper, to whom he signalled his position, course and speed: eleven minutes later, at 4.32 p.m., his leading battleships could see the distant shapes of ships in action—our own battle-cruisers engaging Hipper. Almost immediately afterwards a light cruiser—*Southampton* with her three consorts in excellent station astern of her—was seen approaching the German van, and was fired upon by ships of his first and third squadrons but without effect.

Scheer rapidly digested the situation as Hipper's battle-cruisers swung round to starboard and dropped into station ahead of his battle line. Beatty's battle-cruisers had turned northward, and were presumably endeavouring to escape. The 'Queen Elizabeths' had not yet turned, however, and making a fire-distribution signal (4.45 p.m.) to his leading ships, Scheer ordered them a minute later to open fire. At the same time, he set his fleet onto a pursuing course, turning them in divisions once again to a northwesterly course, straight for the British force. Beatty's battle-cruisers were almost out of his range, but Scheer's leading ships quickly began to concentrate on the Fifth Battle Squadron, and especially on their turning point, as they turned to the northwards some two or three minutes later.

Closing the British squadron rapidly, and with his fleet in quarter line, Scheer decided at 4.53 p.m.—just as the battleships were passing *Lion*—to press them as hard as he could, and ordered the speed to be increased. His leading squadron of 'Königs', his most modern Dreadnoughts, working up to 22 knots, outstripped the rest of his

---

[1] See Scheer's *Despatch, passim: Official Despatches.*

fleet: his slow Dreadnoughts of the Second Squadron in the rear began to drop back.

(ii)

The position at five o'clock was therefore that Beatty had just sighted Hipper's battle-cruisers again and had resumed the engagement, firing at a range of 17,000 yards in indifferent visibility. On the other hand the British battle-cruisers were almost out of sight of Scheer's van, their range being over 22,000 yards. The Fifth Battle Squadron had turned successfully, although under a hail of fire from the High Seas Fleet concentrated on their turning point at 22,000 yards; but the range was closing and soon after the turn, destructive hits were visible on the British battleships. To Scheer's disappointment, none of them was disabled: they passed majestically northwards on their way through a forest of water splashes.

Evan-Thomas, moreover, was quickly in action again. His two leading ships were ranging on Hipper's battle-cruisers, his two rear ships firing at the advancing 'Königs' and rapidly getting their range. Astern of them, the Second Light-Cruiser Squadron was coming round also to the northward. From this position Commodore Goodenough continued to observe and report the enemy's movements, although, for the next half hour, his squadron was continually under fire from the German battleships; none of his ships was hit. With Scheer pressing ahead on a north-westerly course, and Hipper still steering to the southward, firing from the battle-cruisers was resumed soon after the turn; but after *Lion* had fired only a few salvoes at *Von der Tann*, Hipper had turned sixteen points and in the ensuing smoke had been temporarily lost from view. The German battle-cruisers were round to the northward, however, by about 4.55 p.m., and after a six-minute break the British squadron resumed their fire upon them at a range of over 15,000 yards, the German ships quickly replying. The light conditions, however, were still very bad for our gunners in that direction; almost at once *Lion* was again heavily hit, causing a fire which—had her magazine not been flooded and the doors closed—might well have been the end of her.

Before this, at about 4.35 p.m., the 11th half-flotilla of German destroyers under the orders of Commander Schultz, had begun to work ahead of Hipper's scouting group in order to make an attack on the British lines.[1] Having got ahead of *Lützow* by 4.45 p.m. he

[1] Scheer's *Despatch. Jutland Despatches.*

turned sharply to starboard and at full speed advanced to launch an attack upon Beatty's force. Before he could reach his firing position, however, Beatty's battle-cruisers had turned northward, and the Fifth Battle Squadron was obscured. Even so, at 4.55 p.m. Commander Schultz' destroyers fired their torpedoes and hastened back to the disengaged side of the First Scouting Group: none of those torpedoes was so much as seen by the British ships.

After Beatty had turned to the north-westward the range opened but the visibility to the eastward appeared to improve, although still only the enemy's flashes were clearly visible. On the other hand, the German gunners appear about this time to have been handicapped— for the first time—by the sun behind the British force, which, appearing out of low cloud from time to time, shone straight into their eyes. The intermittent firing of these few minutes was, therefore, not without some British success; *Tiger*, firing as regularly as a metronome, hit *Seydlitz* at 5.06 p.m. and four minutes later hit *Von der Tann* as well with a full salvo finally putting her turrets out of action at a range of 18,800 yards. Previously she had also straddled the *Derfflinger*.[1] By ten minutes past five, however, the enemy battle-cruisers could no longer be seen from *Lion* and within a couple of minutes were out of sight of the whole British line. *Lion* and her consorts then ran out of range, speed was reduced to 24 knots and silence descended on the battle-cruisers of both sides.

Two British destroyers now chose, upon their own initiative, to deliver a gallant—but abortive—torpedo attack: *Onslow* (Lieutenant-Commander Tovey)[2] and *Moresby* (Lieutenant-Commander Alison) having provided a screen to the seaplane-carrier *Engadine*, and now rejoining their Admiral's flag, noticed an opportunity to make an attack, and soon after five o'clock, when the range was opening between the big ships, set off together at speed to close Hipper's battle-cruisers. As they did so, they soon came under heavy and accurate fire from the four light cruisers of Boedicker's Second Scouting Group now off Hipper's bow, and both British destroyers were forced to abandon their attack. *Onslow*, turning to port, returned to the British line and rejoined her 13th flotilla; *Moresby*, however, having turned to starboard, sighted the van of Scheer's battle fleet and closing it to within 9,000 yards fired a long-range torpedo, at the 6th ship in the line: it missed. She, then, too returned at full speed and under heavy fire, to rejoin her consorts at the head of the British line.

[1] Keyes. *Naval Memoirs.*
[2] Later to be Commander-in-Chief, Home Fleet in the Second World War.

In the battle-scarred battle-cruisers there was now a lull in the action for some twenty-five minutes: the first real break since the engagement had begun. Officers and men who had been below or in cramped spaces during the fight, came up into the air on deck to stretch their limbs, and take in the scene, to exchange gossip and 'buzzes'. It was a lull which afforded a few minutes also in which to remove the dead, and transfer the wounded to more comfortable surroundings; there was also time to examine and repair ship damage where possible.

At 5.16 p.m. Admiral Jellicoe signalled his position, course and speed, and this information, picked up by the *Princess Royal*, was received in *Lion* at about 5.30 p.m. Unaware then of any discrepancies in either his own or his Commander-in-Chief's position, Beatty calculated that Jellicoe bore about 'north-16°-west' from him, and that by altering course to the north-north-east—some six points to starboard—he would be able to make good contact with the centre of Jellicoe's cruiser screen. At 5.34 p.m., *Lion* therefore hauled round on this new course, the three battle-cruisers following her: ahead of them the First and Third Light-Cruiser Squadrons conformed. Just before turning, however, at 5.33 p.m. *Falmouth*, then some four and a half miles in advance of *Lion*, sighted several cruisers approaching from the north-west.[1] These cruisers were quickly recognised as our armoured cruisers *Black Prince* and *Duke of Edinburgh*, the westernmost ships of Admiral Jellicoe's advance screen: *Black Prince* was then steering eastward to close in upon the screen's centre because of the poor visibility. At 5.36 p.m., three minutes after the sighting, *Falmouth* signalled by searchlight to *Black Prince*:

Battle-cruisers engaged to the south-south-west of me.

At this time, *Black Prince* was thirteen miles due south of Jellicoe, so 'visual communication' had been established between the advanced forces of the Grand Fleet and the Battle-Cruiser Force.

Beatty had eight light-cruisers ahead of him, all of them with a speed of 26 knots or more and when he turned northward at 4.54 p.m. they had been twenty miles to his north-westward—twenty miles nearer to Jellicoe. Even at five o'clock, when they were closing in on their force commander, they were still ten and a half miles to the northward; Beatty had thus lost the opportunity of disposing these light-cruisers as a lookout screen and visual link well ahead of

[1] Rear-Admiral Napier's Report (Third Light-Cruiser Squadron) gives the time as 5.33 p.m., but his signal log gives it as 5.30 p.m.

his battle-cruisers. Had this 'screen' been pushed even ten miles further ahead it would have established 'visual communication' with the Battle Fleet minutes earlier, and to the Commander-in-Chief in *Iron Duke* every minute counted. Unfortunately, when *Falmouth* did meet *Black Prince*, she had no vital information that she could pass on—information as to the bearing and distance of the van of the enemy battle fleet; this was what Jellicoe needed—information in terms of the relative positions between visual links.

Three miles astern of the British battle-cruisers, however, the four battleships of Evan-Thomas' Fifth Battle Squadron could have provided enlightenment, for they had been continuously in action both with Hipper's battle-cruisers and with the van of Scheer's High Seas Fleet since their turn to the north at 5.01 p.m.

To quote a German appreciation of their great rearguard action:

... the Fifth Battle Squadron bore more and more the full brunt of the battle, effectively affording cover to the British battle-cruisers.

Since before five o'clock the divisions of Scheer's battle fleet had been closing the range, his most modern units in the Third Squadron closing it at 22 knots. Already under heavy fire from this squadron, Evan-Thomas found that in spite of his maximum 25 knots he could not open the range on account of the convergence of his and the German course. He knew quite well that he could lessen the punishment his ships were taking if he turned away to the westward out of range; but that, he also knew, would delay junction with Admiral Jellicoe and would uncover the rear of the battle-cruisers. So he held his ground and his stout hulls took their punishment—they shuddered to the shock as enemy shells struck home, and held on their path apparently unmoved.[1] *Barham* and *Valiant* in these minutes were each hit, but astern of them *Warspite* and especially the *Malaya* at the tail of the line were hit repeatedly and suffered considerable damage. At one stage *Warspite* was seen by German watchers to haul out of the line, only to resume her station a few minutes later, firing as steadily as ever. *Malaya*, the last in the line, was heavily hit and developed a temporary list. She was even considering firing salvoes from her starboard six-inch battery into the water to imitate enemy 'short' shots as a ruse to deceive the German fire control and ease the pressure; but before this could be put into effect, a German heavy shell burst in her six-inch gun battery causing considerable damage and loss of life. She held on her way, with the German battleships

[1] During this part of the action most of the casualties suffered by the Fifth Battle Squadron were occasioned; *Barham* had 63, *Warspite* 7, *Malaya* 92 casualties.

concentrating their fire upon *Warspite* and herself, while *Barham* and *Valiant* continued to fire intermittently at Hipper's battle-cruisers whenever they could be seen. The hard hit battle squadron had been ordered by Beatty to prolong the line astern of him, and to the best of their loyal ability they were doing so.

Nor did the Germans during this grim half an hour have things entirely their own way.

> The fire of the battle squadron had been quite effective . . . the *Grosser Kurfürst, Markgraf, Lützow, Derfflinger* and *Seydlitz* had all been hit by them and their salvoes had been continuously falling around the enemy ships that were within range, throwing up tremendous columns of water and showering the German decks with splinters.[1]

During the lull after Beatty had temporarily steamed out of range of Hipper's battle-cruisers, Scheer seems to have imagined from the sounds that the fire of Beatty's battle-cruisers was diminishing under punishment. He therefore ordered 'General Chase' at 5.26 p.m., unaware that his battle-cruisers were still suffering at the hands of the British battleship squadron, and that *Von der Tann* was no longer a fighting unit, and was only keeping her station in Hipper's line to prevent an increased concentration of fire upon her consorts if she fell out.

In obedience to his Commander-in-Chief's orders to chase, Hipper at 5.27 p.m. immediately headed his ships three points to port to close Beatty's force once more and increased speed. The German Battle Fleet's course, slanting north-westward now, brought it directly on to the two crippled British destroyers *Nestor* and *Nomad*. Admiral Scheer in his despatch, somewhat unworthily, commented later upon their destroyer battle:

> Our [the German] *V-27*[2] and *V-29* were sunk by heavy shell-fire; the crews of both boats were rescued under enemy fire by *V-26* and *S-35*. On the enemy's side, two destroyers [*Nestor* and *Nomad*] were . . . so badly damaged that they were left behind . . . The enemy made no attempt to save the crews of their boats.[3]

How little the admiral really understood us: he knew all the tricks of the sea, but little of its traditions. As has been recounted elsewhere *Petard*, (Lieutenant-Commander Thomson) had offered his help to *Nestor* but was ordered to obey the 'Recall' by his Senior Destroyer Officer. A quarter of an hour after that, the officers

---

[1] *Krieg zur See.*
[2] Scheer was wrong: *V-27* was torpedoed by *Petard*.
[3] Scheer's *Despatch.*

and men of the two disabled destroyers could see in the distance 'an apparently endless procession of German battleships' coming up towards them from the south. They dealt with *Nomad* (Lieutenant-Commander Whitfield) first, and there was no reply that could be made by a single destroyer to a dozen German Dreadnoughts firing their broadsides at what soon was little more than a hulk. It seemed to one of the British survivors that the ship was being used for target practice 'and was rapidly being turned into something remarkably like a Gruyère cheese.' Her gallant crew had, however, got the torpedo tubes loaded for the last time, and with the enemy battle line little more than 2,000 yards away—point-blank range—they fired their torpedoes. Then with the riddled ship sinking fast by the stern, the survivors slipped over the side and swam clear, to be picked up by German hands and to spend the rest of the war in a German prison camp: seventy-two officers and men became prisoners of war, eight had been killed.

Nestor's Captain (Commander The Honourable E. B. S. Bingham) perforce had to watch what happened to his flotilla-mate: it left him in no doubt as to the fate in store for his own ship. *Nestor* was lying rather further ahead, and her turn must come next. In the few minutes that were left he and his sub-lieutenant kept all hands busy, throwing confidential books and charts and other secret documents over the side, lowering and provisioning the ship's boats and rafts, and in other mind-occupying tasks. When the approaching German fleet was less than 10,000 yards away, the battleships opened fire on *Nestor* with their 5.9-inch secondary armaments, and within seconds the doomed destroyer was engulfed in a whirlwind of smoke, spray and shrieking shells. There was just time at the torpedo tubes for one final gesture of defiance—the destroyer's gun armament would have been useless against these armoured mastodons. As the torpedo tubes sights came on, the last torpedo was fired, and as her commander reported long afterwards 'was seen to run well'. The end followed swiftly: *Nestor*, holed in a dozen places, began to settle by the stern, listing to starboard. Her captain ordered 'Abandon Ship' and the boats and floats and rafts alongside were promptly filled with the survivors and drew clear. The Commander with his First Lieutenant[1] were ready to take their place in a float—the last to leave the ship— when Commander Bingham asked his First Lieutenant, half jokingly: 'Where shall we go now, Number One?' The other answered: 'To Heaven, I trust, sir.' A moment later the First Lieutenant was hit by a bursting shell as he turned to comfort a dying man.

[1] Lieutenant M. J. Bethell, R.N.

The captain left his ship, and the boat pushed clear. Very soon *Nestor* raised her battered hull erect—her colours still flying—and then slid back to the sea bed. Her crew—lying off in their floats—gave three cheers for the ship, and sang 'God Save the King' as the German vessels headed for them. They too were picked up and became prisoners of war: out of *Nestor's* complement of 86 officers and men, only two officers, including her gallant First Lieutenant, and five men perished. It would indeed have been fitting if at least one of the defiant torpedoes they had fired had found a billet in a German battleship's hull but the Sea Gods were not so disposed.[1]

(iii)

It had been just after 5.35 p.m. when the second of the two destroyers went down. Hipper, with his battle-cruisers in echelon, was then obeying his Commander-in-Chief's instructions to close; Admiral Sir David Beatty was also closing the range on his north-north-east course. The lull in the action was over, and Beatty had already signalled his battle-cruisers to prepare to resume the battle. At 5.40 p.m., the German battle-cruisers suddenly emerged from a thin bank of mist to the south-eastward, and at a range of 14,000 yards the British battle-cruisers poured in a rapid and concentrated fire, salvo after salvo, dropping on and around their enemy. The tricks of light and visibility for a while went in the British favour, and they took full advantage of this. At the same time, Hipper's ships became clearly visible to Evan-Thomas' leading battleships, *Barham* and *Valiant*, who also poured in a devastating fire while *Warspite* and *Malaya* continued to pound at Scheer's battleships whenever they got a glimpse of them. During the next nine or ten minutes, with the fickle sun dazzling Hipper's gunners, the German battle-cruisers suffered very considerable damage, hits being registered on the *Lützow* and *Seydlitz*, and fires breaking out on both these ships; *Derfflinger* was hit in her forward torpedo compartment, causing damage which started flooding, so that the ship was soon seen to be down by the head.

Hipper was, moreover, in imminent danger of having his T crossed by Beatty, who at twenty-four knots was racing to the north-north-eastward and cutting athwart the German track far ahead. Beatty had almost reached the desired position, when Hipper, with half his guns no longer able to bear, was obliged to give ground, leading round to the north-east to open the range. Six miles

[1] Commander Bingham was subsequently awarded the Victoria Cross.

to the south-westward of *Lion*, the two rear ships of the Fifth Battle Squadron—*Warspite* and *Malaya*—kept up their reply to the German battle fleet's fire, hitting *König*—the leading German battleship, and others in her line, and causing the enemy fire to slacken as Scheer turned them more to the northward to conform to Hipper's latest opening movement.

Scheer was undoubtedly a puzzled man at this moment: he knew almost to a yard where Beatty's battle-cruisers and battleships were, yet since around 5.40 p.m. he had been hearing faint sounds of gunfire to the *north-eastward* as well. It seems now that he must have begun gradually to sense that 'something', as yet unseen, lay ahead. At 5.46 p.m. he altered the course of his battlefleet to the northward, directing his leading ship to take guide of the fleet. During the 'chase', the varying maximum speeds of his squadrons had caused his line to straggle very badly; at 5.50, therefore, he reduced the speed of his leading squadrons to 15 knots to enable the line to close up, and his slow pre-Dreadnought squadron to catch up in the rear. Five minutes later, with his line much less straggled, he increased speed again; he was, however, if anything, more puzzled than ever, for the fainter rumble of distant gunfire to the north-east was now joined by the deeper rumble of heavy guns in the same direction. A little later, a signal reached Scheer, delayed in transmission because *Lützow's* wireless had been shot away, which turned his puzzlement into anxiety for it reported that Hipper's light cruisers of the Second Scouting Group were in action with British forces well to the north-eastward.

Hipper's battle-cruisers were indeed in a sad plight at that time: his turn north-easterly to prevent Beatty from crossing the T had been of little avail, and the torment of his battle-cruisers continued until at 5.53 p.m. Hipper was obliged to turn due east, directly away from the guns of the Fifth Battle Squadron, and opening the range from the battle-cruisers. The mists seemed to be drifting and gathering more and more densely in patches around Hipper, yet through it, and from ahead on his new course, he could make out the sounds of gunfire quite distinctly: they were the same sounds Scheer could hear, but Hipper was much nearer to them, and they were very real to him. He was now really 'hard-pressed, and unable to return the [enemy's] fire effectively; the position of the German battle-cruisers was becoming unbearable'.[1] Hipper's flagship, *Lützow*, upon which both *Lion* and *Princess Royal* had been concentrating an accurate and rapid fire with much advantage from the

[1] Scheer's *Despatch*.

changed visibility, had been straddled repeatedly and hit more than once at ranges between 13,000 and 14,000 yards. She was now ablaze and seriously damaged, and at 5.59 p.m. was obliged to draw out of the line. Beatty and his battle-cruisers now had not only the advantage of speed, but also of visibility over their German opponents, and they were making good use of it. Referring to this latter part of the battle, a German eye-witness has said:

> Admiral Beatty, by completely outflanking us in spite of our high speed, accomplished an excellent tactical manoeuvre, and his ships carried out an admirable feat of technique. He accomplished the famous 'Crossing the T', compelled us to alter course, and brought us into such a position that we were completely enveloped by the English battle fleet.[1]

With his flagship burning, Admiral Hipper put his helm over, and swung his battle-cruisers round to starboard in a wide circle, harking back to the support of Scheer and the battle fleet.

To the westward of him, Beatty's battle-cruisers had reached their haven at last. At 5.55 p.m. the starboard wing column of Jellicoe's battle fleet had suddenly come in sight out of the misty background at a distance of only four and a half miles on *Lion's* port bow. Almost at the same time, *Lion* was sighted from *Marlborough*, flying the flag of Sir Cecil Burney, second in command of the Grand Fleet. The Scouting Admiral was home; Evan-Thomas with his battleship squadron also came into sight—firing intermittently—a few minutes later. Between them, they had drawn the pursuing German fleet towards Jellicoe's battle fleet and their joint efforts had forced the German van to turn eastward.

Beatty now hoisted to his ships the flag signal to alter course to north-east by east—right across the front of the battle fleet—speed 25 knots. He clearly had the twofold intention of following the old tactical axiom—'Never lose hold of the enemy's van', and also of complying with the Battle Order to prevent the enemy forces from obtaining information of Jellicoe's movements.

There was, however, still Beatty's primary duty as a scouting admiral to be discharged, for he had been in command of the Grand Fleet's advanced scouting forces. Admittedly, he had not got into 'visual communication' with his Commander-in-Chief as early as he might have done; he had not used the eight light cruisers who had kept steadily ahead of him as an advanced screen to pass in early news of the enemy's movements. Indeed his light cruisers were already heading eastward, merging into the stream of cruisers. They

[1] Von Hase, *Kiel and Jutland*.

had not even been able to comply with Beatty's flag signal at 5.47 p.m. to attack the enemy with torpedoes. Having set no screen, the 'scouting admiral' had had to make direct contact between his flag-ship and the battle fleet. As Beatty turned his squadron to hasten eastward across the van of the Grand Fleet, *Lion's* battle-scarred sides could be seen clearly, her Q turret, bleakly staring over the port side with its guns elevated, and a small fire apparently still smoulder-ing amidships—mute witness to the two and a quarter hours of grim fighting.

Five minutes before *Lion* had been sighted by *Marlborough* the latter ship had signalled by semaphore to Jellicoe: 'Gun flashes and heavy firing on starboard bow (5.50).' The Commander-in-Chief had taken up this point, by a searchlight signal two minutes later: 'What can you see?' To which *Marlborough* had instantly replied: 'Our battle-cruisers bearing south-south-west, steering east, *Lion* leading ship,' adding, five minutes later, also by searchlight, 'Fifth Battle Squadron bearing south-west', as Evan-Thomas and his battleships hove in sight.

Within three minutes *Lion*, as she headed north-eastward across the front, could be seen clearly from *Iron Duke's* bridge, and Jellicoe signalled his 'scouting admiral' direct by searchlight at 6.01 p.m.:

> Commander-in-Chief to Senior Officer, Battle-Cruiser Force: Where is the enemy's battle fleet?

But there was no reply to this vital question; no reply to the question to which the Commander-in-Chief so urgently needed a positive answer. There was no reply, because his scouting admiral did not know; he had not had the enemy battle fleet in sight since just after five o'clock!

5

Interludes and Consequences

ONE of the remarkable features of naval warfare is the way in which Destiny seems inexorably to draw rival fleets of warships to an inevitable common meeting point: Nelson's quest for Villeneuve led him through the length and breadth of the Mediterranean and across the Atlantic and back before an eventual meeting off Cadiz; Rodzhestvensky's fleet steamed over fifteen thousand miles, only to be sunk by Togo at Tsu-Shima in the Straits of Korea: in 1914 a squadron under Graf von Spee had been drawn from Tsing-Tau across the Pacific, while Cradock's force of obsolete British cruisers steamed from the English channel down the Atlantic and round the Horn, to meet off Coronel on the bleak Chile coast.

The distances involved with Jutland were admittedly not as great as these—a mere three hundred miles or so from the Navy's Scottish bases and 250 miles from Germany's Jade River. But with all the vast expanse of the unmined North Sea for their rendezvous the battle fleets of Britain and Germany were now drawn as inexorably as ever to one small stretch of waters above the Fisher and Jutland Banks. As if to mock at mortals' efforts, the Sea Gods on Olympus on this day also provided swirling mists to hide the battle fleets' approach, just as they had given a fretting Nelson headwinds, and just as they had belaboured Cradock with a flurry of politically inspired instructions and a rising gale in which his ships' main-deck guns could not be worked.

Through the early afternoon, Admiral Jellicoe had been advancing steadily with his battle fleet in war cruising formation at fourteen knots towards his 2.00 p.m. rendezvous. By two o'clock he had been by his dead reckoning nineteen and a half miles from the position from which he had previously told Beatty he would head towards Horns Reef.[1] This delay had been occasioned by the necessity

[1] Position by 'dead reckoning' is calculated from course and distance steamed from the last known 'fix' by either celestial or terrestrial observation. The *Iron Duke's* noon position was 58° 09′ North, 02° 59′ East, as entered in her signal log; at 2.00 p.m. her position by dead reckoning was thus 57° 45′ North, 04° 15′ East. In actual fact, her *real* position at that time was four miles nearer to the rendezvous—she was only 15½ miles from it instead of 19½ as had been calculated. This is not an unimportant detail.

of examining passing merchant and fishing vessels sighted en route.

Since the Admiralty's 12.30 p.m. telegram implying that the German High Seas Fleet was not at sea, there had been no clear reason for any especial hurry. This can be seen from signals made by *Iron Duke* to the destroyers at three o'clock, to the effect that they were to 'bank fires' in boilers not required for a speed of 21 knots. Even when *Galatea's* early enemy sighting reports began to reach the fleet flagship there was no immediate reason to change the speed: these reports indicated—at first—only a local brush with destroyers or light cruisers which were apparently withdrawing towards their bases.[1] *Galatea's* later signal reporting that these enemy light forces were steering north and north-west and were apparently chasing her left the situation approximately as it was before, for the positions given suggested that the enemy might be being led towards the Grand Fleet. To be ready for any eventualities, however, as his fleet had only raised steam for 18 knots, Jellicoe had ordered steam for full speed to be raised; neither *Galatea's* further signal 25 minutes after her first, reporting smoke 'as of a fleet', nor her later signal, that the smoke came from 'seven vessels and accompanying destroyers steering north', altered the strategic situation.

They only confirmed that the enemy ships, whatever they were, were making a general north and north-west movement. Jellicoe was undoubtedly of the opinion from this evidence that the British light forces were leading enemy light forces north and westward and in his direction: he could probably also visualise that Beatty, mindful of previous similar experiences, would be working round behind the enemy to cut off their line of escape. Jellicoe had ceased zigzagging in his battle fleet, thereby increasing his fleet's speed of advance, and twelve minutes later, at 2.55 p.m., he had amplified his early steam-raising signal into 'Raise Steam with Utmost Despatch', increasing speed to 18 knots—the maximum speed for which the fleet had steam at that time. A few minutes later, Admiral Jellicoe had almost reached his turning point, and two minutes after three he 'wheeled' his fleet towards Horns Reef, on a south-east by south course as planned.

Having turned to the new course, he now ordered his cruiser screen to assume 'organisation *LS16*'—the line of armoured cruisers to be sixteen miles in advance of the fleet flagship, the linking ships to advance proportionate distances. His intention was clearly to

[1] *Galatea's* 2.30 p.m. signal reported that the 'enemy in sight' was steering south-south-east—i.e. towards Heligoland.

extend the range of visibility of his fleet in preparation for a possible meeting with the enemy light forces.

This order to the cruiser screen to push forward another six miles was likely to place a strain upon such elderly vessels; the battle fleet was already steaming at 18 knots and, within the next half-hour or so, was to increase to 20 knots; the middle-aged armoured cruisers, in 1916, had a best maximum speed of $21\frac{1}{2}$ or 22 knots at most. They would have a hard struggle to claw ahead: had they been in their correct position at the time of Jellicoe's signal ordering them to push ahead, they might well have been almost as far in advance of the battle fleet as the admiral desired by about six o'clock. Unfortunately, even then, at three o'clock, they were considerably astern of their proper station and in consequence were never able to get very much ahead at all.

Hood was already, with the three 'Invincibles', and two light cruisers,[1] twenty miles in advance of the battle fleet. This force was, in fact, actually four or five miles *in advance* of its proper station so that the spearhead of Jellicoe's look-out screen was already over 25 miles ahead of the fleet flagship.

The brilliant but fiery Rear-Admiral Hood, a direct descendant of the redoubtable Admiral Hood famous for his part in the wars of the later eighteenth century, had seen a particular significance in *Galatea's* early reports of the enemy heading north and north-west: he visualised that should they catch sight of any of Beatty's heavier ships, they might well attempt to escape by continuing to the northward into the Skagerrak, and thence home by way of the Kattegat to Kiel, since their southern retreat would be blocked. He therefore ceased zigzagging, and at 3.10 p.m. ordered his ships in company to conform to his movements and increasing to 22 knots headed east-south-east—more towards the Skagerrak, where he could cut off any escape by that channel; two minutes later he signalled 'Action Stations' to ships in company. He felt no doubt that a degree of urgency had been added to his situation by a report from *Indomitable* that German wireless signals could be heard strongly, for he ordered his two light cruisers to keep a good lookout; at 3.10 p.m. he signalled by searchlight, via *Chester* and *Minotaur* in the screen, to the Commander-in-Chief to tell him what he had done; Jellicoe, appreciating entirely the reason for this, saw no grounds for

---

[1] The battle-cruisers were the older 25-knot, 12-inch gun ships; *Chester*, ten 5.5-inch guns, was one of two light cruisers which had been building on Merseyside for the Greek government at the outbreak of war, and which had been purchased by Britain in January 1915. *Birkenhead* had been completed in the autumn of that year, but *Chester* was less far advanced and commissioned only in the beginning of May 1916.

any alteration.[1] It was an excellent example of the liberty of action permitted by Jellicoe to flag officers in his command.

With the main fleet continuing towards Horns Reef, and its spearhead gradually diverging more to the northward, Admiral Jellicoe continued to receive the series of reports from further to the south. None of them materially affected the situation or his appreciation of it. At 3.20 p.m. he increased the fleet's speed to 19 knots nonetheless, and had barely done so when two signals came to hand, one from *Nottingham* and a confirmatory one from *Galatea* reporting five columns of smoke to the east-north-east of them, steering west-north-west. There was some intangible sense of change in these two signals: five columns of smoke did have some resemblance to five battle-cruisers. Jellicoe noted, however, that if their course was west-north-west he was still in an excellent position to deal with them should they come north, and instructed the flag officers of his squadrons to inform their divisions of the position.

Soon afterwards the Commander-in-Chief intercepted a signal from Beatty giving his course as east at 25 knots (3.30 p.m.); this could only confirm any impression that existed that Beatty was still trying to cut off the enemy in sight from their home base. For Beatty's information, Jellicoe, therefore, signalled to him the position, course and speed of *Iron Duke*. Barely ten minutes later, however, the whole situation had swiftly changed, for Jellicoe was reading the signal from Beatty reporting five enemy battle-cruisers and a large number of destroyers in sight at 3.35 p.m.

Events now moved fast. At 3.38 p.m. *Falmouth*, some sixteen miles to the northward of Beatty, reported this enemy—presumably battle-cruisers—as steering south-east at 21–25 knots which suggested that the enemy might now be heading back towards Horns Reef. A signal from Beatty seven minutes later, giving the enemy course as south 55° east, confirmed this, but as his previous signal had given the Battle Cruiser Force course as east, at 25 knots, it seemed he was still in a position to cut the enemy's line of retreat.

Five minutes later, Jellicoe was reading *Lion's* signal: 'Am engaging the enemy.'[2] At once Jellicoe ordered the speed of his fleet

---

[1] Some critics have claimed that Hood's move had been ordered by Jellicoe. This is quite incorrect. Cf. *inter alia* Mr. Carlyon Bellairs, MP, *Battle of Jutland*.

[2] Most of these enemy-report signals had given the position of the reporting ship in terms of latitude and longitude; none of which was in agreement with each other; all that could be deduced was that there was an enemy in a certain area, steering south-55°-east. As an example of the unreliability of signalled positions, *Lion* at 3.45 p.m. reported her position as 56° 53′ North, 05° 33′ East, and at 3.50 p.m. as being 56° 33′ North, 05° 31′ East. But *Lion* had been steaming eastwards for these five minutes at 25 knots, as far as Jellicoe was aware, just over two miles in all; while *Lion's* second signalled position was nearly *twenty miles south* of her first one five minutes before.

and its screen to be increased to twenty knots. This was the maximum obtainable for it would leave only one knot in hand for station-keeping even for his most modern ships.

From the meagre information at the Commander-in-Chief's disposal the picture now presented seemed to be the old one of Hipper's battle-cruisers racing for home with Beatty—who had the legs of them—engaging them and doing his utmost to cut off their retreat. So strategically important, however, did Jellicoe consider it that this enemy battle-cruiser squadron should be overwhelmed—the squadron that had caused us so much trouble and bombarded our coasts—that he decided to reinforce Beatty's battle-cruisers, as he had foreshadowed in his sailing signal, as soon as possible. Jellicoe therefore ordered Rear-Admiral Hood with his Third Battle-Cruiser Squadron to 'Proceed immediately to support Battle-Cruiser Fleet': he also gave him Beatty's last signalled position, and the enemy's course as signalled, to assist him in planning his movements.

The sturdy Hood, however, had already once again anticipated his Commander-in-Chief's intentions: at 3.45 p.m., having inter-cepted Beatty's report of five enemy battle-cruisers in sight, he had at once turned southward on his own initiative to support him.

It must have been obvious to Hood that, even with his battle-cruisers going at their best speed, he could not expect to catch up with Beatty who was apparently steering away from him at 25 knots at least. Jellicoe must have realised this also and naturally his thoughts turned to the sufficiency of the force already at Beatty's disposal. He had heard nothing for twenty minutes, so at 4.15 p.m. Jellicoe signalled direct to Admiral Evan-Thomas of the Fifth Battle Squadron: 'Are you in company with Senior Officer, Battle-Cruiser Fleet?' A quarter of an hour later there was the comforting reply, 'Yes. I am engaging enemy. (1630)'.

Then, suddenly, after some anxious waiting, the wireless crackled and there were two electrifying messages from *Southampton*: the first reported an enemy cruiser in sight to the south-east, steering north-east; this was obviously a new enemy. But the second stated 'have sighted enemy battle fleet bearing approximately south-east, course of enemy north (1638)'. These two signals were of crucial importance, for thus far Jellicoe had undoubtedly relied upon the Admiralty's 12.30 p.m. message that the German fleet was in the Jade River—yet here it was, 180 miles from Wilhelmshaven, in sight of one of his scouting cruisers and apparently only some 75–80 miles away, heading northwards towards the Battle Fleet.

Admiral Jellicoe's immediate reaction to this startling information

When the *Queen Mary* blew up ICE-ADMIRAL BEATTY bserved: 'What's the matter with our bloody ships today?'

Beatty's flagship *Lion* was hit on Q turret amidships at 3.57 p.m. (*above*), but was saved by the presence of mind of a mortally wounded Royal Marines major who ordered the ship's magazine flooded.

was to close the Kattegat and Skagerrak to the escape of possible commerce raiders by ordering the Tenth Cruiser (Blockade) Squadron to move to their eastern patrol line. He then signalled to his fleet: 'Enemy battle fleet is coming north'—the most welcome news his officers and men had heard for many a long month. Shortly afterwards, yet another admirable report came in from Commodore Goodenough in *Southampton*, confirming his own views, and giving details of the composition and formation of the enemy fleet. At 4.50 p.m. Jellicoe informed the Admiralty:

> Urgent. Fleet action is imminent.

(ii)

The arrival of this message in Whitehall set in motion long-prepared arrangements. Tugs were ordered to be held in readiness at the principal east coast ports; docks were cleared at the east coast naval bases and on the Tyne for the reception, if necessary, of any of our ships which might be damaged in action and in need of repair on their return. At the Nore, Admiral Bradford, with his Third Battle Squadron of pre-Dreadnought battleships, signalled to the Admiralty that he was proceeding forthwith with his squadron out to the Black Deep and the Swin to cover the approaches to the Thames and the Narrow Seas, and to join there the Third Cruiser Squadron which had sailed from Sheerness on the evening before.

At Harwich, Rear Admiral Tyrwhitt, leader of the Harwich Force of light cruisers and destroyers, had intercepted the earlier signals and now, with the report of the enemy battle fleet in sight before him, telegraphed the Admiralty: 'Have you any instructions? (1645).'

To the Admiralty the strategic position was still too clouded: Jellicoe's signal advising them of the imminence of a fleet action somewhere to the northward did not necessarily guarantee that *all* the German High Seas Fleet would be engaged. This 'imminent action' might be only a feint to draw off our forces to the northward, towards Norway, while a second powerful German force darted out from the Bight to bombard our East Coast, or to raid the shipping in the Downs and the Narrow Seas, or even to make a sortie into the Thames estuary itself. The only force available to meet this now, since the Channel fleet had been dissipated in Middle East adventures, was the Third Battle-Squadron in the Swin, in support of Commodore Tyrwhitt's Harwich Force and of Admiral Bacon's destroyers and 'Monitors' of the Dover Patrol.

Tyrwhitt, however, was becoming more impatient hourly, and reasonably so: twenty-five precious minutes had passed, since his request for instructions, and still no answer. So he sailed, reporting: 'Urgent. I am proceeding to sea. (1710).'

This at least seems to have galvanised some activity in Whitehall; and a peremptory order went out to him from the wireless masts high above the Admiralty building: 'Return at once and await orders. (1725).' The unfortunate Commodore was therefore obliged to return to Harwich, and wait. Although they could not have known it, it was already too late for Tyrwhitt to start; he could not have arrived on the scene much before 4.00 a.m. next morning, 1st June. But it was an anti-climax for the Harwich Force, and, to some extent, a betrayal of Admiral Jellicoe who had been told by the Admiralty by telegram at 5.55 p.m. the previous evening, 'Harwich destroyers will not be sent out *till more is known.*'

For that matter, Jellicoe also would have liked to know much more, as he steered at his fleet's best speed towards the German High Seas Fleet. His chief anxiety at this time was, he has said, 'the uncertainty which still prevailed as to the position of the enemy battle fleet and its formation.'[1]

Between five o'clock and 5.42 p.m., Jellicoe received no information from any source whatsoever; neither Beatty, nor Evan-Thomas, nor Goodenough, nor *Falmouth*, nor *Galatea* seemed to have thought it so necessary that the Commander-in-Chief should have frequent regular and exact information of the enemy's position during the approach. Then, between 5.42 p.m. and 6.00 p.m., he received a veritable torrent of sighting reports, until, at six o'clock, *Marlborough*, leading the right-wing column of his battleships, signalled to the Commander-in-Chief: 'Our battle-cruisers are in sight, bearing south-south-west three to four miles, steering East. *Lion* leading ship (1800).' Maybe positive news of the enemy was at hand at last.

The spate of sighting reports had done little to clear the picture for Jellicoe. Already *Comus*, in the light-cruiser squadron three miles in advance of *Iron Duke*, had reported gunfire and flashes to the southward at 5.40 p.m.; five minutes later, *Defence* had reported ships in action south-south-west of her. Five minutes later still, gunfire and the sparkle of gun-flashes could be seen from *Iron Duke's* upper bridge, dimly visible through the thickening mists off the starboard bow: they were distant, but they were there none the less.

[1] Jellicoe, *Grand Fleet.*

Jellicoe knew that Scheer and the enemy fleet were approaching, but the vital information that he needed was not forthcoming: where exactly was the enemy fleet's van relative to his own? He *had* to know that.

The rival battle fleets were closing the gap between them at a rate of between 35 and 40 knots. The mutter of guns was growing more insistent from the west-south-west right round the horizon to the south-eastward: Admiral Jellicoe was nearing the battlefield. At 5.40 p.m. only just over thirty-two mist-laden miles separated the two battle fleets. To both Admirals, the position now was anxious and obscure: Scheer was beginning to suspect that *something* lay ahead, but he had no idea of Jellicoe's proximity, much less the direction of his approach; Jellicoe *knew* that Scheer was approaching, and he *knew* his rival's course as well; but he did *not* know how far away he was.

(iii)

To add to the other uncertainties, the arena between the two fleets was now filled with a swirling mist. For the next half-hour, it was to be the stage of several entirely separate episodes, detached from any of the larger British and German formations—five episodes that would tend to make confusion still more confusing. But each of these seemingly localised events made an impact upon the leaders of the two fleets; each was linked in some way with the others, yet none was linked with the main fleets themselves.

Since four o'clock, Rear Admiral Hood's three battle-cruisers—*Invincible* (flagship), *Inflexible* and *Indomitable*—had been hurrying southward to find and support Admiral Beatty: with them were the light-cruisers *Canterbury*—as lookout three miles ahead—and *Chester*—six miles off the flagship's starboard beam; four destroyers—*Shark*, *Ophelia*, *Acasta*, *Christopher*—screened ahead. This compact force was steaming through patches of diaphanous mist; the visibility was deceptively variable. In some directions it was as high as 16,000 yards—eight miles—in others as low as 2,000 yards and even less. It seemed as if they were entering an unreal world, silent except for the break of bow-waves and the usual ship noises—and the low and intermittent mutter of distant guns off the starboard bow.

Although on receipt of *Southampton's* report of the enemy battle fleet in sight Hood had hauled up a point to starboard, this course was still not very realistic. Admittedly, *Lion* had not reported her northerly course to anyone, but it could surely have been assumed that in the presence of the enemy battle fleet Beatty would have reverted to the rôle of 'scouting admiral' and would also be steering in a northerly direction to keep in touch with the north-bound enemy. Had Hood shaped a course more south-south-westerly, it would have led to his bringing support to Beatty; as it was, his south-by-east course was to take him 20 miles to the eastward of Beatty. He was to pass him about a quarter-past-five, with the enemy somewhere in the mists between them.

The course, however, although unrealistic, was destined to be fortunate for reasons unknown to Hood at the time.[1]

At 5.25 p.m. *Chester,* nearer to the enemy than were her battle-cruisers, heard the distant rumble of heavy guns on her starboard bow. Reporting this to the Admiral by searchlight she turned to investigate, increasing speed as she did so. After some minutes distant gun flashes could also be seen through the mist, still to starboard. These were the rear battleships of Evan-Thomas' squadron, firing at Scheer's leading ships. One minute later, on the starboard bow there emerged about 5.36 p.m. the dim shape of a three-funnelled cruiser with what appeared to be two destroyers nearby and perhaps four or five miles away. *Chester* must have been sighted at the same time, for the stranger challenged,[2] using the British secret letter current for the day. The enemy had indeed quickly assimilated the information which *Elbing* had passed back to Hipper at 2.26 p.m. At first the stranger had seemed to resemble the three-funnelled 'Galatea' class, but *Chester's* captain was suspicious, for the stranger's tall after-mast, even seen through the mist, did not look quite right. His own position, moreover, seeming to be open to torpedo attack, he turned to a course apparently parallel (north-north-west) with that of the strangers. As *Chester* turned, two other ghost-like cruisers were seen to emerge from the mists in some sort of quarter-line; *Chester* replied to the challenge.

Immediately, at little more than 6,000 yards, the strangers opened fire. *Chester*—a very recently commissioned ship[3]—returned the fire on their second salvo from her port broadside. It was the last salvo her port guns were to fire than day: for even before they could be reloaded, *Chester* was smothered by the fire from the enemy's

---

[1] A northerly course for the Battle-Cruiser Force could easily have been assumed by Hood from *Southampton's* positions given in her 2.45 p.m., 4.38 p.m. and 5.00 p.m. signals. Hood was not to know then that these positions were on average 9 miles to the eastward of *Southampton's* actual position. There is an interesting comment on the reliability of signalled positions in *Indomitable's* report: 'as usual positions of the enemy by wireless did not agree'.

[2] Rear-Admiral von Lützow, *Skagerrak.*

[3] *Chester* had only commissioned for the first time on 2nd May, 1916 at Liverpool.

5.9-inch guns. Her two foremost 5.5-inch guns were put out of action, her port numbers 2 and 3 guns were disabled, her fire-control was knocked out, and her decks reduced to a shambles, with most of the guns' crews killed or wounded. To make matters worse, a fourth enemy light cruiser now appeared from the mist. Captain Lawson had, however, already decided to get out of range as quickly as possible. His main engines were to all intents and purposes still intact, and turning sharply to the north-eastward he strove to extricate his ship at maximum speed from the perilous position in which she stood.

He had unexpectedly encountered Rear-Admiral Boedicker's Second Scouting Group—the light-cruisers *Frankfurt* (the flag-ship), *Pillau*, *Elbing* and *Wiesbaden*.

In the meantime, Rear-Admiral Hood had heard the gunfire and seen flashes much closer than before, and on his starboard hand—the opening of the engagement between *Chester* and the enemy light cruisers. At once at 5.37 p.m. he turned his flagship, without making any signal, sharply to starboard, and *Indomitable* and *Inflexible* followed her round on to a north-westerly course and towards the sound of the guns. Quite soon, several ships could be made out dimly on *Invincible*'s port bow, apparently engaging a single ship—*Chester*—well ahead of them. The three battle-cruisers, therefore, continued to turn gradually to starboard until *Chester* was fine on the flagship's port bow and was nearing sanctuary. The enemy cruisers were still firing on her, having turned to pursue; they seemed too intent on the matter in hand to notice the approach of Nemesis at full speed, and as *Chester* drew nearer to the shelter of Hood's flagship, the battle-cruisers' turrets were already swinging round menacingly on to her tormentors.

Chester crossed *Invincible*'s bow at 5.54 p.m., turning into safety on the disengaged side. On her escape course, her captain had handled his ship brilliantly, dodging salvo after salvo like a snipe, so that only towards the end did an occasional shell reach her. Down below her engine-room staff had responded superbly to the Captain's demand to 'Give her all she's got!' *Chester* was soon steaming 28 knots, yet she had only reached $26\frac{1}{2}$ on her trials some weeks before. The fact that most of her port battery was disabled, that her electric circuits had been severed, that her range-finder had been hit and blown over the side, had not prevented her after gun from firing steadily on the enemy during the escape. But a grim price had been paid: in addition to the damage already mentioned, *Chester* had four large holes along her side at main deck level, her deck was a shambles;

she had been under the 5.9-inch gunfire of three, then four, enemy cruisers for nineteen minutes, and had been hit eighteen times: in that short time two officers and 33 men had been killed, three officers and 39 men wounded. Among the latter was the sight-setter of a forecastle 5.5-inch gun—Boy 1st Class John Cornwall: after his gun had been disabled by enemy shells and most of its crew killed or wounded, and although mortally wounded himself, he had, true to the traditions of the Royal Navy, remained bravely at his post on the left side of the gun, with his headphones strapped to his head, awaiting further orders—orders which never came for unknown to him the communications had been severed. He was only 16½ years old and he died later from his wounds. For his shining example of devotion to duty, no less than his personal courage and gallantry, he was posthumously awarded the Victoria Cross.

As *Chester* ran across *Invincible*'s bows into safety, the battle-cruiser's 12-inch guns opened fire on her German pursuers: *Indomitable* and *Inflexible* followed suit almost immediately.

The four light cruisers of Boedicker's Second Scouting Group had indeed barely settled down to their pursuit of *Chester* when they had come under fire from another unexpected quarter. Only very faintly visible through the mist to the northward, two armoured cruisers had opened fire upon them with their main armament.[1]

Boedicker, quickly considering it prudent to open the range, turned to the south-eastward, thus still keeping some hold on the flying *Chester* and at the same time making a reply to the opponents in the north, whose fire ceased almost as he turned away. Barely had his flagship *Frankfurt* steadied on the new southerly course, at 5.55 p.m., than three large capital ships—unidentifiable because of the mist—were seen off the port bow, a grim apparition indeed. They were obviously British, and heading straight towards him. Even as he sighted them, their 12-inch guns flashed and at a range of only 11,500 yards the shells quickly began to fall in and around the German light cruisers; the range, moreover, fell rapidly as they were on opposite courses, and the four German ships almost at once were deluged with heavy shell fire and by the battle-cruisers' secondary armament fire as well.

The German ships made such reply as lay in their power, opening the range at 5.56 p.m. by turning almost to south. The enemy flagship *Frankfurt*, with admirable promptness, launched four torpedoes at the three large British ships as she turned but the torpedoes passed harmlessly ahead of them. The alteration of course to the

---

[1] These were *Defence* and *Warrior*.

southward was of little use, however, for the smothering fire continued for several minutes until the opposing squadrons, racing past each other at a relative speed of some 50 knots, faded from each other's sight into the mists. By that time the German squadron had been badly mauled: *Wiesbaden* having been heavily hit almost with the opening salvoes, had been obliged to drop out of the line and with both engines damaged was now straggling slowly away to the northward, badly on fire; Rear-Admiral Boedicker's own flagship *Frankfurt* had been seriously damaged by a direct hit; *Pillau* astern of him had been hit under her bridge and in her machinery compartments putting four boilers out of action and seriously reducing her speed.

News of the incident was already on its way to the German Commander-in-Chief: *Wiesbaden*, as she went limping out of line, wirelessed to Admiral Scheer that she had been disabled and was out of control. At 5.56 p.m., when Rear-Admiral Boedicker had first sighted the British battle-cruisers, he had also reported to Scheer that he was engaging 'heavy enemy forces sighted to the northeastward'. This signal was also intercepted by Vice-Admiral Hipper. By way of contrast it is noteworthy that Rear-Admiral Hood failed to make any report whatsoever either to Jellicoe or to Beatty.

The crushing fire of Hood's battle-cruiser squadron was at its height when Boedicker sighted further dangers ahead of him, for a torpedo attack was developing from the four destroyers who had been in company with Hood. When *Invincible* had turned suddenly at 5.40 p.m., these four destroyers had been ahead: the flagship's turn without signal had left them on the starboard quarter, and they too then altered course to conform. In that position, at about 5.50 p.m., their leader, Commander Loftus Jones in *Shark*, had sighted the enemy on his port bow. Increasing speed and steering towards them to attack from ahead with torpedoes *Shark* and her three consorts, *Acasta*, *Ophelia* and *Christopher* at once came under fire from Boedicker's cruisers, although the latter were still half hidden by the shell splashes falling around them from the fire of the battle-cruisers.

As the Second Scouting Group drew nearer, their fire became more concentrated on the four British destroyers. Undeterred by this, *Shark* was about to turn to make his attack when, in the misty distance beyond Boedicker's flagship and ahead of her, Commander Loftus Jones sighted another enemy light cruiser—*Regensburg*—advancing and surrounded by what seemed a very large number of enemy destroyers. Clearly this new force was moving out to make a determined torpedo attack upon Hood's battle-cruisers, and unhesitatingly *Shark* broke off his attack upon Boedicker's three light cruisers and at 6.05 p.m. headed straight towards the newcomers. This move was sudden, but it was not made before his little division had each fired a torpedo into the already battered Scouting Group—these missed.

Frankfurt was thus left to continue on her way southwards, for the moment, still firing into *Shark* and her three consorts who were also coming under an increasingly concentrated fire from the massed destroyers approaching out of the mists. After about four minutes *Shark*, firing with all guns, turned sharply to launch her torpedoes; her division followed suit. Almost at once, under the concentrated fire of the enemy destroyers, *Shark* was hit in the boiler room and brought to a dead stop. Within seconds, her foremost gun was knocked out, her fore steering gear shattered, and then the after gun was put out of action. Commander Loftus Jones had, however, got off one torpedo at *Regensburg*—which missed—and with his solitary midship gun, in charge of Midshipman Smith RNR, continued to reply to overwhelming odds.

Acasta, astern of *Shark*, had turned to fire but, heavily hit, was obliged to draw away out of action: *Ophelia* turned short to avoid serious damage by gunfire, but unable to fire her torpedoes, also withdrew. *Christopher* was also driven out of action, but managed to fire one torpedo before withdrawing independently. Clear of the mêlée, *Christopher* held on to rejoin her flotilla; *Ophelia* circled round for a chance to renew the attack; Lieutenant-Commander 'Joe' Barron of *Acasta*—though driven away—saw that his flotilla-mate *Shark* was stopped and, under heavy fire, turned back to offer assistance. As he drew near, he could see that *Shark* was very badly disabled, but her Captain—Commander Loftus Jones—sent his old friend away, telling him 'not to get sunk for him.' *Acasta* limped sadly away; she was badly holed, but she was able to steam and to steer, and she had torpedoes still ready to fire.

As *Shark* lay stopped, grievously damaged, her Captain and crew at least had the satisfaction of seeing that they had thwarted, if no more, the worst of the heavy attack that was being mounted against Hood's ships, by now out of sight in the mist.

Commodore Heinrich, the second leader of flotillas, had intercepted Boedicker's signal that heavy ships had been sighted and, on his own initiative collecting the destroyers of the German 6th and 9th flotillas around him, had turned eastward in *Regensburg*, to bring what help he could. As he advanced through the mist, he saw the dim shapes of Hood's force, but could not see its composition. Distorted by mist, it seemed to him that it must be a portion of the British battle fleet, and he seems to have passed the news forward.[1] Before Heinrich had advanced far with his destroyers, however, he was ordered by Vice-Admiral Hipper at 5.59 p.m. to promote an attack on the enemy's 'heavy ships' which Hipper could now hear firing ahead of him, as his battle-cruisers hurried eastward to open the range from Evan-Thomas' deadly 15-inch guns. Two minutes later, Hipper, convinced from the near sound of guns ahead, and from Boedicker's recent enemy-report, that heavy ships were to the north and eastward in the mist, turned south-eastwards and five minutes later swung completely round to the south-west to fall back upon the support of the leading German battle squadrons. When he reached his position off the van, having passed on his information and his appreciation of the situation to Admiral Scheer, he turned back north-eastwards at 6.12 p.m. and was round by 6.16 p.m.

Covered now by Hipper's order, Commodore Heinrich with thirty-one destroyers advanced to the attack, only to find *Shark*'s division of four British destroyers in his path, daring to attack him. The necessity of dealing with them spoilt Heinrich's advance and, by the time *Shark* had been brought to a standstill and her consorts driven off, the best chances of attacking Hood had faded into the enveloping mists.

The second half of the 6th flotilla was diverted to protect the Second Scouting Group and after that to circle round the wounded *Wiesbaden:* this half-flotilla fired torpedoes at the departing British battle-cruisers and put up an artificial smoke-and-fog-screen, by floats around the damaged German light cruiser. The first half of the 6th flotilla, further astern of them, also went on to fire its torpedoes. Twelve torpedoes were fired in all—five of them crossed the track of the three battle-cruisers later on, but were seen and avoided. The 2nd and 9th flotillas went forward to deal with *Shark*, who was still firing with her midship gun as they approached.

It is possible that the German flotillas, with a Pisgah view of deathless renown for the German destroyer Service if only they

---

[1] This impression was conveyed to Scheer (cf. his *Despatch*, reproduced in *Battle of Jutland: Official Despatches*) for he said: 'Several battleships appeared, among them the *Agincourt*. The full strength of the enemy could not be ascertained because of the mist.' *Agincourt* was a battleship that had been building for Turkey at the outbreak of war, and taken over by the British Government; she mounted fourteen 12-inch guns and twenty 6-inch, and formed a formidable unit of the Grand Fleet.

could cripple the British battle fleet presumed to be ahead and eastward, had rushed forward on the Commodore's initiative. Hipper's signal converted the gesture into an order, but in either case, the eastward move of this mass of destroyers was a blunder, for it deprived Scheer of their services for any massed destroyer attack upon the British fleet in the immediate future when such an attack would have been of very great value to him.

The German destroyers, baffled and thwarted, had come out this time to give *Shark* the coup-de-grâce: she had only the one gun firing now, and the enemy's gunfire was very heavy as they drew near. Even with his one gun, Commander Loftus Jones was still in the fight and a shell from it soon brought the German destroyer *V-48* to a standstill.[1] The sight of a German destroyer sinking not so far from them at 6.35 p.m. put new heart, if any were needed, into *Shark's* ship's company and they kept up the fight. One by one the crew of the solitary midships gun fell—killed or wounded—until only two men remained; then one more fell out, and the captain, already wounded in face and thigh, stepped up and took that man's place at the gun. A minute later the gun received a direct hit, and the bursting shell took the gallant captain's right leg off above the knee. Though mortally wounded he continued to exhort the surviving crew of the doomed ship; he was obviously worried about his ship's battle ensign, for the gaff from which it had been flying had been shot away. Midshipman Smith appears to have got another—a new ensign—and to have rehoisted it, where it fluttered bravely in the light breeze. Although his strength was ebbing, the ensign flying once again seemed to set the Captain's mind at rest and he was content. The ship's decks were already awash; a stoker pettyofficer put a life-jacket around his mortally wounded Captain and, aided by the few surviving seamen, they placed him on a floating raft alongside. The Captain told them to save themselves, and they took to the water, pushing his float clear just as two German destroyers raced up to hit the brave *Shark* amidships with two torpedoes.

This was the end: *Shark* sank with her colours still flying. Of all that gallant company, only seven men survived and were picked up after midnight, by the Danish merchant ship *Vidar*, who took them straight to Hull; but not before one of the seven had died of exhaustion. Commander Loftus Jones died on his small floating raft a few hours after his ship went down and the raft floated on into the darkness. Two or three weeks later, his body was washed ashore on the coast of Sweden, and there they buried him in the churchyard in the

[1] The German's crew were rescued by other destroyers and the *V-48* later sank.

village of Fischebaksie, like a true Norseman—with a stone to his head and a stone to his feet. His Sovereign rewarded his immortal heroism posthumously with the Victoria Cross.

(iv)

This was not the end of the episode. The destroyer *Ophelia* (Commander Crabbe) it will be recalled, was driven off by enemy gunfire during *Shark's* original attack. She had however circled round hoping to get another chance to fire her torpedoes. It came almost sooner than her Captain had expected, for looming up out of the mists on her bow she sighted Hipper's battle-cruisers turning from a southerly to a south-westerly course as they fell back to the support of Scheer's battleships. This was an opportunity not to be missed and without hesitation *Ophelia* closed to 8,000 yards and fired a torpedo; although she at once encountered heavy fire from *Lützow*, *Derfflinger* and other battle-cruisers, she withdrew successfully and undamaged, and later was able to rejoin her own 4th flotilla. Her torpedo missed, but the deliberate calm of her attack added to Hipper's anxiety, and helped greatly to confirm his (wrong) view that the British fleet was east of him, for surely one solitary destroyer would not attack battle-cruisers alone and without strong support?

Acasta, steaming slowly and sadly away from the stricken *Shark*, headed northwards in the direction of Hood's battle-cruisers. After a few minutes on this course, her Captain, Lieutenant-Commander Barron, was rewarded also by the sight of Hipper's battle-cruisers on his port quarter: they were now coming up fast *from* the south-westward. Hipper had altered course to the eastward at 6.01 p.m. and further round to south-east at 6.05 p.m., turning about three minutes later to the south-westward with the object of taking station ahead of the leading ships of Scheer's battle fleet. As he sighted them, he had turned again in succession to starboard at 6.12 p.m., his ships coming into line on a north-east course at 6.16 p.m. On this course, they were under fire from some British battle-cruisers to the northward, for Lieutenant-Commander Barron could see the shell-splashes sprouting out of the water around them: *Lützow* was still leading, but she was listing and heavily on fire, and seemed to him to offer an ideal target. *Acasta* turned to the attack and pressed on until he was only some 4,500 yards from *Lützow's* starboard bow; then he fired. The torpedo seemed to hit the German flagship, for there was a heavy explosion, but *Lützow* still continued her course.[1]

---

[1] Post-war reports suggested that the torpedo did not hit her.

She was firing now with every gun that would bear upon her puny attacker and *Acasta* turned away under very heavy fire. Holed, her decks a shambles, her steering gear smashed and her machinery crippled she could now neither steer nor, for the moment, stop her engines: so she careered across the water and through the mists until finally she came to a standstill in the path of Jellicoe's battle fleet.

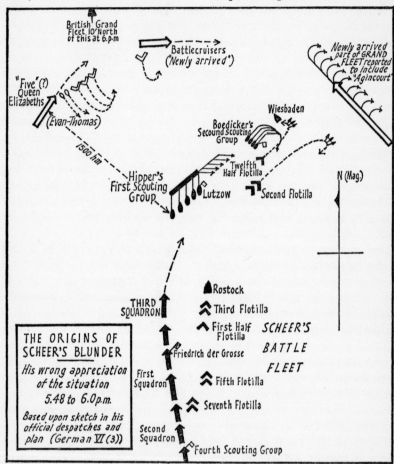

THE ORIGINS OF
SCHEER'S BLUNDER

*His wrong appreciation
of the situation
5.48 to 6.0 p.m.*

Based upon sketch in his
official despatches and
plan (German VI (3))

Nor were Hipper's battle-cruisers persecuted only by *Ophelia* and *Acasta*, from the eastward; on their other—northern—side, Hipper was almost immediately attacked again, by the destroyer *Onslow*. This destroyer of the 13th flotilla attached to Beatty's force, had remained on the battle-cruisers' engaged bow during their run to the northward, and as *Lion* turned eastward after sighting *Marlborough* and the Battle Fleet she was still in the same position off

Lion's bow. Her Captain, Lieutenant-Commander Tovey, now caught sight of *Wiesbaden*, stopped and burning, part-shrouded in artificial smoke and fog, off his starboard bow. She seemed to him to be in a position from which she would be able to fire her torpedoes into Beatty's advancing battle-cruisers, so without delay Tovey, at 6.04 p.m., raced towards her on his own initiative firing as he closed the range from 4,000 to under 2,000 yards.[1] *Wiesbaden*, despite her obvious injuries, pluckily returned this fire as best she could, as *Onslow* pressed in to point-blank range. Tovey then saw that his attack course towards *Wiesbaden* had brought him once more in sight of his old opponents, Hipper's battle-cruisers—now looking somewhat the worse for wear—who were coming towards him on a north-east course. Their leading ship was on fire, and the next two in line seemed rather low down in the water. This was a more worthwhile target and, leaving *Wiesbaden*, he turned to attack them. *Derfflinger's* gunnery officer had seen *Onslow* 'worrying' the injured *Wiesbaden* and at once turned his secondary armament onto the destroyer. Lieutenant-Commander Tovey was, however, determined not to lose a chance, and held on until he was barely 8,000 yards from *Derfflinger's* port bow: he then ordered all four torpedoes to be fired.

Just as the first left its tube, however, a salvo of shells struck *Onslow*, severing her steam-pipes and engulfing her instantly in a cloud of roaring, escaping steam. In the confusion of the moment only one torpedo had been fired: her Captain, under the impression that *all* had gone, and realising that his ship's speed must be falling, decided to withdraw while he could still move ahead, for he was still under fire. His torpedo had missed, but it was quickly reported to him that three torpedo tubes were still loaded. As his withdrawal was taking him close to the *Wiesbaden* again, he fired one at her, hitting her fairly and squarely under her conning tower with a distinct and visible explosion. Even this, however, did not sink the battered cruiser—a tribute to her designers and builders.

Lieutenant-Commander Tovey still had two torpedoes left and ready to fire: he could also now see the head of the German battle fleet coming up behind their battle-cruisers out of the mists some five miles away—yet another target worthy of his torpedoes. His speed was dropping very fast, however, and to turn to an attack course under such conditions was almost to invite destruction. Nevertheless, he turned and attacked the powerful enemy at a range of 8,500 yards, firing both remaining torpedoes. Neither of them scored a hit,

[1] He fired 58 rounds of four-inch.

although the resolution with which the attack had been pressed forced Scheer to manoeuvre to avoid them.

Although holed, *Onslow* remained afloat: eventually, as her feed tanks had been hit, her steam failed altogether and at about seven o'clock she lay still. The thunder of battle had passed away, and the scene had fallen silent. She had taken eight hits, five of them from 5.9-inch shells. The destroyer was now paralysed and drifting, and her crew busied themselves plugging holes as best they could, and with sublime optimism preparing to be taken in tow! At 7.15 p.m., there came to the crippled *Onslow* the destroyer *Defender* (Lieutenant-Commander Palmer), herself hit in the boiler-room by a 12-inch shell and able to steam at only ten knots. Kipling's immortal words have told the tale of the 'cripple' with the 'paralytic' in tow, of how they set off that evening for home—and how they reached it.

The final episode of this 'interlude in arms' was of a very different character from those preceding it.

The armoured-cruisers of the First Cruiser Squadron—*Defence* (Rear-Admiral Sir Robert Arbuthnot), *Warrior, Duke of Edinburgh* and *Black Prince*—and of the Second Cruiser Squadron—*Minotaur* (Rear-Admiral Heath), *Shannon, Cochrane,* and *Hampshire*—between them had formed the battle-fleet's advanced cruiser screen, the former squadron manning the southern arm and the latter the northern.

The Grand Fleet's battle orders clearly defined the functions of these cruisers. They were stationed ahead basically for reconnaissance work, to prevent enemy light forces from 'discovering' Jellicoe's fleet.

Prior to fleet deployment, their primary function was to push ahead and locate the head of the enemy's battle fleet, reporting back to the Commander-in-Chief its position, course and other details. Jellicoe had stationed his cruiser screen ten miles ahead of his fleet as he had steamed across the North Sea. At 3.10 p.m., however, when it had seemed that enemy light cruisers were being shepherded in his direction, he had signalled his cruisers to move their line six miles further on, to a distance sixteen miles from his flagship. Had they increased to their full speed of 22 knots, say at 3.10 p.m., they could have pushed ahead to within a mile and a half of the distance ordered. They had, however, done nothing of the sort: far from drawing ahead, they had adhered to the fleet's speed and even tended to drop back until barely ten miles ahead.

Moreover, at 4.40 p.m., the visibility had begun to deteriorate very quickly, especially on the southern wing of this screen, and the

Senior Officer of Cruisers (*Minotaur*) had ordered ships to close in towards the centre to visibility-distance apart. This could only be done by their steering inwards on a diagonal course, and by doing so these ships dropped even further astern of station. By 5.20 p.m. the cruiser line, by now an irregular double curve, concave on its southern and convex on its northern arm, was on an average only six miles ahead of *Iron Duke*—ten miles behind its appointed station.

They were soon to reap the whirlwind: at about 5.39 p.m., *Minotaur*, with *Shannon* in station astern, then about eight miles ahead and just off the port bow of *King George V*, leading the port wing of the battle fleet, heard distant gunfire three points on her starboard bow. (This was, in fact, the opening of *Chester's* engagement with Boedicker's Second Scouting Group.) At once the two cruisers headed towards the sound: soon they could see flashes in the mist and noted the additional thunder of heavy guns (Hood's battle-cruisers opening fire). About 4.53 p.m. from *Minotaur* could be seen several heavy ships emerging from the mist about nine miles to the south-westward. They were firing hard at an unseen target.

Minotaur at once turned to a north-east course and prepared to engage them. Fortunately, however, they were identified almost at once as Hood's three 'Invincible' class battle-cruisers. *Minotaur* thereafter continued to the eastward, collecting *Cochrane* at 6.15 p.m. and *Hampshire* a quarter of an hour later: the Second Cruiser Squadron was thus reunited in line ahead, astern of their Admiral, and could head for its appointed station four and a half miles on the engaged bow of the battle fleet, from which it was now nine miles too far to the northward. *Minotaur* and her Second Cruiser Squadron had thus contributed nothing to the paltry sum total of information at the Commander-in-Chief's disposal.

Almost seven miles due west of *Minotaur* at 5.40 p.m. was *Defence* (Rear-Admiral Arbuthnot) with *Warrior* in station astern: *Defence* was then about five miles off the port bow of *Marlborough*, leading the fleet's right-wing column. The other two cruisers of this Squadron, the *Duke of Edinburgh* and *Black Prince*, were at the time closing in to take station astern. Just before 5.40 p.m. the sound of gunfire could be heard on *Defence's* starboard bow, and, with *Warrior* at her heels, she pushed on towards it. The flagship was soon able to see flashes, and at 5.50 p.m. three or four enemy light cruisers came out of the mist about $8\frac{1}{2}$ miles away, engaging an unseen target. (This was Boedicker's squadron engaging *Chester*). *Defence* and *Warrior* at once turned to an easterly course, and opened fire, firing three salvoes of main armament guns each.

At this the enemy apparently turned away, for the range opened and the enemy disappeared into the mist. As the six salvoes had all fallen 'short', Arbuthnot decided to push on in pursuit; he had at least succeeded in fulfilling his secondary function—that of preventing enemy cruisers from closing the Grand Fleet for scouting or other purposes.

He turned therefore six points to starboard to the south-westward; *Duke of Edinburgh* and, further away, *Black Prince* gradually closed in to join their flagship. Arbuthnot now—at last—increased his squadron's speed to its maximum of 22½ knots, and at about 6.03 p.m. caught sight of *Wiesbaden*, seven miles distant. Altering course sharply to starboard, he turned until the burning ship was almost ahead. She was obviously disabled, but still limping very, very slowly forward. Arbuthnot seems to have resolved there and then to end the German's career once and for all: his squadron, racing towards her, opened heavy fire upon the blazing wreck. The Admiral seems hardly to have noticed that *Lion*, with her three battle-cruisers astern, was heading eastward towards him at 25 knots on a course directly converging with his own: Arbuthnot held his three armoured cruisers resolutely on their way, firing fast. *Lion*, who had lost sight of her target—Hipper's battle-cruisers—in the mist after their turns away at 6.01 and 6.04 p.m., had suddenly picked them up as the enemy were turning to the north-eastward again at 6.12 p.m., having taken their place at the head of the German battle fleet. *Lion* reopened fire on them about a minute later together with *Princess Royal*, *Tiger* and *New Zealand*. Still Arbuthnot in *Defence* held on, intent only on dealing with *Wiesbaden*: people who saw his advance considered that he was 'impatient to get into action'.[1] His shells had already brought *Wiesbaden* to a stop and at 6.16 p.m., as Hipper's whole line was round, Arbuthnot led his squadron straight across *Lion's* bows, so closely that *Lion* and *Princess Royal* had to haul abruptly out to port to avoid collision. *Defence* and *Warrior* held on their way still firing; the *Duke of Edinburgh*, the third in the line, found she could not get across the battle-cruisers' bows in safety and so remained—fortunately for herself—on the disengaged side of the battle-cruisers.

In full view of the leading British battleships and of our battle-cruisers the two armoured cruisers raced on, deluging *Wiesbaden* with their salvoes; but the volumes of smoke belching from the cruisers' funnels so fouled the battle-cruisers' range that several minutes elapsed before Beatty's force was again able to fire. Within

[1] *Fighting at Jutland.*

a minute of clearing *Lion*, however, heavy shells began to fall around *Defence* and *Warrior*. The guns of *Derfflinger* and *Lützow* and also of the leading German battleships were trained upon them as they advanced and, fury at the treatment being meted out to the hapless *Wiesbaden* stimulating the German gunners' efforts, they all opened fire almost together. It seemed that only at this moment did Arbuthnot realise the appalling peril into which he had led his armoured cruisers, for he could not fail now to see the German battle-cruisers only 6,000 yards from him, or the three leading German battle squadrons at ranges between 8,500 and 12,500 yards away.

He turned sharply westward and *Warrior* followed: watchers in the Grand Fleet, less than three miles to the northward, saw the two ships half hidden by a screen of huge splashes sprouting continually around them. As the German gunners 'found' their targets, both ships were hit heavily again and again and the end came quickly: *Defence* was hit by two heavy salvoes in succession at about 6.19 p.m., one probably from Scheer's own flagship *Friedrich der Grosse*, and the other from Hipper's battered flagship *Lützow*. *Defence* was seen to reel and stagger under the first blow and then to right herself; the second took her amidships, and in an instant she was rent asunder by a violent explosion. A searing flame flashed up and was gone; a huge pillar of smoke leapt hundreds of feet into the air. When the shot-torn *Warrior* passed the spot one minute later there was no trace of her flagship—*Defence* had gone, and with her Rear-Admiral Arbuthnot, 54 other officers and 849 men—in full view of most of the ships of Britain's Grand Fleet.

The enemy's fire was now concentrated upon *Warrior* alone. She was hit again and again but surrounded with splashes she limped westward seeming to bear a charmed life. With the odds that were so heavily arrayed against her, the guns of the High Seas Fleet, she must assuredly have shared her flagship's fate—but for the almost miraculous and quite unintentional intervention of the battleship *Warspite*,[1] distracting the Germans' attention.

[1] See next chapter.

6

Junction and Deployment

THE preliminaries of sea battle were now almost at an end: the brush between opposing light forces had brought the rival supporting groups into contact. A running fight had followed —interrupted by the sudden appearance of the enemy's battle fleet. Covered by Evan-Thomas's four indomitable battleships, Beatty's battle-cruisers had then fallen back—as planned—upon the support of Jellicoe's battle fleet. Scheer had pursued the Battle-Cruiser Force with his whole fleet—blissfully unaware of Jellicoe's near approach.

This unawareness had to be preserved at all cost, or the German High Seas Fleet would have turned about and raced for the sanctuary of its minefields and defended bases with nothing to bar the path.

The overture was thus drawing to its close, and thus far Jellicoe possessed the advantage attendant upon surprise; the curtain must soon rise on main fleets in direct contact.

Battles between 'modern' fleets must inevitably be of relatively short duration for they have to be fought out between the ships that are present, and with the resources in men and equipment, fuel and ammunition—100 rounds per 'big gun'—carried into action by these ships. The opportunities of sea battle are rare in a war—there were only three significant battles in the twenty-odd years of fighting in the long war with France—so that when a chance arises it cannot be suffered to pass, for it may not recur. Furthermore there is a marked difference between land and sea fighting: a defeated army can often be withdrawn, reformed and again put into the line; a defeated fleet, however, has seldom been re-created after a decisive naval action. Modern ships of war, once destroyed, can seldom be replaced in the course of the war and this particular factor inevitably compels a sober approach to battle at sea, and is a curb upon the decisions of the most ardent and impetuous sea commander.

Jellicoe had given long and earnest thought to the problems of battle: he had tested his ideas on the Tactical Board, and had experimented with fleets at sea. He had long known exactly what form battle must take and, like Nelson before him, had 'made his intentions known' to his flag officers and captains in his *Grand Fleet Battle Orders.* Within their compass were to be found instructions covering almost every situation which might arise before, during and after battle; these Orders were supported by numerous diagrams and plans, and the whole was constantly revised as necessary in the

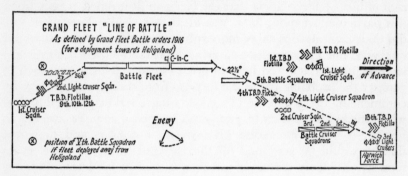

light of experience. The opening paragraph gave the key to Jellicoe's plan for battle:

> Action upon approximately similar courses will be one of the under-lying objects of my tactics, because it is the form of action most likely to give the most decisive result.

This clearly eschewed action on opposite courses, for this is invariably indecisive. The battle was thus to be a gun-duel, fought out with the weapon with which Britain had held her maritime supremacy for over four centuries—a gun duel and in single line of battle. There were well-known disadvantages to this particular fleet formation, but after carefully investigating alternative formations, Jellicoe was of opinion that the single line 'was still the best that could be devised'.[1]

Historically, the drawback to the 'single line' had been its rigidity; Jellicoe's battle organisation had, however, imparted flexibility to it by stationing his two free fast squadrons—the battle-cruisers and the Fifth Battle Squadron—in the van and at the rear of the line. He planned to open his gun-duel at a range outside extreme German torpedo range—12,000 to 15,000 yards at that time—and as far beyond that as visibility would permit to enable the most effective use to be made of his heavier gun armament at a range at which the

[1] Jellicoe, *Grand Fleet.*

lighter German weapons would be relatively ineffective. He purposed in this way first to dominate the enemy's fire-power, and then progressively to close in to a destructive gun range.

He had, however, to take into account the effect of the new and comparatively untried weapon—the torpedo. Torpedo experts in our own fleet were confident that this weapon, in a 'browning' attack used against a line of ships, should be able to achieve 40 per cent of hits. Jellicoe knew that the German fleet relied greatly upon this particular weapon, for it was ideal to a weaker force: not only did their capital ships carry more submerged torpedo tubes than did our own, but their torpedo-carrying light craft—their destroyers—were highly trained and held in great esteem. Jellicoe proposed to counter the probable use of the torpedo from enemy capital ships by commencing the action out of torpedo range, and he planned to deal with attacks from enemy torpedo-craft by special counter attacks. In his line-of-battle formation his own light cruisers and destroyer flotillas would be stationed off the engaged bow and quarter. As soon as an enemy destroyer attack was seen to be developing, our light forces were to move out and break it up. Both light cruisers and destroyers had been given speed and superior gunpower for this purpose. For such enemy destroyers as evaded this breaking-up process and persisted with their attack, the secondary armaments—6-inch and 4-inch—of the battle fleet would be used to keep them beyond torpedo range if possible.

For those daring spirits who, braving this gun barrage, still pressed home their attack and fired their torpedoes, there only remained swift 'avoiding' manoeuvres by the battleships, turning either towards or away from the attack as necessary until the torpedos had passed harmlessly between ships, then turning back to their battle course again. There was no element of trial and error about this manoeuvre: it had been tested by destroyers firing torpedoes with dummy warheads at a line of battleships under all conditions, and there was virtually no known alternative at the time to such 'avoiding' tactics unless the risk of the 40 per cent loss prophesied by torpedo experts was accepted. As the effect of a torpedo-hit upon a British warship thus far in the war had almost invariably proved fatal to the ship, there was every reason to prefer the use of evasive tactics whenever necessary; in point of fact the same conclusion had been reached in the German fleet and in every other navy at that time.

The possibility of having to turn either the whole fleet or part of it suddenly, in order to evade a mass torpedo attack, also opened

up the question of decentralised command, and the need for flag
officers of divisions to take action upon their own initiative.

Quite early in the war, on 10th September 1914, while on a
'sweep' into the Bight, Jellicoe had made an interesting private note
on prevailing conditions:

> The weather conditions . . . were very unfavourable for a general
> action [he had written] owing to the low visibility and the glare caused
> by brilliant sunlight and absence of wind. . . . The conditions make it
> impossible for the Commander-in-Chief in the centre of the Fleet to
> know what is going on in the van and the rear . . . besides being favour-
> able to tactics largely based upon the employment of torpedo craft.[1]

The experience of this day in typical North Sea weather—oddly,
very similar to the weather which prevailed on the fateful 31st May
—had convinced Jellicoe that it was necessary to give considerable
latitude and initiative to his squadron flag officers.

Of late years, it has been almost a fashion to stigmatize these
Battle Orders as a 'system' which robbed subordinate officers of all
individuality. It is difficult to see what greater degree of practical
decentralisation an experienced Commander-in-Chief could have
placed in the hands of his junior flag officers. Any wider scope
could have produced a situation in which every flag officer felt at
liberty to steam around the North Sea at his own whim, and probably to his own peril.

(ii)

Admiral Scheer's plans were fundamentally different from Jellicoe's:
he had no intention of joining battle with the Grand Fleet unless he
was in a position of tactical advantage—and that advantage would
certainly not be conceded voluntarily by so able a tactician as
Jellicoe. In justice to Scheer it must be said that to some extent this
policy was imposed upon him by superior authority, for ever since the
Battle of the Bight, in the early weeks of war, the Kaiser had for-
bidden any movement involving risk to the German main fleet. Even
when the Emperor had approved Scheer's more vigorous naval
offensive, the ban still remained on the use of the battle fleet. Scheer
was thus committed to retiring tactics should he encounter Jellicoe's
fleet, not only because this was the usual procedure of a weaker
fleet but also because of the Imperial edict. Even if by being

[1] Jellicoe, *Grand Fleet*.

decoyed into a trap, or on account of low visibility, he should encounter the Grand Fleet fortuitously he had no intention of fighting it out unless at a tactical advantage. He intended to adopt a retiring movement as quickly as possible and then withdraw at speed to the safety of his bases.

Apart from fully expecting the employment of such retiring tactics, which have always been difficult to counter, Admiral Jellicoe also knew the exact form these would most probably take: he had been provided by the Admiralty Intelligence department with a copy of the confidential Battle Orders issued to the German fleet.[1] If cornered, the German fleet would turn about using a much-practised manoeuvre—the 'battle-turn-away' (*Gefechtskehrtwendung*) —withdrawing under cover, if necessary, of massed torpedo attacks and smoke-screens made by their destroyers. The turn itself was commenced from the rear of the line: as the rear ship began to turn, the ship ahead of her at once put her helm over to turn, and this procedure was followed all down the line in quick succession. It was a risky manoeuvre, especially under fire; but it had been practised assiduously under all conditions, even with bends in the line, and could now be executed with precision and safety.

Jellicoe's ideas of sea battle therefore centred on a gun-duel; Scheer was concerned with avoiding action and with turning away from it under cover of smoke and torpedo attacks, as he retired swiftly to his base. The two concepts were obviously irreconcilable: but the more Jellicoe considered this problem, the more certain he was that if on meeting he could bring Scheer under a swift and overwhelming concentration of gunfire, an initial result might be achieved before Scheer had time to put into effect his turning-away tactics.

With his fleet second-in-command, Vice-Admiral Sir Cecil Burney, his chief-of-staff, Admiral Madden, his flag captain, Captain Dreyer—a gunnery expert of the first order—and other senior officers, Jellicoe had studied the problem from every angle, coming to the conclusion that on meeting the enemy the advance of the British battle line would have to embody two principles—a sudden concentration of fire on the enemy van and an enveloping movement designed to hamper Scheer's retreat to his base. Of these two factors Jellicoe was of opinion that it was most important that Scheer should be prevented from reaching his own waters even if the manoeuvring of the fleet to achieve this end should result in unfavourable gunnery conditions for a time.[2]

[1] These were recovered together with the codes from the German cruiser *Magdeburg*.
[2] Jellicoe, *Grand Fleet*.

It was impossible to foresee the conditions in which the fleets would meet, but Jellicoe had felt that he would be able to achieve his object in the course of his 'deployment'.

Deployment is the important manoeuvre by means of which a fleet is changed from its square cruising formation into its linear order of battle. Nelson at Trafalgar was not troubled with this: his Memorandum had decreed that the order of sailing—his cruising formation—should also be his 'order of battle'. Scheer was able to do much the same, for the negotiation of his swept channels demanded single line ahead, and the possibility of undiscovered British mine-fields beyond made single line the most prudent formation.

Jellicoe's problem was quite different from Nelson's off Cadiz or Scheer's now: he had to bring his fleet across three hundred miles of North Sea, knowing—in May 1916—that it was infested with U-boats. He had to make use of a formation that presented the minimum target to the torpedoes of a marauding submarine, that was compact for purposes of cruising, *and* capable of being converted in a single 'line-of-battle' by 'direct deployment' in the shortest possible time. There was, however, one prerequisite to this swift deployment: the Commander-in-Chief must have prior accurate information of the enemy's position course and speed, in ample time to 'wheel' the fleet[1] so that on sighting the enemy the line of the guides would be at right-angles to the direction of enemy advance. This 'wheeling' might take up to 25 minutes, which emphasised the need for early and exact information: as this manoeuvring took place, however, before fleet contact—even with the enemy battle fleet over the horizon—this time was quite immaterial; as long as the bearing of the guides was correct on sighting with reference to the enemy's advance, the position of the centre of the column vis-à-vis the enemy could be adjusted prior to deployment by 'sidling' the fleet bodily the required amount.

Once in sight of the enemy, deployment into line would require $4\frac{1}{2}$ minutes, and this manoeuvre had been practised again and again by the fleet at sea—as lately as 30th March—and had been perfected. Once the line was formed or forming, Jellicoe contemplated direct-ing its advance in such a way as to envelop the enemy's van, and force a battle on his own terms: if the enemy were to turn away, which was quite likely, he proposed to retain the initiative by altering the course of his battle line so as to prevent the enemy from reaching his own waters. He was not going to allow Scheer to impose

---

[1] i.e. alter the bearing of guides and columns. The enemy's centre is the point taken for measurement of his 'direction of advance'.

a 'chase' upon him and thus let the initiative pass out of his hands into those of the enemy.

Early Intelligence of the enemy was the key to successful deployment; and on this May afternoon, the deteriorating visibility was, if anything, aiding the element of surprise in Jellicoe's approach, and at the same time, by veiling the distance, was reducing Scheer's chance of escaping action. As the Grand Fleet held steadily on its south-east-by-south course at 20 knots, a number of reports of Scheer's reputed position, course and speed reached Admiral Jellicoe. These reports can be separated into four distinct groups: the period of *distant reports* (by wireless) which primarily covered the period 4.30 p.m. to 5 p.m.; the *period of silence*, from 5 p.m. to 5.40 p.m., when virtually no reports reached the Commander-in-Chief; the period of *audible reports* (of gunfire, etc.) from 5.40 p.m. onwards; and the final period of *visual contact* reports which the Commander-in-Chief received between 5.42 p.m. and 6.14 p.m.

Considering first the *distant* reports of the enemy—four from *Southampton*, one from *Champion*, one from *Lion* (passed in from *Princess Royal*), and one from the Admiralty, derived presumably by direction-finding, which gave the positions of the German battle fleet at 4.09 p.m., its course as north-west, speed 15 knots: plotted to a comparable basis with enemy positions derived from *Southampton* and *Lion*, however, this last suggested that the enemy was $12\frac{1}{2}$ miles further to the westward. It was discarded for Jellicoe had, however, good reason to be suspicious of Admiralty reports after the fiasco of the Admiralty's 12.30 signal: in any case, where there was so wide a discrepancy between a direction-finding report and one derived by visual observation from a cruiser, any Commander-in-Chief would presumably prefer that of his cruisers. As it so happened, the position given by the Admiralty signal was approximately correct;[1] the Admiralty signal also contained a strong indication that the course might well be more to the westward than the northerly course reported by the cruisers and *Lion*[2]—but that is being wise after the event.

The general result of these 'distant signals' when worked up on a basis of course north and speed 15 knots suggested that the Grand Fleet, in its cruising formation, using *Iron Duke's* reckoning, would sight the enemy battle fleet either ahead or a little to starboard of the centre of its front about 6.35 p.m. Jellicoe could not, of course, know

[1] Cf. Harper, *The Truth about Jutland*.
[2] The Admiralty signal may be presumed to have originated from a lucky direction-finding bearing on the signal made by Scheer to Hipper when he altered course to north-west in his endeavour to get Beatty between two fires.

that *Southampton's* dead-reckoning position was some 7 miles north-west of her actual position, so that the enemy's expected time of sighting would be some 20 to 25 minutes sooner, and also would be eight miles west of the deduced position.[1]

After this, silence seemed to have closed in on the fleet flagship and Jellicoe's anxiety during this unmerited silence was reflected at 5.13 p.m. in a signal he despatched to Beatty, giving his 'scouting admiral' the position, course and speed of the Grand Fleet; perhaps he hoped that this might produce some sort of answer about the position of the enemy. Unfortunately someone on Jellicoe's staff blundered badly over the wording of this signal. It gave *Iron Duke's* position at 5 o'clock, without stating this fact; the 'time of origin' on this signal, 5.13 p.m., would—and did—justify Beatty's navigational staff in assuming that the position in the signal was that at 5.13. This error, when plotted in *Lion* after its receipt some eight minutes later, would place *Iron Duke*, at 5.13, 4½ miles to the north-westward of her dead reckoning position. The result would be that it seemed *Lion* would meet the battle fleet sooner.

The third period, that of 'audible reports', opened with *Comus*, in the centre of the Fourth Light-Cruiser Squadron line and three miles ahead of *Iron Duke*, reporting by searchlight, at 5.45 p.m., 'gunfire', and, a little later, the 'flashes' of guns three points off her starboard bow, i.e. about south. This Jellicoe rightly assumed to come from Beatty's battle-cruisers who had just reopened fire on Hipper's ships.

Five minutes later a report was received—intercepted from *Defence* to *Minotaur* at 5.46 p.m.—of 'ships in action, bearing south-south-west and steering north-east'. *Defence* was then on *Iron Duke's* port bow and in sight, so that the 'enemy' could be plotted in the fleet flagship as being 45° on the bow. What had in fact been seen in *Defence* was the flash of Beatty's guns as he headed north-eastwards to force Hipper away from our battle fleet.

Jellicoe, however, was inclined to think that this report could indicate the leading ships of Scheer's battle fleet: something was very wrong here, for from *Iron Duke's* bridge the thunder of gunfire could now be heard to the southward (Beatty and Hipper) and south-westward (Evan-Thomas). Shortly afterwards, moreover, occasional gunflashes could be seen dimly through the mist to the south-south-west but still no ships were in sight. As the minutes passed, the gunfire grew louder, and with it Jellicoe's uncertainty increased. Nor did it diminish when at about 5.50 p.m. a signal was received from

---

[1] *Southampton's* signalled positions by dead-reckoning were actually all to the westward of her proper position at the time: 13 miles at 4.38 p.m., 6 miles at 4.45 p.m. and 9 miles at 4.48 p.m.

Black Prince:[1] this signal, timed 5.40 p.m., reported: 'Battle-cruisers in sight south, distant five miles'. The cruiser's position as given in the signal was open to considerable doubt: it could not be reconciled with her proper position in the screen and in consequence there was some doubt as to whether the 'battle-cruisers' referred to could be Beatty's or Hipper's. Jellicoe decided they must be Beatty's.

About the same time, another signal was received from *Southampton*, giving the German battle fleet's course as 'north-north-west'.[2] Apart from the clear indication in this report that the enemy van might now be sighted further to starboard, i.e. to the westward, than had been anticipated, this signal also gave some indication of the Battle-Cruiser Force, since *Southampton* would be in company with Beatty. The position still did not match the growing sound of guns which suggested that the reported positions for the enemy were too far to the southward and that the enemy was nearer than had been calculated.

Four minutes later, a further signal from *Southampton*[3] reported that the enemy battle fleet had reverted to its north course.

This was the last of a difficult series of varied reports, the sum total of which could only be considered as confusing: it had suggested that the enemy was still heading towards the Grand Fleet, though to starboard of the centre, as had been anticipated; and it did nothing to clear up the mystery of Evan-Thomas' or Beatty's position.

There were two other signals during this period—one from *Falmouth* which was not recorded in *Iron Duke* and is therefore of no concern here; and another wireless signal from the Admiralty at 5.45 p.m. giving a direction-finding position with course and speed of the enemy main fleet at 4.30 p.m. This signal was not read in time to be of any use.[4]

By Jellicoe's reasoning, the van of the enemy was about 33 miles south of *Iron Duke* at 5.40 p.m., steering between north and north-north-west at 15 knots, perhaps more: its van was in fact only 27 miles away then, that is to say six miles nearer, and eight miles westward of Jellicoe's estimate. This was largely a consequence of

---

[1] Cf. *Naval Operations*, where it is reported that this signal was received at 5.42 p.m. but not read by Jellicoe until considerably later. Cf. also Jellicoe, *Grand Fleet*.

[2] *Southampton*'s signalled position at that time, 5.40 p.m., was six miles south of her actual position, so the enemy would have been that much nearer to Jellicoe.

[3] *Southampton*'s signalled position was 8½ miles to the northward of her actual position, the enemy was therefore much nearer than expected.

[4] The position given in this second Admiralty signal was apparently only about four miles in error as it happened. The Admiralty's official *Narrative* of the battle gives the time of receipt of this signal as 5.53 p.m., but Admiral Harper in his *Truth about Jutland*, says this signal was not received in time to be of any use. This seems to be more probable.

the Commander-in-Chief having had to rely upon dubious wire-lessed positions. At the Admiralty after the war, in much greater personal comfort and with far less distracting noise than surrounded the Commander-in-Chief on his flagship's bridge, and after long and earnest labours—possibly by many hands—a line of reasoning was produced that would have done credit to a Chancery lawyer to show how Jellicoe 'could' have drawn inferences and assumptions which in the light of the Admiralty's post-war knowledge would have enabled him to arrive at a very close approximation indeed to the exact position, course and speed of the enemy van.[1] Such prescience is happily given to few mortals; the little Admiral *was* mortal with, as Alfred Noyes has said of him, the shrewd brown eyes, the 'gentle heart, the resolute truth in judgment and in act'. Many will assuredly agree with the Rear-Admiral who reading this shaft of Official Wisdom growled: 'We could have done with brains like theirs at sea; but probably they would not have known where to find where that was.'

During the last ten minutes, the thunder of gunfire had grown louder and louder: it was now becoming deafening on *Iron Duke's* bridge: the whole horizon from south right round to south-west and on to the west-south-west seemed to tremble with it. It was at this time, 5.55 p.m., that Jellicoe signalled by searchlight to the fleet's second-in-command, Sir Cecil Burney, in *Marlborough*, to ask what they could see at the head of the starboard wing column.[2]

At 6.01 Jellicoe could see *Lion* heading at high speed eastward across the front of the advancing battle fleet with her funnels belching smoke. Here at last was the answer to his problem, and his search-light blinked to his 'scouting admiral': 'Where is the enemy's battle fleet?' There was no answer, for Beatty did not know; nor as it hap-pened did *Southampton*, from whom a signal was received two minutes later that he had lost sight of the enemy battle fleet. At that time only Evan-Thomas knew where it was, for he was still under fire from their guns.

When *Lion* failed to answer the Commander-in-Chief's question, the conviction that the enemy was going to appear more to the westward than expected was rapidly growing in the Commander-in-Chief's mind: at 6.02 p.m. he signalled the fleet to alter course, by divisions, to south. It was clearly his intention to take ground—'sidle' the fleet—more to the westward to clear up the position: had there been time he would probably have altered the bearing of

[1] Cf., for example, the Admiralty's *Narrative* of Jutland, Appendix G., pp. 108–110.
[2] See p. 91.

guides as well, but with the noise of gunfire growing increasingly loud, he knew that there was no longer time for this manoeuvre, essential to 'direct deployment'; he must now meet the problem of deployment as and when it happened.

There was a moment now to consider the outstanding fact of Beatty's junction with the fleet: *Lion* by *Iron Duke's* reckoning should have appeared on the *port* bow of the leader of the *port* column, *King George V*, but she had instead been sighted off the *starboard* bow of the leader of the *starboard* column, *Marlborough*. There was therefore clearly a navigational discrepancy of at least twelve miles.[1]

Jellicoe was now certain that the German fleet was more to starboard, and that it was very close indeed. At 6.06 p.m. he felt he could 'sidle' the fleet no more, and turned his fleet back to south. He was also becoming sure, although devoid of all 'contact' information, that he would have to 'deploy' on his port wing column if the enemy was going to be sighted soon, maybe twenty minutes earlier than he had anticipated.

As he turned back to his southerly course, *Lion's* searchlight blinked quickly off *Iron Duke's* port bow: 'Enemy battle-cruisers south-east'. Two minutes previously, Jellicoe had again asked his 'scouting admiral' for bread—for news of the enemy *battle fleet*: he had now been given a stone—news of Hipper, which was of relatively minor concern. At this moment, moreover, Hipper was busy turning away to the south and south-west, out of Beatty's sight, in order to fall back upon the German battle fleet.

At 6.08 p.m., convinced now that there was little time left, Jellicoe signalled to his destroyers and light cruisers to take up Disposition Number 1, in preparation for battle: he would thus have flotillas ahead and astern on the engaged side of his battle line, where they could break up enemy destroyer-attacks, and be in good position for making attacks themselves upon the enemy as necessary.

The prevailing uncertainty about the enemy battle fleet's position was now becoming very serious indeed: flashes to the south-westward suggested someone was near, but as Jellicoe was turning back to the south-eastward *Marlborough* to starboard signalled him, by searchlight: 'Fifth Battle Squadron in sight, bearing south-west'. Here perhaps was someone who would supply news of the position of the enemy's battle fleet.

Barham, however, was indeed coming to Jellicoe's aid. He had sighted the enemy battle fleet again at 6.10 p.m., and by visual

---

[1] Jellicoe, *Grand Fleet*. The cumulative error was in fact about 11 miles: *Iron Duke* being 4¼ miles east of her reckoning and *Lion* 6¾ miles west of hers.

signal directed *Valiant* to inform the Commander-in-Chief of this by wireless. The signal reached *Iron Duke* at 6.14 p.m.: 'Enemy battle fleet south-south-east. (1810).' Almost simultaneously and in fact just before this report was received Beatty signalled from *Lion*, at last answering Jellicoe's urgent question: 'Have sighted enemy battle fleet, south-south-west. (1814).' Allowing a reasonable distance for visibility of five to six miles, a position for the enemy van had at last been obtained. Seconds later, *Barham's* bearing could also be plotted. On *Iron Duke's* bridge the signal was reported to the admiral: he walked to the compass, glanced across it towards the south-south-westward, and then over his shoulder towards *Marlborough*. He could see the course taken by Beatty's battle-cruisers, and assumed that the enemy fleet would be following the same course. He was as calm, as unruffled and as cool as always. A pause, while the fates of Country, Empire—even Freedom itself—hung in the balance; then he spoke quite quietly to Commander Wood, his staff signal officer: 'Hoist Equal Speed pennant, South-East!' He was deploying to the south-east.

Jellicoe's Signal Officer at once drew the admiral's attention to the fact that the code book did not contain a simple signal for deployment to south-east: there *was* a way of signalling this but it would involve the use of an unfamiliar signal—undesirable at such a critical juncture. Commander Wood suggested that if the Commander-in-Chief would deploy the fleet on a course one point ($11\frac{1}{4}°$) to *port* of south-east—i.e., to south-east-by-east)—it would have two advantages; firstly a normal and straightforward signal could be made and secondly it would remove any possibility of ambiguity as to upon which wing column—port or starboard—deployment was to take place.

On *Iron Duke's* signal bridge the flags were whisked out of the lockers and bent on to the halyards; there were glimpses of yellow and black and red bunting—and then the signal was fluttering aloft: 'Equal Speed—C L' (Deploy South-east-by-east, preserving the speed of the Fleet)'.

The leader of the port column, *King George V*, thus had to alter course to south-east by east, the ships astern following her in succession. Leaders of the other divisions turned eight points (90°) to port, the ships in their columns following in succession. On arriving at the pivot point, each ship also turned south-east by east, and took station astern of the next ahead. At 6.15 p.m., the 'deployment' signal was made, 'Commander-in-Chief General', by flags and by wireless.

The Grand Fleet's deployment, so long delayed for want of information, was in progress at last—and none too soon, for already some stray 'overs' and 'shorts' intended presumably for the Fifth Battle Squadron were dropping among the ships of the rear divisions. On the bridge of *Colossus*, they were watching particularly the antics of a large yellow shell with a black band painted round it.

It seemed certain that the enemy was quite unaware of Jellicoe's manoeuvre: we know now that they were unaware of Jellicoe's presence there at all. Between the enemy fleet and our own fleet there was, moreover, a thickening pall of smoke merging with the mist which provided an effective curtain. On the British side of this a seemingly infinite number of ships was racing eastward or westward—destroyers, light cruisers, battle-cruisers—all pressing on at utmost speed to reach their allotted battle station in van or rear. Afterwards the fleet dubbed this corner off *Marlborough's* bow 'Windy Corner', for the shells dropped continously through mist and smoke and small craft were being handled there as never before—avoiding collision by inches in their hurry to reach their station.

Lion was leading her battle-cruisers eastward at high speed across the front, and was again engaging Hipper's ships at short range and securing hits; ahead, and to the eastward of him, Beatty caught sight of Hood's three battle-cruisers busily and successfully avoiding five of the torpedoes which Heinrich's destroyers had fired—and signalled them to take station ahead of him as he raced to his place at the head of the British battle line.

Five minutes later, Hood in *Invincible* led his three ships round to drop into excellent station ahead of Beatty.

As *Lion* and her consorts raced ahead, their funnel smoke which at first had masked the rear squadrons in the line began to blow clear and at 6.17 p.m. *Marlborough* opened fire.

At the rear of the line, Evan-Thomas had turned his four gallant battleships along the southern side of *Marlborough* and was forging ahead; it is possible he thought that deployment might take place on the starboard wing, and was preparing, in such case, to take the head of the line as laid down in the Battle Orders. When he realised that deployment was on the port column, he made ready to take position in line astern of *Marlborough's* starboard wing division as he did not intend to mask the fleet's guns by pushing ahead to the van in Beatty's wake. As a preliminary to dropping into his position, he signalled his Fifth Battle Squadron to alter course 16 points to starboard in succession: *Barham* turned at 6.18 p.m. and so later did

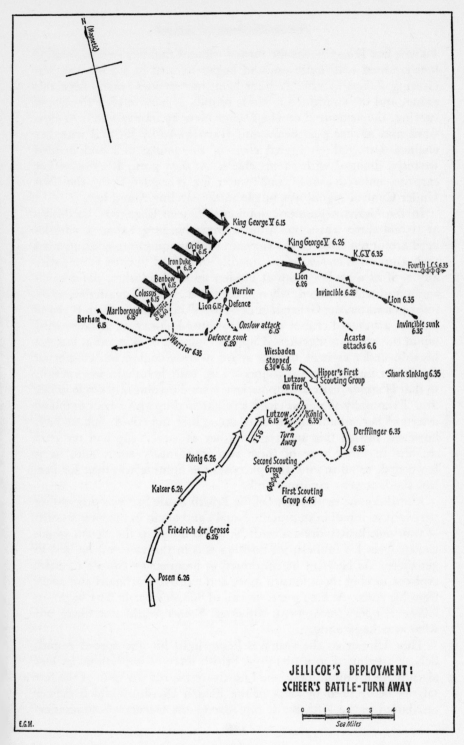

N (Magnetic)

King George Ⅴ 6.15
King George Ⅴ 6.26
K.G.Ⅴ 6.35
Fourth L.C.S. 6.35
Orion 6.15
Iron Duke 6.15
Lion 6.26
Benbow 6.15
Invincible 6.26
Lion 6.35
Colossus 6.15
Warrior
Lion 6.15 Defence
Invincible sunk 6.35
Marlborough 6.15
Barham 6.15
Onslow attack 6.15
Defence sunk 6.20
Warrior 6.35
Acasta attacks 6.6

Wiesbaden stopped 6.30 6.16
Lützow on fire
Hipper's First Scouting Group
Shark sinking 6.35

Lützow 6.15
König 6.35
1.S.G.
Turn Away
Derfflinger 6.35
6.35

König 6.26
Second Scouting Group
Kaiser 6.26
First Scouting Group 6.45

Friedrich der Grosse 6.26

Posen 6.26

JELLICOE'S DEPLOYMENT:
SCHEER'S BATTLE-TURN AWAY

0 1 2 3 4
Sea Miles

E.G.M.

Valiant, but *Warspite*—as she turned—found that her steering-engine had jammed with helm on, and began to turn in a wide arc, just clearing *Valiant's* stern. Neither helm nor engines could check this swing, and she continued to circle round. A minute after she began turning, the armoured cruiser *Defence* blew up barely a mile to eastward and on her port beam and *Warrior*—badly hit and with her engines damaged—straggled clear of the smoke pall and headed westerly, deluged with enemy shells. At 6.23 p.m., *Warrior*, to her surprise, entered almost 'safe' water for *Warspite*—flying the 'Not Under Control' signal was involuntarily circling round her.

In the German gunners' opinion a 'Queen Elizabeth' battleship at 10,000 yards was a much more profitable target than a middle-aged armoured cruiser: the German leading squadrons concentrated their guns on *Warspite*, as she steadily continued to turn as majestically as if at a review. Almost hidden by shell-splashes, she was hit again and again. Even, when at 6.27 p.m., *Warrior* again limped on into open water, the German guns were still interested only in *Warspite* and the armoured cruiser was left to stumble away to the westward out of the action altogether. Captain Philpotts of *Warspite* at last got his ship under control and the spare steering-engine was connected up. Unfortunately, it was connected up with 'helm' already upon it, so that *Warspite* proceeded to make a second involuntary circle under fire. Eventually she drew clear, straightened up and began to follow astern of her squadron, catching up as best she could. Scheer had, however, missed this and reported her as 'sunk': she had received six hits in the course of these two involuntary turns and, as it happened, to all intents and purposes the fighting was over for her. But she was very far from sunk.

Elsewhere the deployment of the British battle line was proceeding perfectly, as it had been practised again and again in the long months of waiting. Beatty drew ahead: he could not help the smoke which trailed from his funnels; his position was in the van and he had to get there. As he went he continued to hammer at Hipper's battle-cruisers, forcing them to turn more and more to starboard and away from his guns. At 6.27 p.m. the van of Scheer's battle fleet began to follow Hipper's movement, although Scheer could not make out what was happening.

That Hipper in the van was being hard hit and forced round, Scheer attributed to a phantom British force of battleships he had already, in his mind, positioned north-westward. In spite of the few salvoes being fired by ships of the Fourth Division—which Scheer attributed to the Fifth Battle Squadron—the German Commander-in-Chief had no idea even yet of what lay beyond the mist-laden smokescreen to north and eastward.

At 6.27 p.m. the British line was in the shape of a large L towards the enemy, who could now be seen, though very dimly. *Iron Duke* had turned to the new course at 6.21 p.m. and was preparing to open fire; the battle line would soon be complete and Jellicoe could already see the results of his instinctive decision to make an indirect deployment on a south-east by east course taking shape. It had achieved complete surprise for the enemy was obviously still unaware of Jellicoe's presence or position, but could not remain in ignorance much longer. As the British line stretched on to the south-eastward, it was crossing Scheer's T—the supreme achievment of the master tactician: it had also given British gunners the advantage of the better light, while themselves remaining hidden from German eyes in the mist and smoke.

Beatty and Hood were pounding at the head of the German line, forcing Hipper steadily round and as our line drew further and further ahead it would overlap and envelop the enemy: it would be well on the road to cutting Scheer's line of retreat. The German admiral had indeed been placed in a very dangerous tactical position.

The smoke of Beatty's battle-cruisers had now drifted clear of our centre battle squadrons and was masking only the second battle-cruiser squadron in the van. Here at the head of the battle line there was considerable congestion, as destroyers and light cruisers and battle-cruisers all raced to take up their positions: Beatty's battle-cruisers were keeping their hold on the enemy van and in the end *King George V* was obliged to haul out to port to give them all room: Jellicoe, realising this congestion, reduced the fleet's speed to 14 knots at 6.26 p.m. but the signal took some time to pass down the line, and resulted in some bunching in the rear, and temporary masking of fire. Up in the van, however, Beatty and the light cruisers were able to press on ahead. Half our battle fleet was now firing; the enemy was replying but their fire was quite ineffective.

The battle fleet and its battle-cruisers were united and the Grand Fleet had deployed into line of battle on the minimum of last-minute information. Jellicoe had secured by his deployment almost every tactical advantage possible, while Scheer on the other hand was in a dangerous position, his T was crossed, and his van enveloped; his battle-cruisers were being heavily battered and forced to bend further away to the southward, his battle fleet was following them. Yet there were, later, critics who thought that the deployment could have been made otherwise. Some averred that it should have been made on *Marlborough*'s starboard wing column, for example—barely 14,000 yards from the enemy's guns; this school of thought argues somewhat obtusely that for Jellicoe to have deployed as he did on the port column was to deploy 'away from the enemy', an entirely meaningless phrase under the circumstances.

Another school—with Mr. Churchill among them—would even have deployed on a *centre* column, thereby throwing half the fleet into semi-confusion, masking the gunfire of some 35 per cent of its ships, while the German gunners got busy on them, and by abruptly meeting Scheer's fleet give Scheer the chance to turn away for home. There have been other critics who would have divided the fleet, sending the Fifth Battle Squadron alone—presumably down one side of the enemy—and the battle fleet down the other, in conditions of visibility well under six miles. Mr. Churchill, indeed, expressed the wish that the 'four' ships of the Fifth Battle Squadron had been sent down the disengaged side of the High Seas Fleet to wipe out the old pre-Dreadnought squadron[1]: an admirable conversation piece, but unfortunately at this stage—because of the damage to *Warspite*—the number of 'Queen Elizabeths' was virtually down to three; Jellicoe did not even know exactly where the German fleet was; and certainly neither he nor Evan-Thomas knew that the 'pre-Dread-noughts' were in company with Scheer at all. Quite apart from this, Evan-Thomas would likely have had a long and perilous journey before he could reach the 'disengaged side'.

When, however, the tumult and the shouting of the amateur tacticians and critics had passed away, there remained the solid achievement of Jellicoe's instinctive deployment. One can ignore the jibe about 'that desperate, pompous business of the Grand Fleet's deployment' uttered by Captain Cowan of the battle-cruiser *Princess Royal*—'Tich' or 'Picture Charlie' as they called this much-bemedalled officer on the mess-decks. With some truth, perhaps, he had added: 'It had ever been beyond my intellect to grasp the value of it.' Better to leave the last word upon this deployment with that great sea captain of the Mediterranean fleet during the Second World War, Admiral of the Fleet Lord Cunningham, who has said of this phase of the Battle of Jutland:

> Had I been in command of the Grand Fleet, I hope I would have been given the good sense to make the same deployment.

Had Jellicoe deployed on the starboard wing column, the Germans would have applauded his decision. The Fourth Battle Squadron

[1] Churchill, *World Crisis*.

contained some of the older 12-inch Dreadnoughts in the fleet, and it is possible that the German Third and First Squadrons would have relished such a move. To quote the German Official Historian:

> One must agree . . . that had he [Jellicoe] acted in this way, he would have led his ships into a position which would have been only too welcome to the German fleet.[1]

The scene at 'Windy Corner' will never be forgotten by those privileged to have witnessed it: with the fleet deploying, the rear divisions opening fire, *Defence* blowing up, *Warspite* turning circles enveloped in shell-splashes, *Warrior* limping through them, and a seeming jumble of ships of all classes hurrying eastward, pressing past *Lion's* battle-cruisers who were still firing heavily as they faded into the mist; the intervening water-space was torn with shell splashes and the seamanship displayed was of an order beyond description. The enemy seemed to be firing at random in the direction of *Marlborough's* division—the battleship *Hercules* was straddled as the deployment signal came down, a reminder of what would have happened had Jellicoe deployed upon *Marlborough's* division instead of *King George V*.

As seen from the Fifth Battle Squadron, turning up at the rear of the battle line 'the general effect outdid the most imaginative picture of a naval battle'.[2]

Some ships in the rear division opened fire as soon as *Lion's* smoke blew clear: at 6.17 p.m., only two minutes after deployment. *Marlborough* saw a 'Kaiser'-class battleship dimly through the mist 30° abaft her starboard beam, and opened fire at 13,000 yards; in four minutes she fired seven salvoes, and after two minutes obtained visible hits with her 5th and 7th. She only ceased firing at 6.21 p.m. when the range was obscured by the burning *Wiesbaden's* smoke fouling the line of sight; whereupon, at 6.24 p.m. (according to a report from her foretop), 'we gave her to the guns . . . and fired five salvoes at her'.[3] Astern of *Marlborough*, the new battleship *Revenge* also opened up with 15-inch-gun salvoes and *Agincourt* astern of her fired a broadside from her fourteen 12-inch guns over the heads of the light cruisers and destroyers hurrying in between.

Behind the veil of smoke and mist, deployment was proceeding smoothly as ship after ship turned to the battle course and dropped into precise station astern of its next ahead. The angle of the L towards the German fleet was outside visibility-range but *Wiesbaden* was not, and as they turned on to the battle course several ships

---

[1] *Krieg zur See, Nordsee.* [2] *Fighting at Jutland.* [3] Ibid.

fired 'warmer' salvoes into the stricken German cruiser: at 6.23 p.m., *Iron Duke*, having turned the corner two minutes previously, was among those who 'cleared the bore' with a couple of 13·5-inch salvoes into *Wiesbaden*. Altogether it seems that about this time some thirteen ships fired between them fifty salvoes into her; *Onslow* had also hit her with a torpedo; yet she still remained afloat for some time afterwards. *Iron Duke* then prepared to locate a better target: it was necessary, however, to exercise great caution, for, owing to the mist being thickened by the smoke of innumerable surface craft moving to their station, and also the smoke of the guns, it was none too easy at this time to distinguish friend from foe.[1]

By 6.30 p.m. *Iron Duke* had found a target for her guns: the range was closing and fire was opened on a 'König'-class battleship 20° before the fleet flagship's starboard beam. Nine salvoes were fired, and six hits were clearly recognised—the distinctive warm red splash made by the shell bursts, which a midshipman aloft in *Neptune*'s top considered 'extremely pleasant to look upon'.[2]

Ahead and astern of *Iron Duke* other ships were also firing as soon as they were able to make out a target, but unfortunately half the fleet was not engaged. The visibility was very bad—now averaging barely 12,000 yards to the southward, its best direction; towards other points of the compass *Iron Duke's* rangefinder could not get ranges even of 9,000 yards.[3]

For the enemy it was far worse, for their own funnel-smoke, reinforced by their gun-smoke as they struggled to reply to the pin-points of gun-flashes which were all they could see, drifted across the range on the light south-west wind, thickening the veil of mist shrouding the British line. Perhaps this accounted for the fact that the German fire was entirely ineffectual at this stage: no British ship was hit at all. On the other hand, despite the slightly better opportunities afforded to the British ships, owing to the vagaries of mist thickening and thinning alternately, their targets were seldom in sight for more than a minute or so at a time. Jellicoe's battle fleet was able during this period to fire only some 50 salvoes, between the time *Marlborough* opened fire at 6.17 p.m. and 6.40 p.m. Forty-two of these salvoes were fired at ships of Admiral Behncke's Third Squadron, of 'Königs' and 'Kaisers', securing some thirteen hits: ten ships between them fired fifty salvoes at the closer target of *Wiesbaden*, many securing hits.[4]

---

[1] Jellicoe, *Grand Fleet*.   [2] *Fighting at Jutland*.   [3] Jellicoe, *Grand Fleet*.
[4] At *Wiesbaden* (in order of firing): *Barham, Revenge, Agincourt, Hercules, Collingwood, Iron Duke, Vanguard, Superb, Canada, Monarch, Conqueror*, and *Thunderer*. At the German Third

By 6.30 p.m. indeed the visibility was so bad that Jellicoe seems to have considered closing the range by altering course of the fleet by sub-divisions three points to starboard. The signal was, however, 'negatived' almost at once and before it was made 'Executive', for such a manoeuvre was seen to be impracticable while the fleet was still in its L-shaped formation.

Sir David Beatty has been unjustly criticised for allowing the smoke from his battle-cruisers to foul the range, consequently preventing Jellicoe seizing an early opportunity to overwhelm the van of the enemy battlefleet at ranges between 12,000 and 15,000 yards. He could not help this pall of smoke, which hung in the air and floated across the range on the light west-south-westerly wind. His battle-station was some miles ahead of *King George V* and he *had* to get there at high speed.

Beatty was, moreover, vigorously engaging the enemy and keeping a remorseless grip upon their battle-cruisers: now that his own four battle-cruisers had been joined by Hood's three, this engagement was rapidly rising to a crescendo of fury. That his funnel-smoke blew sulphurously onto the bridges and control-tops of the battle-ships of the crack-shooting Second Battle Squadron upon which Jellicoe's plan for a concentration of fire depended, was one of those quirks of fortune ever present in sea-fights; the moment passed, and with it the opportunity.[1]

The reduction of speed to 14 knots enabled the van ships and battle-cruisers to get ahead towards their stations, and as they began to clear, the smoke ceased to be such a disadvantage, although it still blew unavoidably down-wind, masking the fire of the four leading battleships.

At this end of the line, the battle drama was, however, fast reaching a climax; and unknown to the participants, tragedy was already maturing. Rear Admiral Hood with *Invincible*, *Inflexible* and *Indomitable* had dropped neatly into station at 6.20 p.m., his rear-ship about half a mile ahead of *Lion*.

As Hood turned into station he caught a distant view of Hipper's battle-cruisers through the smoke, and at once opened rapid fire at

---

Battle Squadron: *Iron Duke* (9), *Hercules* (7), *Marlborough* (7), *Barham* (3), *Orion* (4), *Monarch* (3), *Conqueror* (3), *Thunderer* (3), and *Revenge, Colossus, Neptune* (one salvo each).—*Admiralty Narrative.*

[1] The pressure of the many craft struggling to get ahead close on the starboard bow of *King George V* was so great at this time that she had at 6.24 p.m. already been forced to haul out a point to port, to give more room to ships astern; not until 6.30 p.m. was she able to turn back gradually to the deployment course (south-east by east) of the Grand Fleet.

10,000 yards with three ships of his squadron. Here was a fresh enemy for Hipper—one he could not see because of the smoke and mist: it was an enemy, moreover, who quickly established hits. Hipper's flagship *Lützow* was soon very heavily hit again, and *Derfflinger* was under a 'hail of fire': shell after shell was crashing into her hull and bursting. On the present course the range was closing very fast and, to ease the punishment Hipper began to turn slowly towards east and then further to the southward, coming on to a course which he hoped would be parallel with the British ships. His flagship, *Lützow*, was now badly on fire again; she was flooded below decks and, no longer a fightable unit, hauled out of the line.

Still Hood and Beatty pressed on, retaining their unremitting hold upon the enemy's van: in *Invincible*, Rear-Admiral Hood, standing beside his flag captain, Captain Cay, was watching the fire of his ships, and was telling Commander Dannreuther, his gunnery officer, up in the control-top: 'Your firing is very good. Keep at it as rapidly as you can. Every shot is telling.' Almost at that moment, the mocking Sea Gods must have decided to intervene, for the curtain of mist and smoke which hitherto had veiled *Invincible* from Hipper's gunners was lifted, maybe for just a couple of minutes. *Derfflinger's* gunnery officer, Commander von Hase, could see his opponent clearly at last and immediately trained his guns upon him. Just as another salvo came crashing into his own ship, he fired at 9,000 metres; the salvo was 'over'. Hase corrected and fired again, straddling *Invincible* at 6.32 p.m. with two direct hits and two 'overs'; twenty seconds later he fired again, and a full salvo struck the side of Hood's flagship around and abreast her Q turret. Once again appalled onlookers witnessed the same tragedy that had overtaken *Indefatigable*, *Queen Mary* and, later, *Defence*. The stricken battle-cruiser staggered under the blast, turned sharply out of line to starboard, only to blow up seconds later in a series of rapid, deafening explosions and a sheet of flame. *Inflexible*, astern of her, swerved to port of the great column of dense, greying smoke that mushroomed skywards 'like a cumulus cloud': *Invincible*, torn asunder by the explosions, broke open amidships and the two halves settled almost instantly to stand erect, each towering a hundred feet out of the sea, marking the grave of a very gallant Admiral, his sixty officers and 965 men.

There were six survivors—two officers and four men—who were later picked up by the destroyer *Badger*. They included the gunnery officer, Commander Dannreuther, who had been in the control top and had 'stepped into the water when the foretop came down'; a lieutenant who had been in the conning tower and had been sucked down as the ship sank; a badly-burned Royal Marine whose battle station had been in a gun turret; and three seamen. Until picked up they had been clinging automatically to pieces of floating wreckage. Nothing could more clearly emphasise the attitude of officers and men of the Grand Fleet at this time than the conduct of these survivors who, moments before, had been the victims of such a catastrophe: the commander of the rescuing destroyer said that the rescued Commander came aboard his ship 'as cheerily as if he was simply joining a new ship in the ordinary course of events'. He and his fellow survivors, regardless of the peril of their own position as they clung to pieces of wreckage, had cheered other ships as they passed. *Indomitable* passed them while she was still firing, and the officer of her foremost turret said: 'I have never seen anything so splendid as these few cheering us as we raced past.' There will be fewer still who disagree with that.[1]

Although the determined fire of Hood's and Beatty's battle-cruisers had battered Hipper's ships so that he had commenced to turn away, some of the credit must also be given to the attacks of *Onslow* and *Acasta*[2], for these had already convinced Hipper that some powerful force lay ahead of him in the mists to the eastward. To this impression also, two light cruisers of the Third Light-Cruiser Squadron had added their contribution. Since joining up with the Grand Fleet about half an hour before, they had kept station off *Lion's* bow as the battle-cruisers hurried eastward; they were crossing ahead of the line when Hood's battle-cruisers swung into their station. The flagship of the squadron *Falmouth* (Rear-Admiral Napier) with *Yarmouth* astern were separated by this turn from *Birkenhead* and *Gloucester* who could not get across Hood's bows in time, and turned up on his disengaged side. *Falmouth* and *Yarmouth*, however, held on, noticing how heavily *Lützow* and *Derfflinger* were being hit, and at about 6,000 yards on the bow of the German ships, and in a position of excellent torpedo advantage, both light cruisers fired torpedoes at the head of the German battle-cruiser line; *Falmouth's* appeared to hit *Lützow* amidships. *Lützow* promptly opened fire on *Falmouth* with her secondary armament (5.9-inch) and secured a hit upon her mainmast which did not burst; *Falmouth*

---

[1] *Fighting at Jutland. Invincible* was 596 feet long, and having broken in two pieces in 30 fathoms of water, the inner part of the bow and stern halves came to rest upon the sea bed, leaving about 100 feet at either end above water. Some time after the battle, a warship was sent to examine the wreck and make sure that no secret documents were there to be recovered by the enemy: the halves of the wreck had, however, subsided, and gone to the bottom. Among those lost in the ship were 5 civilians.

[2] See p. 107 *et seq.*

was withdrawing at the moment that *Invincible* blew up. On her way back, however, she noticed Boedicker's light cruisers of the Second Scouting Group emerge from the mists on what appeared to be a somewhat half-hearted reconnaissance and by way of good measure drove them back into the mists again with a few well-directed salvoes.

Almost at the same time the dauntless *Shark* was firing her last torpedo at the oncoming German battle-cruisers before she sank. With single destroyers attacking on either side, with Hood and Beatty hammering him from the north-eastward, with *Falmouth* attacking from the south-eastward—there was every justification for Hipper's confused impression that there was maximum British strength somewhere in the mists, all round and ahead of him—and he turned steadily through east and south.

The leading 'Königs' in the German Third Battle Squadron close astern had also taken part in the reply to the battle-cruisers, but being badly hit by invisible battleships they were glad to conform to Hipper's south-eastwards turn as well. The destruction of *Invincible* was Hipper's culminating achievement, as with his battered ships he turned southerly and out of range: by 6.35 p.m. he was heading west of south.

Scheer had heard the crescendo of gunfire ahead, from his flag-ship in the centre of the line, and at 6.27 p.m. he had felt obliged to abandon a plan to save *Wiesbaden*. He had now turned more eastward to afford some support to Hipper. His difficulty was to determine in what way his support could best be used: although half the British fleet were firing now, it was the leading half, and that irregularly and as the visibility permitted. Scheer could thus get no clear picture of the situation which remained obscure to him, and he was receiving no signals that might clarify it. Range-finding was almost impossible because of the low visibility, and all his gunners could do was fire at the will-o'-the-wisp flashes that appeared in the murky distance: in consequence, without ranges, or any constant point of aim, his fire was ineffectual,[1] and his shells hit nothing but water.

As Behncke's 'Königs' ahead began to bear away to the eastward and southward under pressure, Scheer astern could, therefore, only conform blindly to their general movements. The gunfire ahead was positive and, with no news whatsoever now from his battle-cruisers, Scheer was certain he must be steaming into a trap from

[1] *Official Despatches.*

which he must extricate his fleet at all costs. At 6.34 p.m. he signalled all ships to make the 'battle-turn-away' (*Gefechtskehrtwendung*) to the westward. The manoeuvre had been well-practised, and its procedure was thoroughly well understood throughout the German fleet: in his desperate position, Scheer had no acceptable alternative to this manoeuvre, although it had never been practised under fire and his fleet was not in a straight line, but had two very marked kinks in it—one in the middle of the leading Third Battle Squadron, half of which had already turned to the south-east—and the other further down the line between his Third and First Squadrons.

Despite the difficult conditions, the manoeuvre was accomplished successfully, although there were minor temporary crises. It was a tribute to the skill of the Captains of the German ships that they achieved this turn so well under fire; the whole High Seas Fleet was safely round and steering south-60°-west by 6.39 p.m.

One minute later, Scheer altered his course to west, directly away from his invisible enemies—and also further and further from his road for home. The firing astern died away.

It is some measure of the peril in which Scheer had suddenly realised his fleet to be that he had attempted this desperate manoeuvre under such conditions: it is also proof of his own personal resolution. To cover his turn-away, Commodore Michelsen, in *Rostock*, the Commodore of Flotillas, had ordered his 3rd flotilla and 1st half-flotilla to attack the British line in a north-easterly direction with torpedoes. They were the only fifteen destroyers available, owing to the absence of Heinrich's flotillas which—it will be remembered—had previously been detailed to deal with Admiral Hood and *Shark's* division and were in consequence still far out of station. The fifteen destroyers detailed set off under Commander Hollmann of the 3rd flotilla, but as the Grand Fleet's firing was dying down, Commodore Michelsen thought they would be firing their torpedoes into a void and recalled them. Twelve of them, after laying a smoke-screen, obeyed the recall; three others pushed on, however—*G-88*, *V-73* of the 3rd flotilla, and *S-32* of the 1st. These latter fired six torpedoes at the British battle-cruisers in the van before they too returned.

Four of these torpedoes passed close to *Lion* and *Princess Royal*, but none of them actually hit.[1] As the mists closed in around the German ships, veiling them from the British gunners, the cannonade fell silent.

[1] *G-88* and *V-73* fired one torpedo each; *S-32* fired four.

7

The Belching Guns

BETWEEN 6.35 and 6.40 p.m. the German High Seas Fleet disappeared abruptly and unexpectedly into the mists to the westward. Quite suddenly, all that remained visible of it was the smoke-shrouded *Wiesbaden*, and two or three destroyers which were quickly lost to view in what might have been a smoke-screen but seemed to merge into the general mist. Except for a few salvoes at *Wiesbaden*, en passant, no target remained for the British guns except for a few ships at the rear of the line firing at destroyers.

This was a critical moment in the day battle: Scheer, confused by the obscure situation, had unsuspectingly blundered into the whole Grand Fleet; to quote the German Official Historian:

> Suddenly the leading ships were faced by the belching guns of an interminable line of ships extending from north-west to north-east, whilst salvo followed salvo without intermission.[1]

Scheer's T was being crossed, and, under the fire of Jellicoe's battleships and Beatty's battle-cruisers, his van was taking heavy punishment. This had been the ideal opportunity for Jellicoe to unleash the concentrated gun-power of his centre and van upon the leading enemy squadrons, but for reasons already explained, the opportunity could not be seized. Before it could recur, Scheer's fleet had vanished precipitately into the mist.

To Admiral Jellicoe the enemy's sudden disappearance was entirely baffling: in the poor visibility prevailing, he had not been able to see more than two or three enemy ships at any one time: now even these were lost to sight. His personal impression was that the German disappearance was due to some temporary, local thickening of the mist to the westward, and that Scheer's ships might probably reappear as suddenly as they had vanished. He therefore held on along his deployment course—south-east by east—

[1] *Krieg zur See, Nordsee.*

138

while his last two ships turned the corner into the single line of
battle; his line was finally formed at about 6.42 p.m. as the Fifth
Battle Squadron reached its station.

With the completion of his line of battle, the Commander-in-
Chief was now able to close the range without difficulty, and at
6.42 p.m. he decided to haul round a point to starboard—to south-
east: this would not only close the range and, he hoped, bring
Scheer's ships into view again, but would also, by making as much
to the southward as possible while there was a chance to do so,
improve the British strategic position across the enemy's escape
routes to the safety of their home bases. Two minutes later, the
fleet altered course in succession to south-east by divisions, as the
Admiral considered this would achieve his object more quickly
than by turning the whole line in succession.[1]

There was still nothing to cause the Commander-in-Chief to
alter his personal view as to Scheer's disappearance. As the minutes
passed, however, and the enemy did not again come into view
despite his fleet's closing course, Jellicoe wondered if perhaps
Scheer had also made some small alteration of course to *keep* his
fleet within the protection of the mist. Eventually even this belief
began to fade, leaving only the probability that Scheer had been
making a big turn-away at around 6.35 p.m., when the guns had
lost their targets. This was hard to accept, for the German fleet
orders distinctly described the 'battle-turn-away' as one covered by
mass destroyer attacks with torpedoes, and a smoke-screen. Three
isolated destroyers could hardly be classed as a 'mass attack', and
not much of a smoke-screen had been seen.[2]

In his quandary the Commander-in-Chief preserved the same
unruffled calm which characterised him throughout the battle. In
his heart, however, he must have realised that now, as in the critical
time before deployment, the vital information he needed was not
forthcoming, and must have sensed that his subordinates were failing him. Yet neither then, nor later, in his Despatches, nor in his
memories of this day as he set them out in *The Grand Fleet*, did he
ever hint at this or complain.

Off *Iron Duke's* starboard bow lay a destroyer, stopped and disabled, rolling uneasily in the swell. She was flying 'Not Under

---

[1] The signal to alter course was made by flags and wireless: *Iron Duke's* signal log shows
6.42 p.m., *Benbow's* 6.40 p.m., *New Zealand* 6.42 p.m., while *Marlborough's* Wireless Entry
Log shows 6.41 p.m. The executive signal to turn followed two minutes later.
[2] The battle-cruiser *Tiger's* report after the battle mentioned the destroyers developing
a 'large smoke-screen'. This quickly merged into the misty background.

Control' signals at one yard-arm, and '6-flag'—'Am in Danger of Sinking'—at the other. At her after-mast, the White Ensign fluttered bravely—she was still in the fight.

The destroyer was *Acasta*, last seen limping away, shot-torn and under fire, having tried unsuccessfully, at close range, to torpedo one of Hipper's battle-cruisers. As she turned from this attack, she had at first careered away unable either to stop or to steer; after some minutes her captain, Lieutenant-Commander J. Barron, had got her under control, however, and steering with his engines, headed slowly towards the dim shapes of the advancing British line. Steam was failing down below, however, for the boiler-feeds had been put out of action, and presently she came to a standstill. Over her masthead the opening salvoes raged, and shells whistled as the Grand Fleet deployed into line, a line that had seemed at first to be heading straight at the disabled ship, and then bore away as *King George V* led the van a little to port. Lieutenant-Commander Barron and his men had worked like demons: the proper signals had been set flying, a collision-mat spread down her battered starboard bow, her bulkheads had been shored up forward: in the steam-laden engine-room, the Engineer Officer and his artificers and stokers had laboured to improvise such repairs as would at least get steerage way on the ship, if no more.

By now the Fleet, its battle-ensigns a-flutter, was drawing near: it would pass *Acasta* very closely and, as one of her officers observed, 'it would have been an ignominious end to have been run down by our own fleet—fortunately they all dodged us'. As the fleet drew near, Lieutenant-Commander Barron mustered every man who could be spared upon the tiny after deck. He could see *Iron Duke* plainly: at her fore fluttered the white flag with the Cross of Saint-George, the Admiral's flag; her silent guns trained and elevated over the starboard beam, ready to speak should the enemy emerge from the protecting mists. The group of men on the after-deck of the rolling destroyer stood straight and still—at attention; Lieutenant-Commander Barron's hand went to his cap in salute—the Commander-in-Chief was passing.

High above them, on the extreme wing of the flagship's upper bridge, *Acasta's* men could see the 'Little Man' as he gravely acknowledged their salute. He saw below him a small and battered ship, lying stopped and disabled and down by the head; he could see the collision mat, the signals, the holes in her hull fore and aft, he could see her rolling heavily in the wash of the passing ships, he could also see that from her after-mast the White Ensign was streaming in the breeze. And suddenly his cap was off, held high over his head, a personal salute.

Discipline and protocol had no place in that moment: the sailors hats came off too, and their spontaneous cheers rang out again and again over the waters as the fleet flagship went on her way. After that, *Acasta's* men stood and cheered every ship as it passed.

Acasta did eventually reach home after many adventures; but that is a story which must wait.

(ii)

Admiral Jellicoe was closing the range and holding his place astride the enemy's escape route; if as now seemed likely Scheer had turned widely to the westward at 6.35 p.m. by steering this course Jellicoe was maintaining a strategic position to bar the road back either to the Jade, or via the Kattegat. He had, moreover, removed his fleet as far as possible from the risk attendant upon any mines scattered by the retreating enemy fleet in its wake.

Still failing any information of the enemy, Jellicoe decided at 6.52 p.m. to close the assumed last position of the enemy, and inclined four points (45°) more to starboard: two minutes later, the fleet's course was accordingly altered by divisions to south.

This signal to turn had barely been hauled down when *Marlborough* at the head of the rear division reported that she had just been hit 'by a mine or torpedo'. She had in fact been struck below the waterline, beneath her fore-bridge, flooding her starboard forward hydraulic engine-room, and dieselroom. The ship quickly took a seven-degree list to starboard as A boiler-room began to flood. The battleship yawed a few degrees on either side of her course, just as she was passing *Acasta*, but managed to maintain the fleet speed of 17 knots although the rising water soon put out the starboard fires in the flooded boiler-room; aboard her there had been some doubt whether, as had been signalled, the damage had been caused by mine or torpedo; this was speedily cleared up, however, and the Commander-in-Chief was informed that the explosion had been caused by a torpedo.

Jellicoe had from the first been quite certain that the hit had been from a torpedo, since too many ships had passed over the same water for there to have been a mine. Who had fired it, however, is still a mystery; most probably it came from the battered *Wiesbaden*, her final gesture of defiance. It might, again, have come from the damaged *V-48*.

The tracks of several torpedoes had been seen by the rear squadrons some minutes previously and avoided—by individual manoeuvring or turning away. These had been fired by a small group of destroyers—invisible from *Iron Duke*, but seen and fired upon by the rear ships as they had emerged from the mist, to be driven back by gunfire. It seems that when the German *V-73*, *G-88* and *S-32* returned after firing their six torpedoes at the battle-cruisers they were at once sent out again with another destroyer by Scheer's direct orders to make an attempt to rescue the surviving crew of the *Wiesbaden*. Although they had only two or three miles of water to cover to reach the burning ship, these destroyers were obliged by British gunfire to abandon the attempt and turn back, but not before they had fired four torpedoes towards the rear of our line. These passed through the line, but were avoided with ease. *Wiesbaden* had thus perforce to be left to her fate, and blazing but still occasionally fired into, she heeled more and more to starboard; the few surviving seamen on board, seeing the destroyers turn back, took to their rafts before the cruiser finally plunged, her colours flying, soon after 7 o'clock. There was only one survivor.[1]

Writing of this phase of the battle, the German Official Historian says:

> At a critical juncture, Admiral Jellicoe had to rely solely and wholly upon his own observation.[2]

This was the brutal truth. The actual turn-away at 6.35 p.m. *had* been seen by cruisers off the van of the British battle-fleet, it had been seen by a number of battleships in the rear, from which direction the visibility was better than from the centre, yet none of these ships' captains[3] seemed to have bothered to report this significant occurrence by signal to the Commander-in-Chief, despite the emphasis which had been laid in the Battle Orders on the necessity for keeping the Commander-in-Chief in the centre informed of matters in the rear and the van, especially under difficult conditions of visibility.

It was not to be the only occasion on which Jellicoe's subordinates failed him in this respect. This time they could plead that with only

---

[1] Six officers and 48 men were lost in *V-48*; in *Wiesbaden* 27 officers and 543 men were lost. The sole survivor, Chief Stoker Zenner, clung to a raft for 38 hours, before he was picked up by the Norwegian steamer *Willi*, to be landed at Tonsberg. The Norwegian authorities very humanely decided not to intern him and he was repatriated a fortnight later to Germany.

[2] *Krieg zur See, Nordsee.*

[3] Among the ships which saw the turn-away and failed to report it were *Falmouth*, *Tiger*, *Indomitable* in the van: *Hercules*, *Benbow*, *Erin*, *Marlborough*, *Barham*: there were others also.

one or two ships visible on either side of a target ship, the turn of one did not necessarily imply that the whole line had turned; on the other hand, had each ship sighting the turn reported this immediately, the consensus of these reports would have clarified the position immediately. As it was, by the time Jellicoe began to feel almost certain that a 'battle-turn-away' had been made by the Germans, it was too late for him to take positive action.

The German 'battle-turn-away' in some ways resembled the similar manoeuvre which had been developed by French tacticians over a century earlier, in the closing years of our war with Napoleon: no answer had been found to it then, nor despite careful investigation of the similar problem in the early months of the present war, both upon the Tactical Board and by practical experiment, had any counter been discovered—other than 'immediate, resolute chase'.[1] A chase was quite out of the question, however: the absence of information had cost Jellicoe valuable time, and this must already have given the enemy an added lead of two to three miles.

Before considering the possibilities of pursuit, it is necessary to clear away some of the mist—other than natural mist—with which Jellicoe's critics—less just than the Official German Historian quoted above—have cloaked this phase of the battle. Jellicoe's decisions at this time were not a part of any 'long-resolved policy'.[2] They were the direct consequence of the absence of vital information from his subordinates; they marked no hesitation in getting to grips, nor were his tactics in any way governed by fear of torpedo-attack or of anything else. Presumably the 'long-resolved policy' referred to above was that to which Jellicoe submitted to the Admiralty in October 1914 and again in April 1915—a policy which had been approved at the time by the Sea Lords, and by Mr. Churchill as First Lord:

> If, for instance, the enemy battle fleet were to turn away from an ·advancing fleet, I should assume that the intention was to lead us over mines and submarines, and should decline to be so drawn.[3]

Jellicoe was well aware that his meeting with Scheer had been entirely fortuitous; the presence therefore of any previously prepared submarine trap was therefore extremely unlikely. The memorandum quoted above thus had no bearing on the situation at all, except perhaps as regards mines dropped by retreating ships to

[1] Corbett, *Naval Operations*.
[2] Cf. Churchill, *World Crisis*.
[3] Battle of Jutland, *Official Despatches*.

impede pursuit: this danger Jellicoe had avoided by moving to the southward.

As to the suitability of the occasion for a chase, Jellicoe had put his view on this subject in writing also:

> Nothing but ample time and superior speed can be an answer [to an enemy retreat] and this means that unless the meeting of the fleets takes place early in the day it is most difficult to fight to a finish.[1]

Superior speed and ample daylight were obviously the keys to success in pursuit: but Jellicoe held neither, as far as he knew.[2] Considering only the Dreadnought battle fleets on both sides, and leaving out of account the German 'Königs' and the British 'Queen Elizabeths', both fast squadrons, it is doubtful if Jellicoe could have expected more than the margin of one knot superior speed over the enemy: had he therefore turned to chase at 6.44 p.m., five minutes after the German 'battle-turn-away' was complete, he still would hardly have reduced the range in two hours' chasing, by which time the sun would have set and the light would be going; Jellicoe might also have forfeited his strategic position across the enemy's escape route to Germany and, under cover of darkness, the Germans might easily have turned directly for home.[3] With the evening so far advanced, therefore, a chase was out of the question.

As for dividing the fleet and sending his fast units to harass the flanks—or even envelop a separate squadron of the enemy, this might well have been considered under other conditions of visibility. The possibility of divided-fleet tactics had been accepted in the Royal Navy since 1911: they had been practised by Jellicoe with the Grand Fleet in his 'PZ' exercises (limited tactical manoeuvres carried out by fleets) earlier in the war, but never under conditions of low visibility and failing light, which would militate against any co-ordination or safety in the movement.

That this was a critical phase in the day fight none will deny; that any solution to its problem lay in pursuing the enemy is quite untenable. Apart from the failure of some of his ships to report at once what they had seen, Jellicoe had no idea even of the direction in which the enemy might have turned. Not only were the ships of the line amiss in not reporting what they knew, but, with one

[1] Harper, *Truth about Jutland*; Corbett, *Naval Operations*; Jellicoe, *Grand Fleet*.
[2] Jellicoe still did not know that Scheer, out of sentiment and against his better judgment, had brought Rear-Admiral Mauve's Second Squadron of pre-Dreadnoughts on this operation: they formed the rear of the German line, and had a *maximum* speed of only eighteen knots.
[3] Sunset on 31st May 1916 was at 8.07 p.m. G.M.T.

exception as will appear, there was also a general failure of reconnaissance from cruisers. The activities of the battle-cruisers, from
6.35 p.m. until after 7 o'clock, are of particular interest in this
connection. The Battle Orders defined their primary function in
action as the destruction of enemy battle-cruisers.[1] In addition,
however, they also had the all-important duty of gaining and maintaining contact with the enemy.

Beatty had presumably noticed that our battle fleet had checked
fire, as had his own ships, when their targets vanished at about
6.35 p.m. He could have regained touch with Hipper's ships—
which he knew were not yet destroyed—and, having thus re-
established contact with the enemy fleet, maintained it thereby
complying with the Battle Orders.

Instead of endeavouring to regain contact, however, his First and
Second Battle-Cruiser Squadrons together with the two remaining
ships of the Third Battle-Cruiser Squadron ahead of him, hurried on
ahead of the van of the battle fleet, until by 6.55 p.m. Beatty was
nearly six miles ahead on *Iron Duke's* port bow—that is, further from
the enemy than was the Commander-in-Chief himself. The fleet's
alterations of course at 6.44 and 6.54 p.m. had probably not been seen
from *Lion*, but as the signals to alter course had also been made by
wireless, these would probably have been repeated to *Lion* by one
or other of the ships in company; in any case *Inflexible* received them
and carried them out in the 3rd Battle-Cruiser Squadron, with
whose movements *Lion* with her 1st and 2nd Battle-Cruiser Squadrons appears to have conformed. She had, however, since ceasing
fire around 6.35 p.m. made no move to re-establish contact with the
enemy.

It seems that Beatty, at about 6.50 p.m.—realising that he had
drawn rather far ahead of the van of the battle fleet—decided to
reduce this distance and at the same time take the opportunity of
concentrating his three battle-cruiser squadrons. He signalled to
Inflexible and *Indomitable*, therefore, to take station in single line
astern of *Lion* and her consorts; the 3rd Battle-Cruiser Squadron was
then about three-quarters of a mile ahead and to the southward of
Lion. Two minutes later, at 6.52 p.m. Beatty reduced the speed of
the battle-cruisers to 18 knots.

At 6.54 p.m. *Lion's* helm went over, to turn to starboard—*Princess
Royal*, *Tiger*, and *New Zealand* following her, as she turned a complete
circle to starboard, *Inflexible* and *Indomitable* joining up in station in
the course of the turn. This circular turn was completed at 7.01 p.m.

[1] Cf. Jellicoe, *Grand Fleet*.

and Beatty then led his six battle-cruisers in line ahead at 18 knots on the south course of the fleet. The turn had brought the van of the battle fleet two miles nearer; but it had also wasted seven valuable minutes—for at 7.01 p.m. *Lion* was back in the position she had been in at the commencement of the turn at 6.54 p.m. This valuable seven minutes could have been better spent probing westward for the enemy. The fact that Beatty turned his battle-cruisers to a south course on the completion of their circling suggests, however, that Beatty was not thinking on those lines. Apart from this, there was nothing out of the way in *Lion* leading her consorts on a circular turn.

Unfortunately, after the battle there was some comment within the fleet concerning the apparent inactivity of the battle-cruisers at this time and the circular turn received an entirely unmerited prominence. Beatty's original track-chart for *Lion*, which had accompanied his post-battle despatch, had clearly shewn this circular turn: Beatty, now, however, denied that it had been made and supported this with a second track-chart (dated July 17th, 1916, and bearing his signature) which showed the turn as an S-turn, 180° to starboard followed by 180° to port which at 7.01 p.m. placed *Lion* some 1,500 yards nearer to the enemy. This alteration was made without regard to the fact that track-charts of other ships showed the circular turn, ships' log-books definitely made mention of the circular turn—and there were many eyewitnesses to it. The explanation put forward to account for this S-shaped turn was that Beatty had decided to head westward to look for the enemy; after *Lion* began to turn, her gyro compass had failed so the turn was continued through 180° to starboard and then compensated by a turn of 180° to port: it was further said that at the time the turn was made Admiral Beatty had left the bridge to examine some of the damage done to his ship.

After the war, in the autumn of 1919, when the battle again became the subject of polemic and controversy and Captain Harper's committee was hard at work producing a factual Record of the movements of British ships during the battle, it was natural that this odd incident should come in for close scrutiny. Captain Harper, who had access to *all* written records and factual documentary evidence had no hesitation in pronouncing that a complete circular turn had been made by the battle-cruisers between 6.54 p.m. and 7.01 p.m. This turn he showed on his draft chart and on the draft of the accompanying letterpress: the draft was submitted to the First Sea Lord for approval before going to the printers. Vice-

Admiral Sir David Beatty, commanding the Battle-Cruiser Force at Jutland had, however, become Admiral Lord Beatty—and was now the First Sea Lord. Unfortunately, he clung to his previous completely untenable position. He thus brushed aside once again the accumulated evidence of other ships' logs and track-charts, eyewitness accounts, and everything else. The diametrically opposed viewpoints of the First Sea Lord and Captain Harper on this point led to Lord Beatty insisting that the charts and text of the projected Record be amended to show *his* version of the story—the S-shaped turn: Captain Harper, six foot two inches of robust New Zealand integrity was only willing to carry out this order provided that an explanatory note was included to give the reason for the amendment and upon whose authority it had been made. This was only one of a number of such conflicting issues; in the end, the Record—although its publication had been promised in the House of Commons—was not published.

(iii)

With Admiral Jellicoe closing the last known position of the enemy and starved of information, and with Beatty's battle-cruisers in the van chasing their tails some miles to the southward, a point arises that deserves some comment: Mr. Churchill's account of this phase of the battle contained a particularly regrettable inaccuracy.

> At 6.35 p.m. he [Admiral Scheer] . . . turned his whole fleet about . . . launching a flotilla to cover his retirement by torpedo-attack. . . . Jellicoe, threatened by the torpedo stream, turned away according to his long-resolved policy.

Taking these points *seriatim*, it must be recalled that Commodore Michelsen had certainly mounted an attack by fifteen destroyers, but had recalled these before they even began to develop their attack; three of them failed to answer the recall, held on and fired six torpedoes at the battle-cruisers four miles ahead of the fleet. Only four of these were seen and were avoided. Later, other destroyers, invisible to *Iron Duke*, appeared in an attempt to rescue the crew of *Wiesbaden*; those had been beaten off and in retiring fired four torpedoes at the rear of the British line; these had also been easily avoided. So the 'flotilla' was in reality very few destroyers; and the 'torpedo stream' proves to have been a barely discernible trickle. Above all, Jellicoe did *not* 'turn away' at all at this stage; indeed, he turned to close the enemy progressively throughout the period.

Leaving Jellicoe to his problems, it is convenient at this point to follow Scheer's progress: he had 'turned away' from the British guns after only twenty minutes of intermittent fire. As he told the Austrian naval attaché afterwards, on 17th June 1916, he had advanced north-eastward because he 'thought he ought to assist the *Wiesbaden*', and because the situation was quite obscure to him, for he 'received no wireless reports'. This was correct as far as it went—although he *did* receive reports from Boedicker and Hipper, and was to receive another in the near future from *Moltke*. As Scheer continued to the attaché:

> I soon saw that the leading ships were coming under an overwhelming fire and that I could not risk the fleet on *Wiesbaden's* account.

He had thereupon hastily reversed his fleet at 6.34 p.m., and headed back into the mist—a point he omitted to mention during the conversation.

To his Kaiser and Emperor, his explanation differed slightly, for he now stressed the presence of the British battle fleet on an arc between north-east and east ahead of him. He continued:

> The First Scouting Group and the van of the Third Battle Squadron were warding off the enemy attack. In course of this, they were forced to turn away so sharply that I considered it necessary at 6.35 p.m. to relieve the pressure by a 'battle-turn-away' to the west.[1]

This certainly sounds more realistic: the necessity was to relieve pressure as quickly as possible; but Scheer's idea of the position of the British battle fleet was gravely in error, for it reached from north to north-east only, and that was including the six battle-cruisers who formed its leading edge. In his post-war memoirs, Admiral Scheer's busy pen observed with truth: 'Our action in reversing the course would be classed as a retreat'.[2] The truth emerges, perhaps, from consideration of the condition of Scheer's fleet after his successful turn-away under fire. Hipper's battle-cruisers were then in far worse shape than were Beatty's surviving battle-cruisers: the German flagship *Lützow* was so badly damaged as to be no longer a sound fighting unit and her speed had been seriously impaired; her casualties were heavy, and she was heavily down by the head with her foredeck almost awash. There were several hundred tons of water swilling to and fro inside the hull, she was listing heavily, on fire, and almost out of control: her wireless installation was out of action.

[1] Cf. Battle of Jutland, *Official Despatches*, with Scheer's *Despatch*.
[2] Scheer, *High Seas Fleet*.

Understandably, the gallant Admiral Hipper was loath to leave his comrades in this battered ship, but if the action were to continue it had to be controlled from a ship that could fight. Just before seven o'clock, therefore, he called the destroyer *G-39* (Commander Albrecht) of the 1st flotilla alongside, embarked in her with his staff and set off to find another suitable ship as his flagship. *Lützow* was told to make her way home as best she could, and Scheer allocated the remainder of the 1st flotilla as an escort, as she limped slowly and painfully southward under cover of smoke. Hipper ordered Captain Hartog of *Derfflinger* to assume command of the Group in the meantime, and set off on his quest for a new flagship: it is said that on board the destroyer he turned his back upon his old ship and that there were tears in his eyes.

Derfflinger would not serve Hipper's purposes, for her wireless had also been disabled: she had been heavily hit twenty times with large projectiles, and had 180 killed and wounded on board; she had a great gaping hole forward through which the seas surged in and out and she was down by the head. A few minutes after the 'battle-turn-away' was completed, she had had perforce to stop, for her torpedo nets had been shot away from their stowage on the net-shelf and were trailing in the water—with the danger that they could entangle her propellers at any moment. The gun-crews came out of their turrets and, working feverishly, succeeded in ten minutes in cutting them free; then they went back to the turrets—never to emerge again, as will be seen.

The battle-cruiser *Seydlitz* (Captain von Egidy) astern of *Derfflinger* with twelve large hits on her, was in little better plight: she had also been badly holed forward, by *Petard's* torpedo. There were already some two thousand tons of water in her, and she was awash forward to the level of her middle deck. *Von der Tann* (Captain Zenker) still had no gun-turrets ready for action—and this left only *Moltke* as a fighting unit.

The leading battleships of Behncke's Third Squadron had also suffered heavy damage, considering the short time they had been in action, particularly *König* with five hits, *Grosser Kurfürst* with four, *Markgraf* with three and *Kaiser* with two. Had they not turned away from the British guns their damage would in a very short time have been comparable with that of Hipper's battle-cruisers.

In the brief encounter—for only eighteen minutes of intermittent fire had taken place before Scheer's turn-away compelled the British guns to 'check fire'—there had been sufficient damage done to show Scheer what would be in store for his ships were he to face the Grand Fleet's guns squarely. Nothing is more certain, therefore, than that as he turned into the mist the dominant thought in his mind was to extricate the High Seas Fleet from its unfavourable position, and make for his German harbours as quickly as possible. He had turned originally to a course south-60°-west; by 6.41 p.m. he was on his course, and a minute later, turned the fleet by divisions further to the westward, bringing Jellicoe more astern of him. At 6.45 p.m. he received a wireless message from *Moltke* reporting that the van of the British battle fleet bore east-by-south. This, in combination with his belief that the 'Invincibles', which had wrought such execution on his battle-cruiser van, must be the four battleships, the existence of which the adventures of Boedicker and *Chester* had firmly implanted in his mind, now crystalised his plans of escape. Scheer during the next few minutes must have calculated that if the van of the British battle fleet was bearing east-by-south, then, assuming the British line to be some six to seven miles in length from tip to tail, it would be curving on an arc from east-by-south to east-north-east. Assuming also that the British line would probably be advancing at a speed of seventeen knots in a south-easterly direction, the rear would now be bearing about east-south-east. By shaping a course east-south-east, therefore, he ought to be able to pass *astern of the British fleet* unseen in the mist, and make thence directly for the German base through the nearest swept channel. The sketch which accompanied his Despatch to the Emperor showed clearly his estimation of the formation and position of the British fleet relative to his own fleet at this time; and upon this, no doubt, he based his plan of action.

Having decided that he must head for home in any case, Scheer now lost no time in putting this plan into action. Altering course two points to starboard by divisions at 6.47 p.m.—by way of preparation —he turned his ships together 16 points to starboard eight minutes later. He thus restored his fleet to its original *Keil Linie 3-1-2*, with *König* in the van as 'guide of the fleet', and with *Derfflinger* leading the battle-cruisers on the new east-south-east course. The intention was clear: to pass astern of the British fleet, and head for Germany: even if his movement across the Grand Fleet's rear were detected and he had to fight he would be in a position to cross Jellicoe's T from astern, and, once he had passed to the eastward side of the British line, *his* gunners would have the advantage of the light.

Scheer's explanations of his moves at this time are somewhat complicated. In his Despatch on the battle, he said that to have started for home before dark would only have played into Jellicoe's hands, for the British admiral would then have been able to re-engage him and cut the escape route back to the Bight. The only alternative that Scheer could see was therefore to advance regardless of consequences and make a second attack on Jellicoe's fleet, at the same time hurling all his destroyers into the fray. It is, however, worthy of note here that, as for making 'another attack', Scheer had not made even one yet. An advance, such as this, Scheer explained, would come as a surprise to the British, and would upset their plans for the rest of the day; if the blow were delivered heavily enough, moreover, it would facilitate the German escape during the night.[1]

For the edification of a much wider post-war public, however, Admiral Scheer produced an interesting if less factual variation upon this theme. He now stated that he had no wish to leave it to Jellicoe to decide when he would meet the Germans next morning and that the only way to deprive Jellicoe of his initiative was to compel him to fight a second (sic) engagement by making 'another (sic) determined advance'. The success of the 'battle-turn-away' he had made under fire, Scheer wrote, was an encouragement to advance eastwards regardless of the consequences:

> It would surprise the enemy, and confound his plans, and, if the blow fell heavily enough, facilitate breaking loose [*loslösen*] at night.

A third variation on this theme seems to have occurred to Scheer in the course of his recorded conversation with the Austrian naval attaché. Referring to the period after the battle-turn-away, he then said:

> When I noticed that the British pressure had quite ceased, and that my fleet remained intact in my hands, I turned back under the impression that the action could not end this way, and that I ought to seek contact with the enemy again.

It is hard to believe that a man of such ability as Admiral Scheer could have expected people to believe this sort of thing. To profess, in all seriousness, that he intended deliberately to thrust at the centre of a stronger fleet, whose fire-power he had already felt, and from which he had already promptly turned away, somewhat surprised, it would seem, to find that his fleet was even as intact as it was, was to hurl his reputation to the Four Winds. Yet, as his chief of staff is said to have remarked afterwards: 'If an Admiral had brought about such a position at manoeuvres, he would have been relieved of his command.'

The German Naval Historian quite understandably accepts

[1] Battle of Jutland, *Official Despatches*.

Scheer's explanation—and finds a convenient parallel between it and Nelson's Trafalgar Memorandum. This analogy had undoubtedly been woven into Scheer's Despatch to his Emperor for this very purpose, for Scheer had written: 'Such a manoeuvre would surprise the enemy and upset his plans . . .' In his post-war book he even repeated this: 'The manoeuvre would be bound to surprise the enemy and upset his plans.'[1] The parallel which the German Official Historian drew was with Nelson's comment to Keats on the subject of his famous Memorandum; Nelson had said: 'I think it will surprise and confound the enemy.' The analogy is there—thus far—but it is a pity that the quotation was not given in full, for Nelson had added '*It will bring forward pell-mell battle, and that is what I want. . . .*'[2] A 'pell-mell battle' was exactly what Scheer did *not* want. He only wanted to be able to escape—to 'break loose' during the night as the 'only one way of avoiding' battle, on Jellicoe's terms on the morrow for this he knew must spell disaster—and he had said so.[3]

Taking everything into consideration, it seems, in the light of later knowledge, what really happened was that Scheer, having determined to withdraw, misjudged the position of the British battle fleet's van; on this false basis he set a course to pass—he thought—across the British fleet's rear, unseen in the mists, and thence to make his way home as quickly as possible during the dark hours. This seems to be a much more probable interpretation of what occurred than the various explanations made by Scheer afterwards.

So Scheer turned eastward and headed for home in single line, with his battle-cruisers ahead of him, and with the 3rd, the 2nd, and the 9th flotillas and *Rostock* (the Flotilla Commodore's flagship) in the van. His Second Scouting Group was on the fleet's starboard bow: it made a half-hearted reconnaissance out of the mist, but quickly turned back—unseen.

Scheer had, however, barely started his eastward journey when he was sighted and reported by that 'admirable Crichton' of reconnaissance, Commodore Goodenough: almost alone of Jellicoe's cruiser flag-officers, the Commodore seems to have been completely aware of his primary duty and this he performed consistently and conscientiously throughout the day. In his flagship, *Southampton*, he had been on Evan-Thomas' quarter, when the Battle-Cruiser Force had joined up with the Grand Fleet an hour previously. In con-

[1] Scheer: *High Seas Fleet.*
[2] Nicholas, *Letters and Despatches of Nelson.*
[3] Scheer's Despatch, *Jutland, Official Despatches.*

sequence, his Second Light-Cruiser Squadron was only passing 'Windy Corner' at 6.25 p.m., ten minutes after deployment had begun; it had been 6.40 p.m. before he had reached his battle-station off the battle-line's engaged quarter. Once there he saw what he thought was the enemy turning away at about 6.45 p.m.; how much it had turned or how many ships had turned he could not see. With his Light-Cruiser Squadron at his heels, Commodore Goodenough, therefore, increased speed and promptly turned to investigate. For a while the mists shut the enemy from his sight, but he headed for the position in which he had last seen them and persisted in his reconnaissance. [At about 6.53 p.m. he turned parallel to the course of the British fleet, and three minutes later was rewarded with a hazy glimpse of the enemy now nine or ten miles away on his starboard beam. Continuing on his south-east course, he noticed the enemy begin to turn at 6.58 p.m., and wishing to see which way they were going, altered his squadron's course towards them. At 7 p.m. he could see that they were steering eastward, and in line; he again turned his ships together in order to observe the enemy's movements more closely. His wireless had, however, already spelt out the news (7.04 p.m.) for which Jellicoe had been waiting:

> *Southampton* to S.O. Battle-Cruiser Force: Urgent. Priority. Enemy Battle Fleet steering east-south-east. Enemy bears south-south-west. Number unknown. . . .[1]

As *Southampton* was just in sight from *Iron Duke*, about five miles to the north-westward of her, the enemy's position could be established at once with considerable accuracy, and Jellicoe at 7.05 altered the battle fleet's course (by divisions, together) three points to starboard, to south-west by south, to close the enemy.

Southampton in the meantime had continued to lead her squadron towards the enemy, but coming under heavy fire from *König*, *Markgraf* and *Grosser Kurfürst*, Commodore Goodenough quickly extricated his ships, bringing them into line and withdrawing north-eastward—but still keeping the enemy under observation. He had once again given an example of good cruiser-scouting work.

The battle fleet quickly came round onto its new course—it had now turned through 90° altogether away from its original deployment course and was closing in by divisions in line abreast, a mile

---

[1] There is a record also of a signal received in *Iron Duke* at about 7.00 p.m., from Beatty, reporting: 'Enemy are to the westward.' At the time Beatty was 13 miles from the *nearest* of them (Hipper's First Scouting Group), and there was not thirteen miles' visibility. In any case Jellicoe *knew* that the enemy was to the westward of him somewhere.

apart. At this moment a report reached *Iron Duke* apparently locating a 'submarine' off the flagship's port bow.[1]

In view of this report, the Commander-in-Chief promptly turned the fleet by divisions back to south at 7.09 p.m.[2] This would bring the reported submarine ahead—the accepted manoeuvre for such a situation. This turn back to south, moreover, left Jellicoe's divisions more nearly in line ahead, which was of some significance, because, just before he turned, enemy destroyers (part of the flotillas about two miles ahead of the enemy fleet's van) had been sighted emerging from the mists to the south-westward. They were reported at 7.08 p.m., by *Benbow*, Vice-Admiral Sturdee's flagship, at the head of the column next to starboard of the fleet flagship; a minute later *Benbow's* 6-inch battery opened fire on them.

The turn to south, therefore, not only brought the reported submarine ahead; it also put the fleet into a more convenient formation for any subsequent manoeuvre that might be required in the enemy's presence, as well as bringing the battleships' A-arcs to bear in the direction from which it was anticipated the enemy would be sighted. As Jellicoe turned to south, the correctness of his move was confirmed, for he could see broad on his starboard bow the dim form of an enemy light cruiser with numerous destroyers (the 18th and 11th half-flotillas) ahead of her, advancing out of the mist.[3]

Once again the great fleets were drawing together, and Jellicoe's battle fleet was again ready in all respects. Ahead of its van *Southampton's* signal at 7.04 seemed to have awakened the battle-cruisers to their responsibilities, and Beatty had turned from his southerly course in which his circling adventure had left him, and was turning gradually round at eighteen knots to the south-south-westward, the course which *Southampton's* signal implied would be one upon which he could regain touch with the enemy. In the van also, Rear-Admiral Napier was leading his Third Light-Cruiser Squadron westwards across the bows of *King George V*: *Calliope* and her fast Fourth Light-Cruiser Squadron, on the fleet's port bow, were also moving across. The destroyer-flotillas were, however, still on the

---

[1] *King George V* reported a submarine ahead of *Iron Duke* at about 7 p.m., and *Duke of Edinburgh*—some three and a quarter miles on the flagship's port bow also reported at the time (7.01 p.m.) a submarine on her port bow. Beatty had also reported the presence of a submarine at 6.44 p.m. These reports could not have referred to the same submarine. There was justification for considering the possible presence of a submarine. There were, in fact, no fewer than 30 recorded reports of submarines among the ships of the fleet between 3.35 and 10 p.m. that day: yet we *now* know there were none there at all. —Cf., Jellicoe, *Grand Fleet*.

[2] The exact time of this alteration is uncertain: from the plotted positions it seems that 7.09 was the most likely time.

[3] Corbett, *Naval Operations*.

fleet's disengaged bow: it had been difficult for both light cruisers and destroyers to get into their proper station on the engaged bow, with the fleet continually altering course inwards. These light forces, however, had a sufficient margin of speed to have reached their position, and they should have used it, for it was likely that their presence on the engaged bow would be required very soon to deal with developing enemy destroyer attacks at least.

It has been said that at the rear of the British line, by reason of the lesser smoke interference, the visibility was generally better than in the centre or in the van. Thus, just as the fleet's turn to south was completed, *Hercules*, the third ship of the rear division— last but four in the battle line—sighted off her starboard bow a German battle-cruiser (*Seydlitz*) heading eastward; the battleship's turrets at once trained round. *Colossus*, leading the fifth division, almost at the same time sighted *Derfflinger*, and her turrets trained round also. As the German battle-cruisers gradually cleared the mist one by one and came clearly into view, battleship after battleship trained their guns, ranged—and opened fire on them. Soon afterwards, behind the First Scouting Group, the 'Königs' and 'Kaisers' could also be seen advancing, then *Friedrich der Grosse* leading other battleships, all of them heading eastwards.

The rear division of the British battle fleet, being nearer, came into action first. *Marlborough*, despite her list and her torpedo damage, was still very much 'in the line': from 7.11 p.m. onwards she fired fourteen salvoes in six minutes at *König*, at ranges of 11,000 to 9,800 yards, hitting her four times and setting her on fire, until she was seen to turn out of the line for a while. *Revenge* also opened fire with her 15-inch broadsides on *König*, but seeing that *Marlborough* was already making 'good practice' on her, shifted her target to the fourth ship in the line, fired thirteen salvoes and then transferred her attentions to a battle-cruiser. *Hercules*, astern of *Revenge*, had first sighted the battle-cruisers, and took the second of these, *Seydlitz*, as her target hitting her with the fifth and sixth salvoes. Astern again, '*Agincourt* the mighty' opened a heavy fire on ships of the German Third Squadron at 11,000 yards firing twelve salvoes, and securing effective hits.

In the meantime, for good measure, *Revenge* fired a torpedo at the *Von der Tann*—but it missed. As the enemy came into view of the fifth division, these began to fire upon the enemy battle-cruisers, and *Colossus* and her division all poured a heavy fire upon these ships at ranges between 8,000 and 9,000 yards: the enemy's reply was ineffectual. At the tail of the line, the Fifth Battle Squadron was also coming into action, engaging the enemy's battle-cruisers, and increasing the volume of British fire-power.

Beatty, heading south-westerly and still several miles ahead of the van, did not sight the enemy until about 7.12 p.m. But two minutes later, his squadron, too, was busily firing at Hipper's battle-cruisers at ranges between 18,000 and 20,000 yards.

By this time, *Iron Duke* also had opened fire—at 7.13 p.m., upon a 'König' battleship, and the remaining ships of the centre and the leading divisions opened fire as the enemy came into view at ranges between 14,000 and 17,500 yards. They chose targets as they presented themselves, whether battleships or battle-cruisers: they were all the enemy. By 7.13 p.m., most of the British fleet was engaged.

The cannonade was indeed tremendous for the short while that it lasted—it was probably the greatest that will ever be fired at sea. The 6-inch and 4-inch guns of the centre and rear divisions were also firing heavily upon the advancing German destroyers; the enemy capital ships were being repeatedly hit with heavy shells and were coming under an ever-increasing pressure from the concentration of fire-power which Jellicoe's line was developing.[1] At 7.12 p.m. the Commander-in-Chief had signalled *Marlborough* and the fifth division to take station astern in line of *Iron Duke's* division, thus withdrawing them from possible danger of torpedo attack as well as strengthening the fleet's concentration of fire. At the same time, Vice-Admiral Sturdee, whose ships had been using their secondary armament since 7.08 p.m. against a small destroyer attack ahead of their starboard beam, assuming that the destroyers had just fired their torpedoes, turned his division at 7.07 p.m. by use of the 'preparative' flag[2] two points *away* from the attack. According to Scheer, the attack had been made by some six destroyers firing six torpedoes; three were avoided by *Colossus*, *Agincourt* and *Neptune*, and the other three are believed to have passed somewhere near the Fifth Battle Squadron unseen. Sturdee was, moreover, anticipating the Commander-in-Chief's intentions and was

[1] 'Regular Distribution of Fire' by separate divisions was impracticable, because of the vagaries of visibility; so each ship 'chose its own bird' and fired at this target.

[2] The 'Preparative Flag' was a code flag used as a special and urgent single-flag signal to be used when manoeuvring ships in line that were menaced by a torpedo attack. It indicated that squadron addressed was to turn by subdivisions (2 ships) two points *away* from the direction of enemy attack, leaders of subdivisions turning together, ship astern of them turning in succession. Correctly used this signal would so turn the line that the experts' expectation of 40 per cent torpedo hits was reduced, mathematically, to less than 2 per cent probable hits.

taking his divisions to form line astern of the flag. Four minutes later at 7.16 p.m., Jellicoe ordered Jerram, with his Second Battle Squadron in the van, to form ahead of *Iron Duke* at full speed, himself reducing the speed of the fleet temporarily to fifteen knots to enable him to do so. Jellicoe's sure tactical instinct had shown him clearly that, with his fleet coming into single battle line, Scheer's T was once more crossed, his van was enveloped and the British gunners had all the advantages of the light.

The battle fleet was, indeed, having its turn during the ten minutes between 7.06 and 7.16 p.m., while a growing concentration of accurate fire beat down on the leading German ships. Their battle-cruisers especially came under a crushing fire.[1]

For the second time that evening, Scheer had blundered headlong into the centre of Jellicoe's fleet: his van was enveloped, his T crossed and his road home barred. If, as he later told the Austrian attaché, he had only steered eastward to seek contact with his enemy, he had certainly succeeded. If, as he wrote in his memoirs, he had intended to fight a second engagement—he was succeeding in that, to his discomfort. If, as he told his Emperor in his Despatch, his eastward course would 'surprise' the enemy, he was wrong: it was Scheer who had been taken by surprise.

Scheer's predicament was indeed now more perilous than before: his leading ships were being remorselessly battered by an enemy discernible only from his gunflashes—and these seemed to form an almost continuous flickering orange light right round the horizon ahead, from port to starboard. His best ships in the Third Squadron, the 'Königs' and 'Kaisers' were being hit, his flagship was under fire, and even the leading ships astern of the flagship were being straddled. In his desperate plight, Scheer quickly recognised that the only hope of avoiding destruction lay in yet another emergency 'battle-turn-away' by his ships, and at 7.11 p.m. he hoisted the green signal flag for this turn—again to starboard—supplementing it with parallel orders by wireless and searchlight. At the same time he directed all his destroyers to advance and lay a smoke-screen and to attack the British line as cover for the main fleet while it turned.[2]

---

[1] *Derfflinger*: fired at by *Benbow**, *Superb*, *Colossus**, *Neptune** and *Revenge**. *Seydlitz*: fired at by *Royal Oak*, *Bellerophon*, *Collingwood**, *Hercules**, *Revenge**, *Agincourt*, *Barham** and *Lion*. *Von der Tann*: fired at by *Valiant**, *Malaya**. *Lützow*: fired at by *Orion*, *Monarch* and *Centurion* firing at over 19,000 yards. The leading division of 'König' and 'Kaiser' battleships was fired on by *Iron Duke*, *King George V*, *Agincourt*, *Revenge*, *Marlborough*, *Royal Oak*, and *Monarch*—all of whom noted hits—among others. The * denotes those ships which noted hits.

[2] Scheer seems to have been unaware that the Commodore of Flotillas had at 6.52 p.m. already committed his 6th and 9th flotillas to an attack.

Just as Togo had done at Tsu-Shima, Jellicoe's guns were holding Scheer's van in an inexorable grip and extending their pressure down the German line progressively as each enemy ship emerged from the mist. Already, under this pressure, the leading battle squadron—Behnke's third—was beginning to bend away to the southward.

Within a minute of hoisting the 'turn-away' signal, however, Scheer seems to have realised that the destroyer-attacks he first planned as tactical cover could not possibly have the desired effect early enough to save his leading battleships from almost certain destruction. Some other urgent means must be essayed—something that would distract the enemy's fire quickly: something, moreover, that must be provided very soon. Only too clearly the German Admiral saw that if he was to save his battleships he must offer up his battlecruisers as a sacrifice to the British guns: this would almost certainly, he felt, draw the fire of the British fleet upon them, and away from the van battleships, two of which were now on fire.

By making a desperate, 'forlorn-hope' dash at the British centre, his battle-cruisers might gain him the time he needed so desperately in which the German battle fleet could be turned away into safety.

At 7.12 p.m.—with the green 'battle-turn-away' signal still flying, Scheer hoisted in his foretop the appropriate code-signal to his battle-cruisers—'9-pendant, R-flag': 'Battle-Cruisers: attack the enemy immediately regardless of consequences.' The last sentence is how the purport of the signal would perhaps have been prosaically conveyed in the more phlegmatic British signal-code-book. The Germans, however, with their unfailing gift for the theatrical gesture, have since enlarged the purport of *'Standart R'* in the German signal-code—*'ran an dem Feind'*—as: 'close the enemy and ram. Ships will fight to the death!'[1]

The battle-cruisers thus called upon to sacrifice themselves to retrieve Scheer's blunder had been under heavy fire for some minutes and had suffered further damage: they were, indeed, in very poor shape for such a desperate venture. Nevertheless, Captain Hartog of *Derfflinger* lost no time in getting his four battle-scarred ships into line ahead. Apart from injury received during the afternoon at the hands of Beatty and Evan-Thomas, they had suffered heavy hits during the twenty minutes between the British deployment and Scheer's first turn-away: *Lützow* had then been rendered un-

---

[1] Cf., Hase, *Kiel and Jutland*.

serviceable by nine more hits; *Derfflinger* had received four hits; and *Seydlitz* two. As they formed up for their great 'ride' *Derfflinger* had one turret damaged, her wireless out of action, and a shell bursting in her port engine-room had cracked the turbine casing filling her engine-room with scalding steam until artificers and stokers had located the damage and patched it. *Seydlitz* had only two turrets now in action; she had a five-degree list, as well as being down by the head; her secondary armament had mostly been put out of action and fires were raging in her casemates and elsewhere above the upper deck. Below decks one of her shellrooms was partly flooded and the shell-room crew laboured to shore up the surrounding bulkheads to keep back the inflow of water. She was being steered now from her steering-engine. *Moltke* was relatively the least damaged, but astern of her *Von der Tann*, with heavy shot-holes in her sides, still kept place in the line, although half her turrets were virtually out of action again.

The spirit of the surviving personnel in these ships was, however, quite unimpaired: at the commencement of the afternoon action, when first heavily hit, 'the men were very subdued, but when it was realised that the hits were not affecting the fighting efficiency of the ships—the men's spirits rose and it was difficult to keep them quiet'.[1] This was the spirit which the self-effacing and brilliant Vice-Admiral Hipper had strenuously inculcated in his officers and men by his personal leadership and by constant exercise and training in the Baltic training ground: his squadron's gunnery was of a very high order; his ships and men were familiar with battle tactics, and had even practised this very manoeuvre of 'forlorn-hope' to which it was now to be committed. The answer to all Hipper's arduous training came in the spontaneous upsurge of morale to new high levels when the battle-cruisers' crews knew that the 'attack' signal was flying. In *Derfflinger* and *Moltke*, in *Von der Tann* and *Seydlitz* the sound of men singing '*Deutschland über Alles*' and '*Die Wacht am Rhein*' floated up the voice-pipes and through the rents in their decks and hulls: down below in *Seydlitz*, the stokers, forcing up the steam-pressure, shot their shovelfuls of coal into the furnaces and rang their shovels on the steel deck to shouts of '*D'rauf Seydlitz! D'rauf Seydlitz!*'—the terrible 160-year-old battle cry of General Seydlitz's Dragoons as they had charged at Rosbach and Zorndorf.

When the signal to attack the enemy had first been hoisted, Vice-Admiral Hipper in the destroyer *G-39* had just gone alongside

[1] Gunnery officer of *Lützow*, *Journal of the Royal United Services Institution*.

Seydlitz to see if she would be suitable as his flagship. She had, however, some 2,000 tons of water in her, and her wireless had been shot away. He had found that she would not do, and the destroyer had then moved towards *Moltke*. Captain Albrecht, commanding *G-39*, was just turning up to go alongside *Moltke* when the 'attack the enemy' signal was hauled down and the *Moltke*, as the range closed, quickly came under fire. Hipper, for the destroyer's safety, ordered her commander to withdraw and the Admiral was obliged to watch from a distance the agony of his ships during the next few minutes, wishing no doubt that he could have shared it with the officers and men he had trained so well.

As the attack signal was hauled down, Captain Hartog of *Derfflinger* unhesitatingly led his ships directly towards the point between the van and centre of the British battle line, closing the range fast as he did so; almost immediately they came under an increasing and heavy fire. Eleven British battleships turned their guns on *Derfflinger* and *Seydlitz*, to be joined after 7.18 p.m. by the guns of Beatty's battle-cruisers, firing at long range off the enemy's starboard bow.

Monarch and *Orion* of the Second Battle Squadron concentrated at long range also on the burning *Lützow* as she endeavoured to withdraw to the southward out of action with her small destroyer escort and, despite the protective smoke-screen they had laid down for her, four heavy shells hit *Lützow* in rapid succession. Her B turret was put out of action and the electric circuits to her after turret were severed; her charthouse was shot away: another shell burst through her upper and protected decks between the after-turrets, exploded in the battle casualty-station beneath and wiped out doctors and wounded, destroying instruments and dressings. Heavily on fire now, her smoke drifted down across her sister ships as she limped on, though ever more slowly now, to the westward, to get out of range.

For the four battle-cruisers closing the enemy in line, a fierce, unequal engagement now developed.

The gunnery officer of *Derfflinger* has recorded:

A perfect hail of projectiles beat on us. A 15-inch shell [from *Revenge*] pierced the armour of 'Caesar' turret, and exploded inside . . . nearly the whole gun-house crew was killed. The shell set on fire two cartridges; the flames spread down to the working chamber where they set fire to four more, and then to the handling-room where yet four more were ignited. The burning charges emitted great tongues of flame which shot up as high as a house; but they only blazed, did not explode as had

In worsening visibility, battle-cruiser *Tiger* opens fire at high speed, with *New Zealand* firing astern of her.

Invincible blows up after a direct hit from *Derfflinger*. The gush of fire bursting out of the exploding forward magazine is clearly visible and the main mast is already falling. Minutes later, only the upended bows and stern remain.

REAR-ADMIRAL THE HON. HORACE HOOD,
commanding the Third Battle-Cruiser Squadron, was
lost when his flagship *Invincible* blew up (seen above
from *Inflexible*, 500 yards astern of her).

been the case with the enemy.[1] This saved the ship, but all but five of the seventy men in the turret were killed. . . . A few minutes later, a 15-inch shell hit the roof of 'Dora' turret, and the same horrors ensued. Again the charges nearest were set on fire, roaring up to the sky like funeral pyres. With the exception of one man, the whole [turret's] crew of eighty were killed instantly; the enemy had our range to an inch.[2]

Derfflinger was hit on her bridge and on her armoured conning-tower, by a shell which tore off great pieces of armour, flinging them round the ship.

Seydlitz, Moltke and *Von der Tann* also suffered heavily, and *Seydlitz* was soon even more down by the head than before.

Seeing their agony, after it had lasted only three minutes, Scheer signalled to his battle-cruisers, varying their 'death-ride' to an order to 'manoeuvre off the enemy van'. This at least permitted Captain Hartog of *Derfflinger* greater freedom of movement, and he hauled round to the southward, parallel to the British line. His advance had, however, closed the range by nearly 3,000 yards, and his punishment continued for a while longer.

The dash of the devoted German battle-cruisers brought some brief respite to the van of their battle fleet. The British fire was, however, steadily increasing in volume, and Scheer, realising that he dare not wait any longer, at 7.17 p.m. hauled down the signal for a 'battle-turn-away' 16 points to starboard. Already there was some 'cover' for his leading destroyers were beginning to lay a dense smoke screen: this would spread and shield his manoeuvre from the watching eyes in the British fleet.

Nothing reveals more clearly the perilous position into which Scheer had directed his fleet than the decision to make his 'battle-turn-away' under such difficult conditions, for not only was it being made under heavy fire, but his Third Squadron was already sharply angled to the rest of his line. The word-picture he afterwards painted[3] for the consumption of his emperor and the German people was one of the German High Seas Fleet advancing regardless of consequences and, with destroyers and battle-cruisers, doing its utmost to force an unwilling British fleet to fight. The British fleet,

---

[1] This was because at the battle of Dogger Bank, in January 1915, a similar shell-burst had almost caused an explosion in *Seydlitz* which could have blown up the ship. The risk of total destruction from this cause was recognised and adequate preventive measures were at once provided. But for this, *Seydlitz* would almost certainly have blown up at this time, as had the three British battle-cruisers.

[2] Hase, *Kiel and Jutland.*

[3] Scheer's Despatch, *Jutland Official Despatches.*

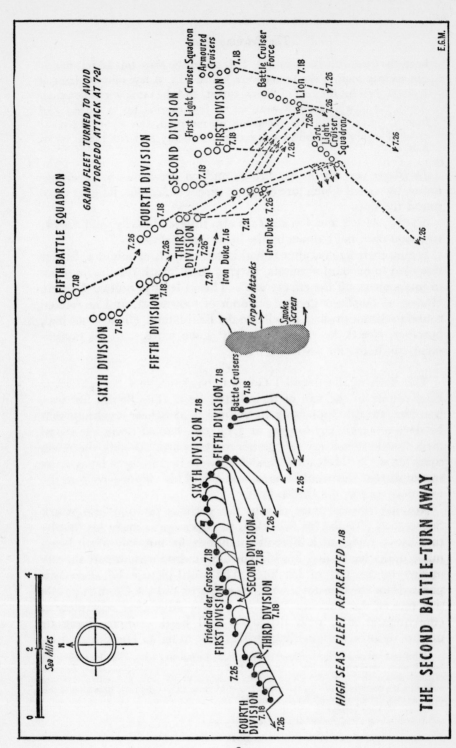

THE SECOND BATTLE—TURN AWAY

according to Scheer's Despatch, turned and ran, leaving only an empty void for the destroyers to attack; Scheer thereupon, his object achieved, and with his brave flotillas by his side, had withdrawn to the westward—oddly enough away from the German bases—to await nightfall.

The gunnery officer of *Derfflinger*, however, having been in the thick of the day's fighting and also having taken part in the 'death-ride', took a very different view and one much nearer to the truth.

> Admiral Scheer [he wrote] had realised the danger to which we [the German fleet] were exposed. The van of our fleet was shut in by the semi-circle of the enemy . . . We were in a regular death-trap [*im absoluten Wurstkessel*]. There was only one way to escape from the unfavourable tactical situation: to turn the line about and withdraw on the opposite course. Before everything else, we must get out of the dangerous enemy envelopment . . . unnoticed and unhindered. The battle-cruisers and destroyers had to cover the movements of the battle fleet.[1]

So the turn-away—the second turn-away from Jellicoe's fleet—was essayed and was achieved, but only by good luck and by the skilful manoeuvres of individual German captains. To quote the German Official Historian:

> The fleet flagship [*Friedrich der Grosse*] and ships of the Third Battle Squadron had to proceed at slow speed close to one another and almost in line abreast. Some had to stop or even go astern: they had little way on, and were bunched together.[2]

König helped to ease the situation by hauling out of the line to the westward and making a smoke-screen; the fleet flagship had to turn to port to give room, Scheer wrote after the war, 'to get through and save the ships ahead of the flagship from a difficult situation'. His turn to port might well have thrown out the whole line to the westward, had not Captain von Natzmer of *Ostfriesland* astern of the flagship promptly put over his helm and turned to starboard without waiting for his next astern, *Thüringen*, to commence the turn—thus breaking a strict rule in his manoeuvre which had been made to avert risk of collision. By doing so he forced every ship behind him to turn to starboard, and disaster was averted, but only narrowly. This was the state of confusion to which Scheer's second precipitate turn had reduced the well-drilled German fleet.

By 7.21 p.m., however, the whole German battle fleet was round

---

[1] Hase, *Kiel and Jutland*.
[2] *Krieg zur See, Nordsee.*

and its battle-cruisers were withdrawing in its wake. *Lützow* also was slowly circling round into the shelter of her main fleet. To *Derfflinger* and her consorts the withdrawal had brought welcome respite, for Beatty's squadron had also been just getting their range—as well as the ships of the Grand Fleet. Turning to comply with the order, Captain Hartog swung his ships round together and at last was able to draw out of range. While his ships had hitherto been clearly visible to the British gunners, they had had only rare glimpses of their enemy. But in one of these, at 7.16 p.m., either *Derfflinger*[1] or *Seydlitz*, had straddled *Colossus* again and again, twice hitting her; this was their only success. One shell entered the superstructure of *Colossus*[2] bursting in her port 4-inch battery, wounding two men and setting fire to some boxes of cordite: another hit her signal deck but did not burst. A third shell, bursting 'short' abreast her fore superstructure, wrecked the charthouse and starboard searchlights and wounded three men.

As they turned to rejoin their fleet, these battle-cruisers at least had the knowledge that they had done all that had been asked of them. The fleet had turned, and the destroyers were already beginning to lay the smoke-screen which would hide Scheer and his battle fleet from their enemies.

Scheer had extricated his fleet without disaster. Whatever the Admiral chose to tell his Emperor or the German people afterwards, his adventure had been a surprise to him and not to Jellicoe: it had done nothing to facilitate his 'breaking loose' at night; it had not disturbed Jellicoe's plans; and, far from 'falling heavily enough' upon the enemy it had recoiled entirely upon the High Seas Fleet itself.

[1] Most probably fired by *Derfflinger*: *Colossus* at first thought *Seydlitz* was responsible.
[2] *Colossus* was the only battleship hit at all after deployment.

8

Prelude and Fugue

A T 7.20 p.m. *Iron Duke*'s guns checked fire, as did the guns along
the line: once again their targets had suddenly vanished from
sight. To the Commander-in-Chief in the centre this was
especially frustrating at this time, for his fleet's firing upon the
enemy van had been nearing a peak of concentration. Looking
westward, however, the dark, heavy, smoke-charged mists seemed to
be growing noticeably more dense, and Jellicoe was inclined to
attribute the enemy's sudden disappearance to the local thickening
of them.[1] This belief, moreover, had reasonable ground for support
for some minutes afterwards due to continuing, if intermittent, fire
from the main armament guns of ships in the rear divisions: presumably these ships could see the enemy more clearly than could the
Commander-in-Chief.

That the apparent thickening in the mist to the westward was in
reality a smoke-screen that had been laid by enemy destroyers, and
was drifting slowly down wind, shutting out effectively what was
going on behind it, Jellicoe did not know; *Tiger* and other ships who
had seen the screen being laid had not reported it. For that matter,
a dozen captains of ships down the battle-line astern of *Iron Duke* had
actually *seen* what was going on behind the smoke-laden mist, but
had not troubled to inform their Commander-in-Chief. In consequence he was once again being left to rely 'wholly and solely'
upon his own very restricted observations. Beyond assuming that
when the temporarily thickened mists thinned once more the targets
would reappear, he had at the moment to concern himself with
another pressing problem—the obvious development of enemy
destroyer-attacks just before the starboard beam.

Groups of destroyers had been seen dimly to the westward ten
minutes earlier, and by 7.12 p.m. a light cruiser (*Regensburg*) with
apparently a large number of destroyers around her, could be made

[1] Jellicoe, *Grand Fleet*.

out clearly from *Iron Duke*'s bridge: there were two distinct columns of destroyers in the middle distance, apparently advancing to the attack, one of them ahead and a little to the northward of the other.

This was a move Jellicoe had fully expected from the German fleet—a torpedo attack made by massed destroyers, most probably by separate flotillas following each other in waves in rapid succession. Jellicoe had long known that the German navy placed great faith in the ability of their destroyers to carry out high-speed torpedo attacks for tactical ends.[1] Not only was the German destroyer service extremely efficient and well-trained, but information had filtered through to the Grand Fleet that it was burning with zeal to regain its position of high favour in the eyes of the German public, a position which had more recently been usurped by submarine commanders.

Jellicoe's general information suggested that at the selected moment at which the German fleet chose to put to sea, some 78 destroyers would be available to accompany the fleet.[2] Of the destroyers with the German High Seas Fleet, some 50 per cent could be expected to mount six torpedo-tubes apiece, firing twenty-eight to thirty-knot 19.5-inch torpedoes, having a running range of between 12,500 and 15,000 yards and carrying a charge in each warhead of 250 to 300 pounds of high explosive. To a great extent the torpedo as a weapon of mass attack was novel and untried. In the Russo-Japanese war, 1904-5, it had been used but had achieved barely 5 per cent of hits. Since then there had been great developments in British torpedoes, and it was reasonable to assume that the German Navy had made similar improvements. The considered and almost unanimous opinion of British torpedo experts before the 1914-18 war, and during its first two years, was that although a precarious weapon if fired at a single ship, if fired at a *line* of ships, there was, as has already been mentioned, a 40 per cent chance of obtaining a hit.

A new menace had thus been added to naval warfare, a menace made more real by the facility with which a destroyer could proceed swiftly to a position of advantage ahead and there fire her torpedoes, by the subsequent almost invisible approach of the torpedo itself, and by the extreme vulnerability of ships to this form of attack. Whereas the vitals of a warship—her engine- and boiler-rooms and her magazines—were afforded reasonable protection from gunfire

---

[1] 'There can be no doubt that the fullest use will also be made by the enemy of surface torpedo craft'. — Jellicoe's letter to the Admiralty, 30th October 1914. *Official Despatches.*
[2] He assumed the High Seas Fleet's total destroyer force to be about 88 boats which, allowing for 10 per cent refitting etc., would leave 78 or 79 for duty. Actually there had been only 61 available on this occasion, and three of those had already been sunk.

damage by armoured topsides and protective decks, the torpedo explodes its charge on contact with a ship's unarmoured and unprotected underbody. At this date the damage resulting from such underwater explosion was generally considered as being very likely to disable a ship and almost certainly impair her speed; it might well prove fatal.

As far as the use of the torpedo in a simultaneous massed attack by a large number of destroyers was concerned—firing between them literally a shoal of torpedoes—there was no data at all from which conclusions could be drawn: as an instrument of war the massed torpedo attack was entirely a 'novel and untried weapon'.

The three phases of current British procedure for countering this form of attack have already been mentioned: the first phase—the *frustration*—of the enemy attack while still in embryo by our own light cruisers and destroyers breaking up the enemy attack; the second phase—the *deterrent*—the secondary armaments of ships of the line used to keep the attackers, if possible, outside effective range for firing their torpedoes—9,000 to 10,000 yards; and the third and final phase—*avoidance* once the torpedoes had been fired—by making appropriate evading manoeuvres in any threatened parts of the battle line and, whenever necessary, by individual ships, to ensure that the torpedoes expended their venom harmlessly in open water and not against ships' sides.

This third phase of *avoidance*, by reason of its extreme finality, had been the subject of intense investigation and practical experiment: as a result certain clear-cut rules had been established; if torpedoes had been fired from a point anywhere between 30° before the beam and right ahead of the target ship, the latter should be *turned towards* the torpedo's firing point; if, however, torpedoes were fired from a position anywhere between 30° before the target ship's beam and right astern, the target ship must be *turned away* from the firing point. For maximum safety it was necessary to know both the exact time the torpedoes were fired and also the exact position from which they had been fired although it was appreciated that this information might not be obtainable under conditions of poor visibility.

It is necessary to emphasise that there was nothing permissive or optional about the character of any avoiding action that had to be taken; the manoeuvres set out above were the accepted methods in use in 1916 by our flag officers and captains of ships and were incorporated as instructions in the Battle Orders; precisely similar avoiding tactics were employed in the German Navy and in the French, Italian and American Fleets.

As such avoiding manoeuvres had usually to be made at short notice and very swiftly, simple visual signals—such as the 'Preparative Flag'—had been evolved for the purpose, and a special instrument had been supplied to ships to ascertain the minimum amount of turn needed to ensure safety. Realising also that the whole purpose of these avoiding manoeuvres was to encourage the torpedo to use up its energy in empty water. Jellicoe preferred to manoeuvre his line by subdivisions of two ships together thereby vastly increasing the ratio of water-space to ship-target and thus reducing the experts' estimated assessment of 40% obtainable hits to rather less than 2%; this small percentage could be reduced to zero by the skilful handling of individual ships as necessary.

With a long line of ships as the enemy's target—a line such as the twenty-four battleships comprising our battle-fleet—there was the additional problem of how much of the line was really vulnerable to a particular attack and should adopt avoiding tactics; in most cases the centre and rear had to be considered as within the danger zone but the generously wide decentralisation of command which Jellicoe's Battle Orders accorded all squadron and divisional commanders enabled them if necessary to make their own decisions to alter course or to hold on regardless of the movements of the rest of the fleet.

In considering the advantages of the various defensive measures in use in the Fleet at this time for dealing with enemy torpedo attacks one must not overlook the attendant disadvantages. To turn towards an enemy torpedo attack—if made within the prescribed bearings—could be sound in principle but to turn towards a carefully organised *succession* of such attacks could easily bring the avoiding fleet into a position of both tactical and strategical disadvantage; similarly, a turn away must inevitably involve the turning fleet in loss of ground and thus, if in the presence of the enemy fleet, in opening the firing range. From this argument it is a short step to the obvious use of a torpedo attack as a means of imposing a course of movement and manoeuvre upon an enemy—or else; this was well appreciated by both sides, it had been used by both Beatty and Hipper already during the afternoon's battle-cruiser engagement.

The enemy destroyers seen approaching at 7.15 p.m. were sighted about 40° before the starboard beam of *Iron Duke*; as the fleet was steering southward this bearing rapidly drew aft, until both the impending attacks came within the category marked for 'turning-away'. In one important respect the fleet was not in a good position, for the first-stage arrangements—for breaking up such an attack before it could develop—were not working. The destroyers and light cruisers, which should already have been positioned on the British fleet's engaged bow had not yet been able to get into their stations, owing to the fleet's continual alteration of course to starboard. For that matter none of these units thus far had made any 'full-speed' attempt to do so. Nor did they use any especial initiative to haul across the van of *King George V* in order to break up the attacks. At 7.22 p.m. Jellicoe had to signal direct to the Fourth Light-Cruiser Squadron: 'Proceed at utmost speed and attack the enemy's torpedo vessels.'

Admiral Jellicoe was thus left to rely entirely upon ship-fire, and later the turning alternative. Already a number of ships, *Royal Oak* and *Barham*, *Iron Duke* herself, *Neptune*, *Marlborough* and others were firing their secondary armament; this seemed to make some slight impression, causing the attackers to steer zig-zag courses—but they still pressed on.

To get the extent of the torpedo attacks made upon the British fleet at this time into perspective, it is first necessary to go back in time over a few minutes. The *first* destroyer attack had already been launched on *Regensburg's* instructions: Commodore Heinrich had detached part of the 3rd flotilla, consisting of three boats reinforced by two others from the 1st flotilla[1] to attack the centre and rear of the British battle line. As these emerged from the mists at about 7.00 p.m., three torpedoes were fired and the destroyers would then have withdrawn: at 7.05 p.m., however, the fleet, quite unaware of this small attack, turned together three points towards it, to southwest by west; four minutes later the ships turned back together again to south. The result of this turn was to bring the fourth division into the danger zone, and the destroyers seem then to have tried another shot. Those who had not yet fired, *V-73* and *G-88*, pushed on, and between them fired three more[2] torpedoes. Their advance had, however, brought them under the fire of the fifth and sixth divisions; *Colossus* even opened up on them with 12-inch as they turned and hurried out of sight. Sturdee, assuming they had fired at him, when they were about two points before the beam, very rightly hoisted the ('Preparative') signal for his division to turn two points *away* from the attack. In point of fact, neither the firing time nor the firing point had been noticed on account of the mist, for before the division could turn three torpedoes (fired at about 7.00 p.m.) were being avoided by the individual ship-manoeuvres of *Colossus*, *Agincourt* and

[1] Cf., *Hercules* Report: 'five or six'. Admiral Scheer in his memoirs said there were six.
[2] According to Scheer's plan, these were fired at 7.15 p.m.

Neptune (between 7.08 and 7.10 p.m.). The three torpedoes fired at about 7.15 p.m. were not seen by anyone.

This *first* attack achieved nothing, therefore, and as Jellicoe was already summoning the Fourth Battle Squadron to form astern of *Iron Duke*, it rather helped that manoeuvre. It could, however, have been a warning to *Castor* and her flotillas to cross to starboard ahead of the Second Battle Squadron and be ready to break up any other attacks which might be coming.

Iron Duke saw the *second* enemy destroyer attack begin to develop shortly after 7.10 p.m.: this was being made by a part of their 11th half-flotilla. The watchers did not, however, see the effective smoke screen being laid which, between 7.17 and 7.25 p.m., drifted steadily down the range obscuring the view. Through this smoke six destroyers appeared at high speed just on *Iron Duke's* beam at 7.20 p.m. 7,000 yards away, and began turning fast to starboard; during the turn they fired no fewer than 11 torpedoes at 7.23 p.m., withdrawing, at high speed under the fire of the battleships of the centre and rear divisions. The Fourth Light-Cruiser Squadron was firing across at them, but was not yet in a position from which it could break up this attack. After 7.22 p.m., and after the Commander-in-Chief's signal, *Calliope* with her Fourth Light-Cruiser Squadron moved across, followed by *Castor* (Commodore of Flotillas) leading out the 1st division of our 11th flotilla; these light forces now took up a position from which to deal with the third attack which was already developing.

As the second attack drew nearer it was clearly seen to be one requiring a 'turn-away'. Unfortunately, the Battle Fleet could not turn immediately. Some minutes earlier, Jellicoe had ordered the Second Battle Squadron to take station ahead of him, and *King George V* and her Squadron had inclined across at maximum speed; by 7.22 p.m. the rear ships were overlapping the leaders of *Iron Duke's* division, and before *Iron Duke* could turn to port and away from the torpedo attack the Second Battle Squadron had to be turned to make room. Jellicoe promptly signalled the Second Battle Squadron to turn four points to port together to clear his ships, and a minute later he turned the rest of the fleet together, two points away from the attack (at 7.22 p.m.). *King George V* and her van division were most unlikely to be the targets of an attack from the bearing on which the destroyers had turned; two minutes later therefore she turned back to the south course of the fleet. The rest of the fleet turned by sub-divisions, to south-south-east opening the water-space between the ships.

The *third* attack was now reaching its climax: it was being delivered by five boats of the German 17th half-flotilla. There had originally been six, but one of them had already been sunk by gunfire; two others had been damaged by shell-fire—but were still carrying on. The fleet's barrage was now tremendous, and was being assisted by the guns of the Fourth Light-Cruiser Squadron.

As the enemy destroyers dashed through their smoke-screen and turned on to their firing course, it was seen that another two points to port would be necessary to avoid the torpedoes and Jellicoe accordingly by 'Preparative' signal again turned his fleet—with the exception of the van—two points to port by subdivisions (making a four-point alteration in all), to a course of south-east.

The 17th half-flotilla fired ten torpedoes at 7.25 at a range of 9,000 yards: the destroyers then made off, harried by gunfire all the way. That the battle fleet should have been left to its own gunfire and manoeuvring capacity to defend itself against these two last attacks is beyond comprehension.

(ii)

As the Grand Fleet held on its way south-eastward, the torpedoes began to appear between the lines of ships at about 7.33 p.m. Even so, several ships had individually to take evading action; to avoid being hit, but the torpedoes were nearly spent and all were avoided. Three were sighted by *Marlborough*, two by *Revenge*, two by *Hercules*, two by *Agincourt*, one by *Saint Vincent* and one by the destroyer *Oak*. Within the next two minutes, nineteen of the twenty-one that had been fired were accounted for. There had been no hits, although their aiming had obviously been good.

As the danger now seemed to be past, Jellicoe, having preserved his ships intact by using the accepted manoeuvres, turned back five points to starboard, to south-by-west, a point nearer to the enemy than his original course had been; this was a course that would close the enemy and, perhaps, clear up a situation which was completely obscure.

A minute later, Jellicoe ordered his ships to form line ahead. Since he still believed that the enemy was just behind the thicker mist to the westward, he was forming his battle line in readiness for another meeting.

Thus, while his line straightened out its 'wrinkles' due to the avoiding action taken earlier by individual ships, he took 'guide of the fleet', and at 7.40 p.m. signalled a 'Recall' to the destroyers of the first division of the 11th flotilla. He then turned the fleet another three points to starboard, closing the enemy still more sharply, on a south-west course, directing *King George V* and her division to conform to this course and take station ahead.

Jellicoe was quite unaware that while he had been successfully avoiding the consequences of the last two attacks, three more had been mounted for his greater discomfort. The *fourth* 'attack' became, literally, the one that never was: it was developed by ten of the German 2nd flotilla, the most modern destroyers in the German fleet—large boats mounting six tubes apiece and carrying a strong armament of four 4.1-inch guns. *Regensburg* had held them on leash, to follow on after the attacks by the 11th and 17th half-flotillas. They were sent off to the attack but almost at once became entangled with the battered German battle-cruisers as the latter turned back: *Regensburg*—seeing that their attack was being sadly diverted, then recalled them, deciding to keep them in hand for use later on if an opportunity arose. The *fifth* attack was mounted by six of the German 3rd flotilla, which had only just returned from attacking Sturdee's division (the first attack). This 3rd flotilla headed away from *Regensburg* at about 7.30 p.m. arriving in the arena some five or six minutes later. They found nothing but a misty void; they also saw a division of British destroyers—part of our 12th flotilla— steering to the southward, which opened fire, driving them westward and back to Scheer's fleet. One of this flotilla, *S-32*, pushed on ahead, however, and was rewarded by the sight of some shadowy shape of a capital ship five miles away to the eastward; her commander launched one torpedo and turned back at high speed to join the rest: this torpedo was probably the one seen and avoided at 7.45 p.m. by *Revenge*. The *sixth* attack was even more abortive: it was developed by eleven boats of the 5th flotilla, who had been screening the German Second Squadron at the far west end of the German line when Scheer had ordered all destroyers to attack. They had therefore had to steam five miles down the German line to reach the arena at all, and were even later in turning to the attack; they saw nothing at all, except our light forces moving southward; coming under fire at once they abandoned their effort and returned at high speed to their own fleet.

It has been necessary to list these various attacks, both actual and abortive, because of the widespread misapprehension that existed after the War that only two attacks were made on Jellicoe's fleet: the last three were threats numerically larger than those which had preceded them, but Jellicoe had removed his fleet from their reach. In all these attacks between 7 p.m. and 7.45 p.m., 28 torpedoes had been fired: 23 of them had been seen and avoided—spent—at the end of their run; no ships in the Grand Fleet had been so much as grazed, yet the aim had been good. The Germans had lost one destroyer—*S-35*—and had two (*S-52* and *S-36*) if not three more damaged by shellfire.

Per contra, the battle fleet had by turning away undoubtedly opened the range by 1,750 yards in the centre, 1,250 yards in the van (since *King George V's* Division had not made the second turn-away but had turned to the course of the fleet at 7.28, as soon as *Iron Duke* was clear) and by 3,800 yards at the rear; this latter was due, however, to the swinging of the line as it reformed ahead. This opening of the range was an unavoidable sacrifice; it had spared the disablement or loss of eight or even more capital ships, had Jellicoe not turned away. In the course of the six attacks, the German destroyers had demonstrated the importance of this form of diversionary attack as a means of imposing a tactical limitation upon an enemy's freedom of manoeuvre. Their attacks had also once and for all stripped from the surface torpedo attack the myth of 'unanswerable menace', with which our torpedo experts had dressed it up: the mountains had been in labour and had brought forth a very small mouse. It must be realised, however, that until 7.30 p.m. on this May evening, this could not have been known.

'Might-have-beens' have little value, but it is not unreasonable here to assume that had the Commodore of the British flotillas (Commodore Hawksley) in *Castor* and the Senior Officer of the Fourth Light-Cruiser Squadron (Commodore Le Mesurier) in *Calliope*, shown a little more initiative and understanding of their *raison-d'être* in the van, they could have been in amongst those twelve enemy destroyers and broken up their attacks with ease, if not preventing them altogether.

In fairness to Scheer, however, the attacks had not been made as he had intended: at 7.21 p.m. he had ordered all available destroyers out to attack to cover his withdrawal and there should have been 49 destroyers ready to respond to their Admiral's call. Unfortunately, the Second Leader of Flotillas, Commodore Heinrich, in *Regensburg*, had at 6.52 p.m. on his own initiative despatched six boats of the 6th flotilla ('11th half-flotilla'), six of the 9th flotilla ('17th half-flotilla') and six of the 3rd flotilla (including *S-35*, left over from the 1st flotilla) to attack Jellicoe's battle fleet: Heinrich was presumably acting on the assumption that Jellicoe would be in pursuit of the German fleet.

When Scheer in the emergency of his second 'battle-turn-away' ordered his flotillas to make a mass-attack to cover his withdrawal, all that were actually available were the 2nd, 5th and the 7th flotillas. Thus Scheer, who by ordering massed destroyer-attacks was relying upon the menace of a *shoal* of torpedoes to cover his withdrawal, was reduced to the protection of one solitary torpedo, as the result of his own orders at 7.21 p.m. The others had been fired as the result of *Regenburg's* intuition.

Scheer had, however, been able to break off the engagement and turn his fleet about, for which he could thank the smokescreen his destroyers had set up. Jellicoe's turn-away had not aided Scheer's 'battle-turn-away': that had been completed *before* the British Fleet had begun to turn away from the torpedo attacks. The smoke-screen had first caused Jellicoe to lose immediate contact, and the failure of his captains to report what they had seen, aided by the turn-away from destroyer attacks, had aggravated this. That Jellicoe would endeavour to regain it Scheer was quite certain, and he almost hoped that Jellicoe would come after him in pursuit, for that would at least enable the German fleet to keep ahead until dark and then turn direct to the nearest swept channel and home; moreover, if he did pursue, Jellicoe would have to sacrifice his position across the Germans' road home.

One thing puzzled Scheer: he could hear the sound of intermittent heavy gunfire astern for nearly ten minutes after he had turned his fleet westward and this made him think he might be pursued. His returning flotillas were, however, able to inform him that they had seen no sign of pursuit astern: on the other hand, the destroyers of the 11th and 17th half-flotillas were also able to confirm his fears that the whole Grand Fleet was now lying between him and his base.

Scheer seems to have done some very quick thinking, in the quarter of an hour or so after receiving this information and after turning south-west. If Jellicoe was not chasing him, then he was probably manoeuvring in such a way as to force the German fleet further and further westward, probably with some plan in mind of re-engaging in the hour remaining before dusk. Jellicoe, Scheer considered, would probably follow this up with destroyer attacks designed to drive the German fleet always further westward—further from its home bases—delaying the start of any night retreat and lengthening its distance until the German Fleet could only reach the entrance to its swept channels *after* daylight: by that time the Grand Fleet would be waiting in its path to give battle.

Scheer realised only too clearly that every four miles that such tactics could succeed in forcing him further to the westward would add another half-hour to the time needed for his homeward journey, and would, therefore, increase Jellicoe's chance of forcing battle on British terms, at daylight the next morning—with all the long day ahead in which to fight it out to a conclusion. Scheer was under no delusion as to what the outcome of such an action must be: his Third Battle Squadron, with some of his best ships had lost much of its fighting value and was getting short of ammunition—the *König*, in particular, was down by the head and damaged; his battle-cruisers were barely capable of fighting at all. An action next morning with all the day ahead would at best result in the near-annihilation of the German High Seas Fleet.

Admiral Scheer, therefore, resolved to keep his fleet in close order, and push on southward while there was yet time.

> Should we succeed in checking the enemy's enveloping movement, and in reaching Horns Reef before them [the British fleet] we should retain the initiative for the next morning. With this object in view, all destroyer-flotillas had to be used for attacking during the night, even at the risk of having to do without them in the new engagement which might be expected at dawn. The main fleet itself had to make for Horns Reef, in close order by the shortest route; and to maintain this course in defiance of all attacks of the enemy.[1]

This was the German Admiral's Despatch afterwards, as he presented it to his Emperor; and the last paragraph accorded very closely to his actual plan, for Scheer did not contemplate any battle at all the next day.

In order to steer as closely to the route for home as was possible —without courting further engagements—Scheer turned his fleet to South at 7.52 p.m., steaming at sixteen knots. At the same time he stationed the destroyers of his 2nd flotilla and 12th half-flotilla five or six miles to the eastward to be in a position to give early warning of any British approach. His fleet was in a somewhat loose three-column-formation at the moment: the 'Kaisers' and 'Königs' of the Third Squadron were moving up into station astern of First Squadron to form the centre column: two and a half miles off the starboard bow of the latter were the pre-Dreadnoughts of the Second Squadron. As a result of the last 'battle-turn-away' all units were in reversed order—*Westfalen* leading the First Squadron, and *Schleswig-Holstein* leading the Second Squadron. A mile off *Westfalen's* port bow were the battered battle-cruisers of Hipper's First Scouting

[1] Admiral Scheer's *Despatch*.

Group with the three surviving light cruisers of Boedicker's Second Scouting Group ahead of them; *Lützow* had rejoined its Group and was trying nobly to keep up with the others, but would obviously soon have to give up the struggle. Ahead of the fleet were the five untouched but older light cruisers of Commodore von Reuter's Fourth Scouting Group—three miles in advance of the pre-Dreadnoughts. Hipper, himself, was still on board the destroyer *G-39*, looking for a new flagship.

(iii)

While Scheer was thus planning to keep out of Jellicoe's sight and reach, Jellicoe was trying equally hard to regain contact with him. As soon as the torpedo danger was past, at 7.35 p.m., Jellicoe had turned his fleet five points to starboard (south-by-west). That Jellicoe still believed the enemy to be lurking behind the thickened mist seven or eight miles to the westward is clear from his signal at 7.31 p.m. to *Castor*—at the time chasing enemy destroyers to the north-westward—warning him not to go 'too near' the enemy battle fleet. Obviously Jellicoe then presumed it to be still somewhere near, although out of sight in the mist: no doubt the Commander-in-Chief had vivid recollections of what had happened a few hours earlier to the unfortunate *Defence*, when she had suddenly come into view of Scheer's battleships. Jellicoe must still have had the same belief fourteen minutes later, when he signalled to his destroyers: 'Tell *Castor* to come back.'

Convinced that the enemy were still close at hand, he had at 7.36 p.m. ordered his squadrons to take station ahead and astern of him and had again formed his line of battle in readiness to meet Scheer. With his line formed, at 7.45 p.m. he closed another three points to starboard by divisions (south-west) to hasten the meeting, for sunset was now barely twenty-five minutes away. His new course was heading towards the point at which Scheer had last been seen in the mists, and by steering thus Jellicoe was deliberately throwing overboard the objections adumbrated in his letter to the Admiralty in October 1914 and, unknowingly, giving the lie to those critics who were later to hint that he was averse to closing his enemies.

It is incomprehensible that none of the captains whose ships had seen the enemy's big turn-away between 7.18 and 7.20 p.m.—and must now have realised that the Commander-in-Chief was striving to regain contact at the earliest moment—should have told him what they had seen. Instead, like Brer Rabbit, they 'lay low and said nuffin'. This was the second display of lack of understanding that

During Scheer's second battle-turn-away *Seydli*z came under heavy fire from seven battleships for several minutes. Ravaged by fire and shipping 5,000 tons of water, she still returned from Jutland, the seas reaching the top-most fish of the crest painted on her bows.

The Battle of Jutland;
6.30 p.m.: in low visibility
Iron Duke (Jellicoe's flagship)
opens fire; astern of her are
Revenge and *Superb*.

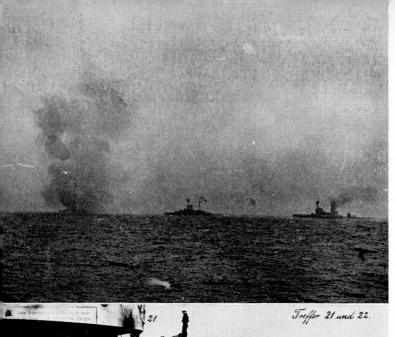

Many of the British shells
broke up on impact with
their targets and did little
more than scorch the armour
plate. *Centre:* such hits on the
side of *Seydlitz*. *Below:*
fragments of a British 15-inch
armour-piercing common
shell recovered by *Seydlitz*,
compared with a German
'capped' 11-inch shell.

a Commander-in-Chief in position in the centre of the fleet might not be able to see all that others in the rear could see. It is of interest to establish who some of these silent spectators were, for some of their ships' names, moreover, may occur again in this story under somewhat similar circumstances: *Marlborough* (Captain Ross); *Hercules* (Captain Clinton-Baker); *Saint Vincent* (Captain W. W. Fisher); *Temeraire* (Captain Underhill); *Valiant* (Captain Woollcombe) and *Malaya* (Captain The Honourable E. D. Boyle). There were no doubt others also: some of them had noticed the German fleet's first turn-away, and had been silent about that too.[1]

The position was still obscure, but after two or three minutes on the new south-westerly course—which at the moment happened to be parallel to that of the German fleet and some fourteen to fifteen miles from its nearest ships—a valuable signal was received by wireless from *Lion* via *Princess Royal*: 'Enemy bears from me north-west by west, distant ten to eleven miles.' The signal was timed 7.30 p.m. and gave *Lion's* position and her course—south-west—and speed, eighteen knots.[2] *Lion* by this time was out of sight from *Iron Duke*, and her signalled position could not be reconciled with that of *Iron Duke*: Jellicoe therefore presumed that *Lion* would have been at 7.30 p.m. in her station in the van about six miles to the south-westward of *Iron Duke*. The signal gave no 'enemy course', but it could be inferred that Beatty would probably be steering in approximately the same direction.

This report contained a definite indication of the enemy's position. Unfortunately, a few minutes later, a second report timed 7.45 p.m., arrived from *Southampton*—whose reports hitherto had always been so excellent. This time, however, it confused the issue badly, by giving the enemy's course as north-west at 7.15 p.m., when Jellicoe knew they must have been steering eastward. The situation therefore remained as obscure as ever, except that Jellicoe now knew that the enemy was no longer in close reach, in the mist, but had drawn well out to the westward.

At 7.59 p.m. Jellicoe received another signal from Beatty, who,

[1] The following extracts are from the Captain's Reports, etc., included on the Battle of Jutland *Official Despatches*: *Marlborough*, 'The enemy battle fleet in sight was observed to turn eight points until their sterns were towards our line'; *Hercules*, 'They then withdrew'; *Saint Vincent*, 'The enemy had turned eight or ten points away, disappearing into the mist'; *Royal Oak*, 'enemy turned away into mist'; *Benbow*, 'enemy observed turning away to starboard'; *Valiant*, 'enemy's battle fleet now altered course together away from us and broke off the action'; *Temeraire*, '[Target showed her port side on opening fire] then turned away until stern on, continuing to come round to starboard and disappeared'; *Malaya*, 'Owing to the battle fleet's having turned away . . .'

[2] This signal, received in *Iron Duke* at 7.40 p.m., was in the Commander-in-Chief's hands presumably some five or six minutes later.

M 177

still continuing to steer south-westward with his squadron, had found the enemy becoming too indistinct for firing. This time the signal was *en clair*, and by searchlight, so there was relatively little time lag: 'Leading enemy battleship bears north-west by west, course about south-west. (1945).'[1] This signal posed an awkward problem: on the face of it, it was similar to the previous 7.30 p.m. signal except that the enemy was now specifically described as the 'leading enemy battleship', the enemy's course being given definitely as 'south-west'; in all probability, this was only an enlargement of the previous signal. Jellicoe, however, had no means of knowing that, at 7.45 p.m., Beatty was nearly *thirteen miles* from the nearest enemy ships, and that these were *battle-cruisers*, not *battleships*. The nearest enemy battleship was more than fifteen miles away from Beatty and must have been out of sight.[2]

Taking this signal at its face value, however, Jellicoe now considered that he was not closing the enemy sharply enough, and at 8 o'clock altered the course of the fleet by divisions, another four points inwards, to west, still steaming at seventeen knots.

It is unfortunate that at least at eight o'clock Sir David Beatty had no definite idea as to the position of the enemy van, for at that time he ordered the light cruisers in company with him[3] to 'sweep to the westward and locate the head of the enemy's battle line before dark. (2000)'.

Jellicoe had no means of knowing that his battle-cruisers by eight o'clock were out of touch with the enemy van and this makes the next signal which Jellicoe received from his colleague quite inexplicable. At 7.54 p.m., a *ciphered* wireless signal arrived from *Lion* (via *Princess Royal*); this had to be deciphered and passed to the Commander-in-Chief, who read it, presumably, some minutes after eight o'clock:

> Urgent. Submit van of battleships follow battle-cruisers. We can then cut off the whole of enemy's battle fleet. (1950).[4]

When the existence of this signal became known officially upon the postwar publication of the Jutland *Official Despatches* and signals,

---

[1] This signal was passed by *Lion* to *King George V* and from the latter visually to *Iron Duke*.

[2] It is difficult to understand how Beatty could have seen even the nearer battle-cruisers clearly enough to have estimated their course for, according to the report written by the Captain of *Lion* after the battle, 'the enemy was still not sufficiently visible to open fire, and this continued until 8.21 p.m.—*Battle of Jutland, Official Despatches*.

[3] The First and Third Light-Cruiser Squadrons.

[4] With regard to the receipt of this signal, Sir Julian Corbett has said, 'It was in the Commander-in-Chief's hands soon after eight o'clock.' *Naval Operations*.

in 1920, it attracted considerable public interest. This extraordinary signal, as it stood, was meaningless and misleading: the whole enemy battle fleet was *already* cut off from the only thing which mattered to Scheer—the easy escape route to its German bases. If Beatty was suggesting that with his six remaining battle-cruisers and eight battleships he could envelop Scheer's whole battle fleet—excluding the battle-cruisers and the damaged *König*—it was surely rather an ambitious programme. How, moreover, was the Grand Fleet's van squadron, the Second Battle Squadron, to *find* Beatty's battle-cruisers not knowing their position and having no visual link with them? Again, how long was Beatty prepared to wait for their support? He was already six miles ahead of them, and were the Second Battle Squadron to hasten to him at their maximum 20 knots it would take an hour and more before they could come in sight of the battle-cruisers and by that time the light would be almost gone.

Although Jellicoe did not know that Beatty no longer had the enemy in sight he would not turn down a colleague's request. He had presumably read the signal at about 8.03 p.m. or 8.04 p.m.; then, no doubt, he would have consulted the chart to see how the proposal fitted in with the relative positions of the various units at the moment. He signalled by searchlight to *King George V*: 'Second Battle Squadron follow our battle-cruisers.'

This signal was received and logged in *King George V* at 8.07 p.m. It must have puzzled Vice-Admiral Jerram as much as the cause of it had puzzled Jellicoe; the Senior Officer of the Second Battle Squadron was ordered to follow ships he could not see, and whose position he did not know: a possible visual link—*Minotaur*—had been dimly visible some five miles away to the southward but even she was passing out of sight into the mist at 8.10 p.m. Jerram, therefore, stayed where he was, until the situation became clearer to him and continued to steer the same course as the rest of the fleet. At 8.18 p.m., however, he heard gunfire to the southward and although this is at best a very dubious indication of direction, Jerram took a chance and, signalling to his Squadron at 8.19 p.m. (by searchlight) 'Follow Me', at 8.20 p.m. hauled round two points to starboard towards the sound of the guns.

A minute later, he called Beatty by wireless, asking for the latter's position, course and speed.[1] Getting no answer to this inquiry, Jerram continued blindly west-south-west as the best course he could steer, as there was now no visual link through which he could

[1] Corbett, *Naval Operations*.

communicate with the invisible battle-cruisers. In the meantime Jellicoe, also hearing the gunfire, had altered the course of the fleet (by divisions) to west-south-west, so that *King George V* and her Second Battle Squadron were in effect still pursuing the same course as the fleet, although a little further to the southward.

The visibility during this critical time between eight and eight-thirty, when the fleets—unknown to each other—were converging sharply, is of great importance. The average visibility was between 10,500 and 9,000 yards in a north and south direction, and between 13,000 and 15,000 yards perhaps, in a westerly direction. For just about fifteen to twenty minutes around sunset (at 8.09 p.m.) there was quite good visibility to the westward and slightly north of westward; *Orion* caught a momentary glimpse of enemy capital ships to the westward, and the officer in *Iron Duke's* B turret also got a momentary glimpse of nine battleships in the distance, dead ahead, at 8.25 p.m.—Scheer's First Battle Squadron.[1]

One explanation that has been advanced for Beatty's extraordinary submission is that he wanted the support of a battle squadron, so that when he did sight the enemy van it would be dealt a heavy blow that would send it reeling westwards just at dusk. Had the wording in any way suggested such a plan, it would have been a different matter: it did not, and could not at the time the signal was despatched, for Beatty had no real idea where the enemy van was or when it would be sighted, or that Scheer was fearful of being driven westward especially at dusk.

Mr. Churchill dealt with this incident in his *World Crisis* somewhat typically: opening his comment with an unfortunate innuendo, 'Beatty, however, still sought to renew the action'—as if to imply that Jellicoe did not. Mr. Churchill continued:

> At 7.47 [Beatty] sent the much-discussed message to the Commander-in-Chief, 'Submit that the van of the battleships follow me; we can then cut off the enemy's fleet'.

The message—in cipher—was timed 7.50 p.m., *not* 7.47 p.m., it was received in *Iron Duke* at 7.54 p.m.; it had to be deciphered, written out and passed to the Commander-in-Chief' The message, as mentioned above, could not have reached the Admiral's hands until shortly after eight o'clock.

> A quarter of an hour was allowed to pass [Mr. Churchill's narrative continued] after Jellicoe received Beatty's signal before he sent the

---

[1] At a range of about 17,000 yards. Cf. *Official Despatches*.

necessary order—and that in no urgent terms—to the Second Battle Squadron. Vice-Admiral Jerram, commanding that squadron, did not . . . ask the *Minotaur* for the *Lion's* position . . . . Thus the *Lion* and her consorts were alone in the last, as in the first, encounter of great ships at Jutland.

It must be observed that Jellicoe's signal to the Second Battle Squadron to follow the battle-cruisers was received in *King George V* and 'logged in' at 8.07 p.m.,[1] three or four minutes at most after Jellicoe had seen the signal: Jerram could not ask *Minotaur* for a position, for the latter ship was running out of sight after 8.10 p.m.; the final insinuation that Admiral Sir John Jellicoe had left his battle-cruisers in the lurch, is, perhaps, best consigned to the limbo of things better forgotten.

(iv)

With Jellicoe turning to the westward at 8 o'clock, and Beatty steering south-south-west on a closing course in search of the enemy, events were likely to move apace at both ends of the line. At the southern end, Beatty had directed his light cruisers to locate the head of the enemy's line before dark. *Falmouth* and *Inconstant* had at once altered course south-westward at speed: *Falmouth* had spread his Third Light-Cruiser Squadron on a line of bearing north and south with the ships a mile apart, and had then turned this line of search to steer west. By 8.09 p.m., he had enemy ships in sight to the northward. He reported this at 8.10 p.m. to Beatty, but within five minutes the strangers could be identified as five light cruisers—*Stettin* (flagship), *München*, *Stuttgart*, *Frauenlob* and *Hamburg* —the enemy's Fourth Scouting Group heading southward. Turning his line to a parallel course, therefore, and increasing speed to 25 knots, *Falmouth*, at the north end of his search-line opened fire on them at 8.17 p.m. at a range of 9,600 yards. The remainder of his squadron promptly closed in on their flagship, opening supporting fire as they came within range.

Falmouth and her three consorts were bigger cruisers: they had a protective armour belt and they mounted eight 6-inch guns apiece; they were also faster than the five older unprotected ships of the Fourth Scouting Group, mounting only ten 4.1-inch guns apiece. The contest was, therefore, likely to be somewhat unequal. Nevertheless, the German ships immediately replied vigorously to *Falmouth's* first salvoes and the action continued on parallel southerly courses.

[1] *Battle of Jutland, Official Despatches.*

Barely a minute after *Falmouth* had opened fire, other guns could be heard very close and to the north-eastward. The Fourth Light-Cruiser Squadron had also suddenly come into action. *Castor* (Commodore 'F') with his 11th flotilla, having now reached a position about two and a half miles on the port bow of *King George V* sighted smoke to the westward at about 8.08 p.m., and a minute later enemy destroyers were observed advancing. The Commodore at once signalled to the first half of his flotilla to attack these destroyers—now bearing north-west—and led off at speed to intercept them. They appeared to be steering a southerly course, with the object of attacking the van of the battle fleet: three minutes later *Castor* signalled to *King George V* 'enemy destroyers bearing north-west'.[1]

Advancing at utmost speed, the Commodore soon made out at least a dozen enemy destroyers to the north-westward, and reported this by signal to the flotilla-leader *Kempenfelt*, and also to the light cruiser *Calliope*, leading the Fourth Light-Cruiser Squadron a mile and a half to the southward. *Calliope*, realising that *Castor* might perhaps need help at once signalled the first division of her Fourth-Light-Cruiser Squadron—*Calliope*, *Comus*, and *Constance*—to follow her and set off to support *Castor* and the destroyers. Turning in pursuit herself, she increased to her utmost speed and at 8.18 p.m. opened fire. The 6-inch guns of *Castor* and the other three light cruisers were too much for the German 12th half-flotilla, and firing some of their torpedoes they swiftly fled north-westward, hotly pursued by the Fourth Light-Cruiser Squadron and destroyers.[2]

At 8.18 p.m., therefore, there was considerable medium gunfire to the westward and also to the south-westward of *Iron Duke*, suggesting that some contact with the enemy had been made with the light forces again.

Admiral Scheer now saw clearly what he must do: the entrance to the Amrum Bank swept channel was still 120 miles away and 16 knots was the best speed he could expect to make; hampered as he was by damaged ships, it would take $7\frac{1}{2}$ hours at that speed to steam the distance. If this passage could be made during the dark hours, and if he could be certain of arriving off Horns Reef at or before dawn—2.30 a.m.—Scheer felt that he had a reasonable chance of getting his Fleet home without being brought to action.

---

[1] This signal did not reach *Iron Duke* till 8.26 p.m.

[2] Of these torpedoes, two only were sighted later at about 8.25 p.m. by *Agincourt* and *Benbow* in the rear battle squadron.

To be later than that would be to risk encountering the British fleet in the early daylight, and, despite the fire-eating views he expressed later to his Emperor, this was the last thing Scheer really wanted to happen. As, therefore, he *must* reach Horns Reef by dawn, he could not afford to be pushed now any further to the westward.

When it was dark enough, Scheer intended to 'probe' with his destroyers and locate the rear of the British fleet; then he proposed to slip past it, out of sight, and head directly for Horns Reef. He would not seek a night fleet action any more than any other contemporary sea commander would have done but should he inadvertently find a British force barring his night-path, there is no doubt that he would try to cut his way through it, relying upon the excellence of his fleet's night-fighting equipment, the careful training his officers and men had received in night-fighting, and the initiative always inherent to the surprise that his action would create. The fleet with the initiative and surprise is most usually successful in the unskilled mêlée of this sort of night action.

It was still too soon to start direct for Horns Reef, so he steered south, which was close enough for safety at present: to ensure a clear route, free from unwelcome British attentions, he not only intended to grope at dusk for Jellicoe's position then, adjusting his own course of advance as necessary, but to divert British attention while he was slipping past the rear of their line, he proposed to launch a series of destroyer attacks during the dark hours.

To facilitate his Admiral's plans, Commodore Michelsen (*Rostock*) delineated certain clear sectors for the night operations of German destroyers. His colleague, Commodore Heinrich (*Regensburg*) had already forestalled him, for all destroyers in the 2nd flotilla and the 11th half-flotilla having more than one torpedo remaining were already under orders: the remainder Heinrich had ordered to report to Commodore Michelsen for fleet screening and other duties. Heinrich had allocated Commander Schurr's 2nd flotilla to an east-north-east/east-south-east sector and Commander Schultz's 12th half-flotilla to an east-south-east/south-east sector with orders to set off at 8 o'clock within their allotted sectors and attack the British battle fleet at 8.45 p.m.

Commodore Michelsen, not wishing to countermand his subordinate's arrangements, took over the remaining destroyers, and allocated them as seemed best for the protection of *Lützow*, for anti-submarine screening, and disposed of the remainder—those with the most torpedoes left—to form a broad inverted V ahead of the fleet van and to commence probing and attacking the British line at 9 o'clock.

These were excellent dispositions—geometrically—and well suited to the purpose, but they lacked an essential pre-requisite; although destroyers had been directed to attack, none had been detailed for reconnaissance—to find the British fleet *for* the attackers. In consequence of this, and also because they started off to the attack too soon—and *found* the British fleet much nearer than they had expected it to be—the first series of attacks designed for 8.45 p.m. failed.[1]

Commander Schultz's 12th half-flotilla, heading south-eastwards within its sector, sighted the British line unexpectedly almost ahead at about 8 p.m., and steered south-south-westward to the attack. This flotilla was sighted by *Castor*, and the destroyers of the first division of the British 11th flotilla who moved out and headed them off; *Calliope*, *Constance* and *Comus* then came up in support firing rapidly, so the Germans launched torpedoes at the head of our line and fled north-west, hotly pursued.

A little later a division of Commander Schurr's 2nd flotilla, probing within its own sector for the rear of our fleet—and again too soon—sighted Goodenough's Fourth Light-Cruiser Squadron in its station off the fleet's western quarter: these soon drove the enemy destroyers away with well directed 6-inch salvoes—forcing them to rejoin the remainder of their flotilla well to the westward.

Neither of these attacks therefore made the slightest impact upon the battle fleet or upon its movements: the first of them did, however, have an unforeseen result, *Calliope*, with *Comus* and *Constance* in company, was chasing the enemy destroyers at utmost speed when at 8.26 p.m. she suddenly saw, coming out of the mists some four miles ahead, a line of enemy battleships. Almost at once two of them—*Prinzregent Luitpold* (now leading the Third Battle Squadron) and *Kaiserin*—opened rapid fire on her. Undeterred, however, *Calliope* (Commodore Le Mesurier) turned to an attacking course, closed the *Prinzregent Luitpold* to 6,200 yards and at 8.30 p.m. fired a torpedo at her (which missed) before turning sharply away. An extremely heavy fire was now directed upon the British light cruiser and her consorts by the two battleships, with *Kaiser* and even

---

[1] Michelsen allocated the 18th half-flotilla to the least vital sector (south-west/south-south-west), then the almost unused 5th flotilla to the south-south-west/south-by-east sector, and the 7th flotilla to the south-by-east/south-east sector. These sectors were drawn out from a centre point in 56° 25′ North, 5°30′ East, where Scheer expected to be at about 9 p.m.: the 5th and 7th flotillas would thus be the spearhead of an advance on a general south-by-easterly course.

Scheer's flagship joining in. The light cruisers speeding away and dodging the salvoes as best they could. *Calliope* was hit five times: two guns were disabled and her casualty-station wrecked, but she got back to the Fleet in safety, with 10 of her complement dead and 23 wounded; she then went at once to her place in the van.

The gun-flashes of this encounter had been visible all along the British battle line: *Royal Oak* and *Monarch* had even seen *Calliope* being hit, and at 8.38 p.m. Jellicoe signalled by searchlight to *Comus*: 'Who are you firing at?' He was told at once: 'Enemy's battle fleet west.'

At long last Jellicoe had *something* from which to deduce the enemy fleet's position relative to his own. During *Calliope's* engagement, she had been about $4\frac{3}{4}$ miles west-by-south of *Iron Duke*, the flashes of the enemy's guns bearing about west-by-north: this tended to place enemy battleships about eight miles to the westward of Jellicoe's flagship at 8.30 p.m. Assuming that *Lion* was also in action ahead of *Iron Duke*—holding firmly on to the enemy van—this gave a location for the German van; working back from this, and allowing Scheer a line five miles long suggested that the enemy might be steering south-south-west and that *Calliope* had been engaged by rear ships. This reasoning placed Jellicoe eight miles from the German line and on a slightly converging course. For while *Calliope's* action had been in progress, there had been important developments further southward. *Falmouth* (Rear-Admiral Napier) and her squadron had barely settled down to their running gun duel with von Reuter's five cruisers, when Beatty, with his six battle-cruisers, racing up fast towards the sound of *Falmouth's* guns again sighted four German battle-cruisers; beyond them, moreover, was the German pre-Dreadnought squadron all steering southward out of the mist. *Tiger* opened fire on the German battle-cruisers at 8.21 p.m.; *Lion* and *Princess Royal* opened fire a minute later at closing ranges of 10,000 and 9,500 yards; *New Zealand* and *Indomitable* quickly joined in and within three minutes an accurate and rapid fire had developed right down the British battle-cruiser line, some ships firing upon the pre-Dreadnoughts, others at the enemy's battle-cruisers. The latter were clearly visible, but were already in such a battered condition that their reply was quite ineffectual: it is doubtful if *Seydlitz* fired at all, and *Von der Tann* could not reply; *Derfflinger* had only four guns in action. From the start the German battle-cruisers were hampered by bad light and poor visibility: they could only see the flashes of Beatty's guns, and after three minutes hauled sharply round to the south-west to open the range. The armoured hulls of the old pre-

Dreadnoughts in the meantime having held on their southward course were able to give their battle-cruisers some protection, and into this shelter *Derfflinger* led her force, turning sharply to the north-west and running out of sight. The pre-Dreadnoughts thus justified the risk which Scheer had taken in bringing them with him for they had undoubtedly saved *Derfflinger* and her consorts from further grievous punishment.

As soon as the German battle-cruisers had drawn clear, the old battleships turned to starboard and also drew westwards out of range.

It had been a brief encounter—destined to be the last that day—but it had been most effective. Of the old German battleships, *Schleswig-Holstein*, *Schlesien* and *Pommern* had each been hit; the battle-cruiser *Seydlitz* had again suffered serious damage; *Derfflinger* had opened fire with the four guns from her two remaining turrets, but had soon been reduced to firing two guns, for a hit on one of her turrets, glancing off its armour, had buckled the turret-training-race, putting this turret also permanently out of action. As they turned westward, the German battle-cruisers could no longer be regarded as battleworthy units.

On our side, *Princess Royal* was hit once, but no serious damage was done, and she promptly launched a torpedo at the enemy—which, however, missed.

The action between *Falmouth's* Third Light-Cruiser Squadron and von Reuter's Fourth Scouting Group also ended abruptly at about the same time—the enemy light cruisers refusing to take the punishment of the British fire any longer, and altering course sharply four points to starboard into the mist at 8.28 p.m.; they were hotly pursued by *Falmouth's* squadron and ran out of sight at 8.38 p.m.

The sudden dying down of the firing to the southward puzzled Admiral Jellicoe at the time, for there had been no news from *Lion*. Jellicoe had, however, heard the battle-cruiser's guns and seen their flashes far to the south-westward. Unaware that there were now only six of the original nine battle-cruisers, he felt that they could maintain their hold on the enemy van.[1] Certain that he was now close to the enemy, Jellicoe turned the fleet at 8.28 p.m. to south-west, once again into line of battle.

Scheer's fleet had indeed been only eight miles away and on a sharply converging course when, despite his determination not to be forced to the westward any more, he had found himself compelled

[1] The Commander-in-Chief was not told of the loss of *Queen Mary* and *Indefatigable* until the morning of 1st June.

to give ground. First his battle-cruisers had turned westward, then his pre-Dreadnought squadron, and finally his Fourth Scouting Group—all had been forced to the westward under British guns. Unaware of Jellicoe's position, and fearful lest his T might again be crossed, he felt obliged to turn west-north-west, and then south-west, giving ground with his whole fleet: before Scheer felt it safe to turn back to a southerly course again he was nearly four miles farther west than he had started.

Although the firing ahead and to the south-westward had died down, it now broke out right astern of the British fleet. Commander Schurr's 2nd flotilla had been moving slowly in, in strength this time, to attack the Fifth Battle Squadron from the rear. *Southampton* was still there, however, with her Second Light-Cruiser Squadron, barring the way. *Southampton* at once engaged the intruders, who turned away, and the light cruiser squadron set off in hot pursuit, hurrying them until they turned westward out of reach of Commodore Goodenough's guns. Thus both the enemy destroyer attacks made on the British rear had failed—as dismally as the attack on the van. The German 2nd flotilla, moreover, was driven so far to the north-ward in its hurried flight from Goodenough's guns that it could not make any serious attempt to regain its fleet, and consequently withdrew out of action; these were Germany's biggest and most modern destroyers. Later, joined by Commander Hollman's 3rd flotilla which seems to have lost its way, they made their way home to Wilhelmshaven—but via the Skagerrak, round the Skaw, to Kiel and thence through the Canal.

Just before nine o'clock, with the light beginning to fail quite quickly, Jellicoe received three signals. One was from *Lion*: 'Enemy battle-cruisers and pre-Dreadnought battleships bear north-34°-west, distant ten to eleven miles, steering south-west (2040)'; the second was from *Falmouth*, reporting: 'Battle-cruisers unknown, bearing north, course of enemy west-south-west (2045)'; and the last was from *Southampton:* 'Urgent. Am engaging enemy destroyers, bearing west from me. Number unknown (2055).'[1]

None of the reporting ships' positions given in these signals could be reconciled, but Jellicoe no doubt considered that he had already located the enemy with sufficient accuracy. The one significant feature in all these signals, however, was that the enemy in sight was reported to be on some westerly course. These indications confirmed

---

[1] Later, at 9.10 p.m., *Southampton* added as a rider to this, 'Enemy reported in my 2055 has been driven to the north-west (2110)'.

Jellicoe's view that the enemy was seven or eight miles to the northward and westward, and apparently steering still more to the westward; he was certain now that he was still right across their road home. There was, however, a flaw in this reasoning: unknown to Jellicoe *Lion*'s signalled position was over six miles northwards of her actual position: the enemy's van as fixed from this signalled position was, therefore, some six miles further to the southward than Jellicoe had estimated.

A curious incident at this time was later to aggravate this erroneous estimate of the enemy's position. *Caroline* and *Royalist*—the second division of *Calliope*'s Fourth Light-Cruiser Squadron—were steering the course of the fleet, south-west, about 1¼ miles on the starboard bow of the leading battleship *King George V*. In this position, at about 8.45 p.m., *Caroline* (Captain H. R. Crooke) sighted to the north-westward[1] ship-shapes, which he at once recognised as battleships; ten minutes later, Captain Crooke now quite sure that the ships sighted were *enemy* ships, reported this to the nearest Flag Officer—Vice-Admiral Jerram—in *King George V*: 'Three battleships, north-west, about 8,000 yards, apparently old battleships.'

Having done this, *Caroline* ordered *Royalist*, who was astern of him, to attack with torpedoes. It was still quite light enough for them to see what they were doing, but *King George V*, however, was certain that the ships they had sighted were our own battle-cruisers: by searchlight signal he negatived the torpedo attack at 9.06 p.m. Happily, *Caroline* and *Royalist* had already attacked one minute earlier, firing their torpedoes, before they received this 'Negative': *Caroline* had fired two torpedoes and *Royalist* one, all, however, without success. As they turned away after firing, both light cruisers came under very heavy gunfire from 'our ships'; this lasted for some minutes and this 'welcome' was plainly visible on the bridge of *King George V* and other battleships of the leading divisions.[2]

Jerram's subsequent explanation of this affair was that one of his officers, recently joined from our Battle-Cruiser Force, was sure

[1] Fourth Light-Cruiser Squadron Track Chart shows the bearing as 305° (N42W, Magnetic) (Chart 12a, *Official Despatches*). *Falmouth* was reporting enemy battleships steering west-south-westwards at about the same time.

[2] *Caroline* had promptly and respectfully replied to the Vice-Admiral's 'Negative'— also by searchlight—'These are evidently enemy ships'. An observation is appended to the Admiral's report upon this incident (*Official Despatches*, p. 114) relating that after Crooke had signalled, the Vice-Admiral replied: 'If you are quite sure—attack!' This latter signal is not recorded in the list of signals given in Appendix II of the *Official Despatches*, however. *Comus* had also come in for a share of this gunfire as she had moved out to support *Caroline* and *Royalist*.

that they *were* our ships. It is, nevertheless, incredible that even in the light prevailing anyone could mistake any of our battle-cruisers for a ship of the German First Battle Squadron. *Caroline* had repeated to *King George V*—and she was much nearer—that the ships were evidently enemy: Captain Crooke had every reason to know that for he was fired upon. *Castor*, also up in the van, saw these ships and at 9.15 p.m. reported them as enemy ships. On the bridge of *Orion*, the leading ship of the second division of the Second Battle Squadron, the enemy ships were also recognised.

Three things are particularly striking about this episode. Firstly, that enemy ships should fail to be identified in the calm contemplation of a battleship's bridge, and of a flagship's bridge in particular. Secondly, that *Castor* having realised that these were enemy ships, did not at once engage them with her destroyer flotilla. Thirdly, why, after *Caroline* was fired upon as she turned away and was kept under fire for some minutes, did none of the leading battleships open fire or make any move to see what was the truth of the incident —that *Caroline* and *Royalist* had sighted and engaged, unsupported, the German First Battle Squadron? As for *Castor*, when the enemy opened fire on the two light cruisers, she turned her flotilla away from them, 'expecting the fleet to fire upon them'. Any doubts *Castor's* Commodore might have had, however, must surely have been dispelled when at about 9.16 p.m. the leading enemy ship was observed to fire a starshell: that type of night illuminant had not yet been supplied to any British ship. *Castor* still made no move, reporting afterwards, 'as the fleet held their fire, I could not attack, as it was not dark enough to make an attack unsupported by fire from the fleet'.[1] The 'battle-cruisers' turned away to starboard, and were lost sight of.

From the fragments of information that reached him, Jellicoe had deduced an approximate position for the enemy van—pending more accurate information which he felt sure would come to hand— as being about seven or eight miles to the north-westward of him: this would serve as a basis for his own night dispositions pending other, later, information.

He had, moreover, by now formed a fair estimate of Admiral Scheer's probable intentions. During the day, the German Admiral had consistently refused battle and turned his fleet away whenever confronted by our battle fleet. It was to be expected therefore that he would use the brief summer hours of darkness to effect his escape while yet there was time. That he would not deliberately seek a

[1] *Official Despatches.*

night fleet action was virtually certain, and Jellicoe correctly assumed that Scheer would be shepherding damaged capital ships.

Jellicoe equally had little intention of indulging in night battle. Night actions must be fought under the inevitable difficulties of recognising friend from foe, and at a close range which reduces gunnery skill to the low level of the mêlée. The day-fighting had shown Jellicoe that the gunnery of his battle fleet was on the whole superior to that of the German battleships, and that the surface attacks by torpedo craft were not the menace they had been made out to be. Having met the enemy so late in the afternoon, and in poor visibility, he had not had the ample time and light to fight to the conclusion he sought. The morrow would have all the day's daylight ahead, and if he could intercept Scheer's fleet at day-break, and before the German ships could reach the shelter he was certain they would seek, Jellicoe felt a decision could be reached.

An important factor had to be considered—the particular swept channel through which Scheer would take his fleet. In many parts of the Heligoland Bight both German and British mines had been laid, and swept up and laid again: it was usual to consider the waters to the southward of 50° North Latitude and to the eastward of the meridian of 6° East Longitude, as a 'mined area'. Through this zone there were known to be several definite channels, or 'ways' which the Germans kept swept clear of mines, some more regularly used than others.

The Commander-in-Chief, at that time, had been informed by the Admiralty of the *general direction* only of these channels: even this information could not be considered wholly reliable;[1] it is open to serious doubt, moreover, whether Jellicoe had ever been given more than the *approximate* location of the seaward exits of these swept channels. It is most important, therefore, that the reader should bear in mind that Jellicoe did not possess the neatly-drawn post-war plans, showing—usually in red—the precise location of enemy minefields and channels and their exits, which have become available since.

Apart from four principal 'swept channels', there was also a fifth route by which Scheer might consider making for home and safety—he might seek escape round the Skaw, the tip of Denmark, and then through the Kattegat down to Kiel. Jellicoe dismissed the possibility of this; the weather frequently encountered off the Skaw was no place for damaged ships down by the head. It was quite possible that the escape route round the Skaw might be used by enemy

[1] Admiralty's *Narrative*.

destroyers and light craft—but Jellicoe was primarily interested in the bigger fish—the German battle fleet.

The easternmost of the four swept channels was the *Amrum Bank* channel, entered about 15 miles south of Horns Reef; the second, the *North Heligoland* channel, had its sea entrance about thirty miles west of the Horns Reef light-vessel; the third, the *Ems* channel, was entered through several mouths to the northward of the West Ems river, and thence along the north side of the Frisian islands. There was also a fourth route, which the Germans used on occasion, but entrance to this was reached on a south-easterly course through a known gap in the British minefields about 35 miles north-west of Heligoland, and thence by a short swept channel running west from Heligoland itself.

From the Germans' assumed position at 9 o'clock, the distance to the seaward entrance of the Amrum Bank channel was about 100 miles—six and a quarter hours' steaming at 16 knots; to the Heligoland-North channel, it was 74 miles, or four and a half hours' steaming; to the little-used Heligoland-West channel, it was 170 miles, or ten and three-quarter hours at 16 knots; to the entrance to the Ems channel it was 190 miles—12 hours' steaming.

Considering the steaming-times involved, account had to be taken of the fact that sunrise on 1st June would be at 3.09 a.m., and that it would be beginning to get light by 2.30 a.m. with some possibilities of more mist and poor visibility. Scheer had, therefore, approximately five and a half hours from nine o'clock to cover most of the ground to any of the swept-channel entrances under cover of darkness.

This fact brought the Heligoland-North channel to the fore (this was the one which Scheer had used to reach the North Sea the day before, although this was not known at the time). Should Scheer choose the eastern-most escape route (the Amrum Bank channel), five-and-a-half hours of steaming could take him to Horns Reef by first light, but this left him just about an hour to steam in growing daylight the fifteen miles to the entrance of the Amrum channel: this possibility could equally not be overlooked. Nor was it possible to dismiss either the little-used Heligoland-West channel or, for that matter, the more remote Ems channel. Scheer when last seen had been reported to be on a west-south-westerly course, so that the more westerly escape routes, though less likely, were quite within the bounds of possibility.[1]

---

[1] As the Admiralty did not direct Tyrwhitt's force to proceed to sea until 2.52 in the morning, they could not possibly have been in a position to interfere with Scheer's going either to the Ems channel or the Heligoland-West channel, had he been so minded.

In all this, it must be realised that Jellicoe had no possible means of knowing, or even guessing, which route Scheer might take. He decided, therefore, that if he steamed south during the night and until dawn at 2.30 a.m. on June 1st, he would be in a position to bar the way to the nearest route—the Heligoland-North channel—also in a good position from which to turn westward at first light to cut the enemy's escape if he was favouring either of the two southern routes, or to turn eastward toward Horns Reef, some two hours' steaming away. On such a southerly course, the Grand Fleet could act as a barrier to all four possible escape routes.

Jellicoe has frankly recorded his night intentions in his Despatch:

> I therefore decided to steer to the southward, where I should be in a position to renew the engagement at daylight and should also be favourably placed to intercept the enemy should he make for his base by steering for Heligoland or towards the Ems, and thence along the North German coast.

None of the flag officers in his fleet saw any reason then or since to dispute the sagacity of this decision: if other information came to hand during the night watches his plan could be modified. Beatty held similar views:

> I assumed that the enemy were to the north-westward and that we had established ourselves between him and his base . . . our strategical position being such that it appeared certain that we should locate the enemy at daylight under most favourable circumstances.

Jellicoe said 'I rejected at once the idea of a night action between heavy ships', and gave his entirely adequate reasons. Beatty also observed 'I did not think it proper or desirable to close the enemy battle fleet during the dark hours'.[1]

At one minute past nine, Jellicoe turned his fleet by divisions to the south.

[1] *Official Despatches.*

9

No Bugles Blare

By three minutes past nine o'clock, the British battle fleet was steering south in columns of divisions with their guides on a quarter line of bearing north-east/south-west.

Admiral Sir John Jellicoe's first task now was to bring his fleet into a formation suitable to the peculiar conditions of night-cruising, in low visibility and in the vicinity of a shrewd enemy. To do this, he purposed to complete his fleet disposition for the night so that every unit would know its own station and each other's, and as far as possible to do this in daylight and by visual signal. He had to keep constantly in mind the great problem besetting any night operation in the presence of the enemy—the difficulty of recognising instantly friend from foe, since warships—like black cats—tend to look alike in the dark; the strain and tension engendered by peering and staring into an eerie darkness can almost be felt, and peoples itself in the imagination of the look-out with lights and shapes.

Like wary cats, the inhabitants of the undistinguishable shapes watch each other: neither wishes to be the first to speak or to make the secret challenging recognition signal until the last moment. Challenge an *enemy*; the immediate reply will be a hail of shells from every gun that will bear, and one's own gunners and the commander on the bridge blinded and dazzled by the fierce white probing beams of enemy searchlights flashed into their eyes. Challenge a *friend*: the immediate reply will be the proper lights for that hour of night, or the Morse letters if they are correct. One can *feel* the sudden relaxation of tension, can almost hear the ship breathe again.

From the control position, the order passes: 'All guns check—check—check.'

With this problem of recognition uppermost in his mind, Admiral Jellicoe closed his battle fleet into a more compact formation (Organisation No. 2)—in column of squadrons in line, leaders abeam to port: columns were to be a mile apart, probably the maximum visibility distance as the night wore on. The signal was made 'General' at 9.17 p.m., by flags and by low-power wireless for the information of every unit. Jellicoe had already signalled the night course of the fleet—south—to the senior officers of all squadrons and flotillas. The night-organisation of the battle fleet was completed by half past nine; the Battle Squadrons, having formed into three columns a mile apart, with the powerful Second Battle Squadron ('King Georges' and 'Orions') on the western side, the side nearer to the enemy, and the three ships of the Fifth Battle Squadron on the eastern side.

The Commander-in-Chief's anxiety as far as his battle fleet was concerned was for the rear division of the First Battle Squadron—*Marlborough* (flagship), *Revenge, Hercules* and *Agincourt*. The first of these, leading the division, was making a desperate struggle to maintain her station in the line; she had informed the Commander-in-Chief an hour and a half earlier that with her A boiler-room flooded, her maximum speed was now only 17 knots—the speed of the fleet. So *Marlborough* would have no margin for manoeuvring, and in reality she was hardly doing her full seventeen, although her stokers were now working knee-deep in water to keep the port boilers fired. By 9.30 p.m. she was already a mile and a half astern of the other part of the First Battle Squadron, led by *Colossus*. The Fifth Battle Squadron, coming up from the rear, was intended to make a column on its own; but tried to take station astern of *Marlborough's* division and then, finding her dropping back, pressed ahead.

Of Jellicoe's light-cruiser squadrons, Commodore Goodenough's Second Light-Cruiser Squadron, which had chased the enemy destroyers westward, turned to the course of the fleet at high speed and at 9.30 p.m. was astern of the Second Battle Squadron, when Goodenough intercepted a signal from *Lion*, giving the latter's night disposition; he proceeded to take up a position covering the rear, about $6\frac{1}{2}$ miles on the starboard quarter of *King George V*, steering the same course as the rest of the fleet. Commodore Le Mesurier's Fourth Light-Cruiser Squadron formed line ahead off *King George V's* starboard bow.

At 9.35 p.m. Admiral Beatty signalled the Commander-in-Chief by wireless and the Senior Officers of the nearest Battle Squadron (the Second), of the First, Second and Third Light-Cruiser Squadrons and to *Champion* (Captain [D], 13th flotilla)—again, on the same principle as Jellicoe, a signal for general information—giving his position, and his course (south) and his speed, seventeen knots. He had neatly dropped into position about eleven miles west of the battle fleet, prolonging his line by putting *Minotaur* and the five armoured cruisers two miles astern of him. Six miles on his starboard bow, he stationed Commodore Sinclair's First Light-Cruiser Squadron, and Rear-Admiral Napier's Third Light-Cruiser Squadron. Nothing could more clearly have shown his complete understanding of the Commander-in-Chief's intentions than this admirable disposition of the battle-cruiser forces at Beatty's disposal. He was, as he said in his Despatch afterwards:

> Carrying out the Commander-in-Chief's wishes. . . . My duty in this situation was to ensure that the enemy fleet could not regain its base by passing round the southern flank of our forces.[1]

He also considered that the enemy was well to the westward and contemplated asking Jellicoe's permission at daylight to sweep further to the south-westward to seek for Scheer. The British barrier to Scheer's escape now had a front of some 22 miles, covering the enemy's road home to the Heligoland-North, the Ems, and the Heligoland-West channels. Two more steps remained to be taken: to cover the possibility of Scheer's escape by way of Horns Reef and the Amrum Bank channel. *Abdiel* (Commander Curtis), the fast fleet mine-laying destroyer, was given special orders at 9.32 p.m. 'If there is time before daylight, lay mines in position [ordered] . . . and then proceed to Rosyth.' *Abdiel*, with her cargo of mines, had been on the disengaged side of the fleet during the evening actions, her crew 'sitting on their eggs'. She now set off at 31 knots (at 10.15 p.m.) and held on unseen by anyone, south-south-eastward, until at 12.30 in the morning she sighted the Horns Reef lightship. Thence she made for 'the position ordered'.[2] Fifteen miles, at 215° from the Vyl light-vessel, she reduced speed, and laid a line of forty mines, ten to the mile, on a south-9-east course; then turning to south-34-west, she laid another forty mines at ten to the mile. The mines were staggered in each line, for *Abdiel* steered a zig-zag course, and they were set at a low-water depth of 15 feet. The work was complete by four minutes past two and *Abdiel* set off back to Rosyth: the mines had been well and truly laid.

The laying of this minefield would, Jellicoe considered, reinforce the work of the three submarines—*E-50*, *E-26* and *D-1*—which had already been sent to their stations—4, 12 and 20 miles respectively west (True) from the Vyl lightship, and were just arriving there.

[1] *Official Despatches.*
[2] This minefield was originally designed for Operation M—Jellicoe's projected plan for enticing the German High Seas Fleet up into the Skagerrak, a plan which would have been carried out on 2nd June but for the intervention of the Battle of Jutland.

Jellicoe did not of course know that the Admiralty, in sending them out, had failed to ensure that their orders were changed before they left Harwich: their existing orders unfortunately required them to sit on the bottom until daylight *on 2nd June*; they, therefore, saw nothing of what happened on the night of 31st May–1st June.[1]

Jellicoe had one more disposition to make—simple, but perhaps the most brilliant of all in its conception: at 9.15 p.m., he signalled 'Destroyers take station astern of battle fleet, five miles (2115)'. The signal was made by wireless on power, as the units were widely scattered; it was in code, and addressed to all Senior Officers of squadrons, to commanders of battle-fleet divisions and to Captain (D) 11—Commodore Hawksley in *Castor*, who was also the Commodore of Grand Fleet Flotillas.[2] This was another example of making a 'General' signal for the information of those people likely to be most concerned.

This disposition effectively placed the fleet's destroyers where they could not be the cause of mistaken identity during the dark hours, between themselves and our battleships or battle-cruisers; it placed them in an ideal position from which to protect the rear of the battle fleet from any attempted enemy night attack upon it and, per contra, from which to attack the enemy line; and above all, by stationing the massed destroyers astern it prolonged the British line northwards. The effective barrier our fleet thus now presented to Scheer's escape was a mobile mass 23 miles in width, and eight miles in depth. It would have been difficult to devise a better barrier on the basis of the information available to the Commander-in-Chief.

As a clinching nail to this edifice, Jellicoe signalled at 9.48 p.m. to Beatty, the Senior Officers of all squadrons and divisions, and to Captains (D) of all flotillas—to everyone in fact—the reference position of *Iron Duke* at 9.45 p.m.: 'Latitude 56°26' North, Longitude 5°47' East, course south, speed 17 knots (2145).' If every unit in the command were now to adjust their dead-reckoning to fit in with *Iron Duke's* 9.45 p.m. position, there could be no further difficulties in regard to the accuracy of signalled positions and it would facilitate moreover a swift reforming and closing up of the fleet and its flotillas and outlying squadrons at any time necessary during the

[1] The orders for these submarines were issued in connection with Operation M: they were required to remain on the bottom until daylight on 2nd June, attacking any ships on the surface after that time.

[2] This signal did not apply to the flotillas screening Beatty's battle-cruisers. The time of despatch was 9.27 p.m.

night or early morning. In the light of after events it does not seem that all Senior Officers addressed by this signal passed on its contents to the individual ships under their command: furthermore, from a perusal of the Ships' Reports, and a consideration of problems that arose later, even those ships that *knew* the reference position did not make the best use of it.

Jellicoe's night disposition reveals the master hand: but it fell short of perfection in several very important details. Firstly the disposing signal to destroyers should have been made to all flotillas, not only to the Commodore—or else he should have been instructed to see that all flotilla-leaders were apprised of the general disposition of our own ships. Secondly, the destroyers themselves, and for that matter the rest of the fleet, should have been given some idea of the assumed position of the enemy, and of his expected moves of escape. Thirdly, though this should not have been necessary in view of the general instructions contained in the Grand Fleet's Battle Orders for destroyers to lose no chance of attacking the enemy, more emphasis might perhaps have been laid on the significant offensive powers of destroyers at night.

Jellicoe and his staff must share the responsibility for the absence of this information and for the signals not having been given to individual destroyers: it was a shortcoming that Commodore (F) might, of course, have noticed and remedied on his own initiative, but he did not. The destroyers therefore turned round and steamed outside and between the lines of the battle fleet to take up their stations astern: the 11th flotilla astern of the Second Battle Squadron, the 4th astern of the Fourth Battle Squadron and *Iron Duke*. For some reason, *Champion*, with her 13th flotilla and small portions of the 9th and 10th (close eastward of her), took station astern of *Marlborough's* division, and the 12th flotilla then took up its post east of them again. The 11th and 4th flotillas were getting in position by 10 p.m.; but the 13th, 9th and 10th were soon troubled, for as *Marlborough's* division dropped more and more astern of station, *Champion* dropped back to keep her distance from *Agincourt* while the 12th flotilla, at the eastern end of the destroyer-mass, conformed and fell back also.

(ii)

While Jellicoe had been making his night-dispositions, Admiral Scheer had not been idle: with only six hours left until sunrise, time for him was now very valuable. He had peremptorily checked the westward drift of his fleet at 8.46 p.m. by ordering a south-south-easterly course for the whole fleet, directing it to form single line with the pre-Dreadnoughts leading for the time being.

At 9.14 p.m., he issued two orders by wireless to his fleet: firstly, the fleet was to assume a new disposition, the pre-Dreadnoughts turning round to take station astern of the First and Third Squadrons. This would put the undamaged First Battle Squadron in the van for the journey home, with *Westfalen* (Captain Redlich) leading the line; the battle-cruisers were to be in the rear. Boedicker's Second Scouting Group, reinforced by *Rostock*, was to take station ahead of *Westfalen*, and the Fourth Scouting Group (von Reuter's) was to manoeuvre off the fleet's bow. The 7th and 5th destroyer flotillas, with others, were to work ahead of the fleet and in a broad V-shaped formation with its arms between south-south-west and south-east, to probe for the enemy, and to attack the British battle fleet. The destroyers would receive any support they needed from the two nearby groups of light cruisers.

His second order directed the fleet to advance towards Horns Reef at about 9.30 p.m.; but an executive signal would be made—the course to be south-south-east-$\frac{1}{2}$-east[1], at sixteen knots.

While the German line was being formed, Beatty had passed $4\frac{1}{2}$ miles ahead of it, without seeing it, at about 9.20 p.m.; *Minotaur* and her armoured cruisers had been even nearer at 9.17 p.m., when *Shannon's* masthead light had revealed their position. Scheer had a very fair idea where the battle-cruisers and armoured cruisers were being stationed for the night, before he ever set out on his Odyssey.

The British battle fleet had to be found as a preliminary, and found with some accuracy: that was to be the duty of the destroyers and the light cruisers. *Westfalen's* turn of 16 points to drop in astern of the Third Battle Squadron had, however, to be delayed while *Minotaur* and her armoured cruisers were in sight; but the turn was soon completed after that. At 9.36 p.m., Scheer finally directed his fleet to steer the course ordered, at sixteen knots, adding: 'This course is to be maintained.'

The destroyer flotillas, given the important task of probing ahead and attacking the rear of the British battle fleet, were under a great handicap from the start. Commander Michelsen had restricted them to a maximum speed of eighteen knots, for they had 'dirty fires' and at any greater speed these could have caused sparking and funnel-flames. Since the Grand Fleet's speed was 17 knots, and the destroyers started from well astern of them, their chance of finding Jellicoe's fleet was going to be very slender.

[1] i.e. South-28°-East Magnetic.

Commander Heinicke's 5th flotilla, searching the sector south-south-west/south-south-east ahead of the advance, found nothing to report, and returned to *Westfalen's* side again. Commander von Koch, with the 7th flotilla and responsible for the south-by-east to south-east sector had started unluckily by being fired upon about 9.32 p.m. by the ships of his own 3rd Battle Squadron. No damage was done, however, and von Koch pushed on south-eastwards until,

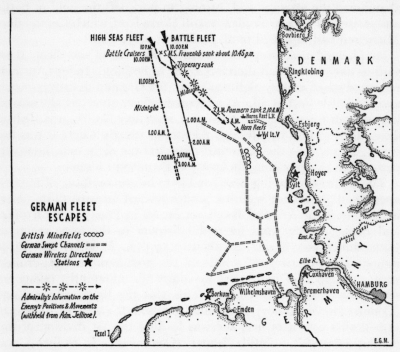

at about 9.50 p.m., he sighted several hostile destroyers on his starboard bow, barely a mile away, steering northward; as it seemed that they had not seen him von Koch did nothing to disclose his position and eight minutes later he fired four close-range torpedoes at them for good measure, before turning away into the dark. He had been lucky enough to see *Tipperary* (Captain Wintour) leading his 4th flotilla to its allotted night station in rear of the British fleet. At about 9.59 p.m., this flotilla turned sharply to south—to the course of the fleet: the torpedoes that had been fired at them, therefore, passed harmlessly astern and to the northward. As the rear destroyers of the division turned, however, *Contest* (Lieutenant-Commander Master), *Garland* (Lieutenant-Commander Goff) and *Fortune* (Lieutenant-Commander Terry) clearly saw the enemy and opened fire on them as they ran off out of sight. *Contest* reported this to Captain (D4), Captain Wintour; but, unaccountably, he made no effort to chase, and held on southward, the course of the fleet.

This failure to grasp the opportunity and pursue undoubtedly emboldened Commander von Koch to try again; but in scudding away from *Contest's* three rounds, he had dropped so far astern that at eighteen knots he could not catch up again. He eventually abandoned the attempt and, turning to port, left the field of battle and steered for a 2 a.m. rendezvous off Horns Reef, which Commodore Michelsen had signalled to all flotillas at 10.32 p.m.[1]

As planned destroyer attacks upon the rear of our fleet, these various movements had therefore come to nothing. Indeed, at their restricted speed of only eighteen knots, the German destroyers never saw our battle fleet at all. As a German officer observed afterwards, 'throughout the night, our destroyers, searching for the great British fleet, failed to find it, although they knew exactly where it was last seen'. To say that they searched *throughout* the night was, however, perhaps an exaggeration, for many of them went home.

The destroyers having been unable to locate anything of import-ance, the light-cruiser scouting groups pushed forward to do better if possible. Rear-Admiral Boedicker set off in *Frankfurt*, with *Pillau* and *Elbing*, to see what he could discover in the same sector as Commander von Koch. At about 9.45 p.m. *Frankfurt* and *Pillau* sighted, three-quarters of a mile on the port hand, a light-cruiser, with a number of destroyers in company, apparently taking up station on a southerly course. This was the light cruiser *Castor* (Commodore Hawksley), the flotilla-commodore's ship, with her own 11th flotilla astern of her: she was leading the 1st division of this flotilla; *Kempenfelt*, a flotilla 'leader' (Commander H. Sulivan), was leading the remainder.

Rear-Admiral Boedicker, realising he had not yet been seen, hauled his light cruisers away a little and was careful not to switch on searchlights or to open fire, 'to avoid drawing the British des-troyers after them [the German cruisers] towards [Scheer's] battle fleet'.[2] He then fired three torpedoes, at 1,200 yards range, and

---

[1] This signal was: 'First Leader of Flotillas [Commodore Michelsen] to all destroyer-flotillas. Rendezvous with our own main fleet by 2 a.m. at Horns Reef, or make passage around Skaw. (1032).' This signal was intercepted by a British monitoring station, deciphered at the Admiralty's Room 40 by 11.15 p.m., but *it was not sent on to Admiral Jellicoe*, despite the vitally important mention of Horns Reef as the dawn rendezvous. Again, by some carelessness in Room 40, the phrase 'with own main fleet' was omitted from the deciphered signal as passed to the Admiralty Operations Division for action.— Cf. Corbett, *Naval Operations*.

[2] *Krieg zur See, Nordsee.*

waited to see the result: they all missed. Boedicker could, however, afford to bide his time, so after swinging away for eight or nine minutes he turned back, having now been joined by *Rostock* and *Hamburg*, and drew in again. This time, at about 10.04 p.m., *Castor* saw the strangers—several cruisers apparently in line ahead to starboard—but assumed them to be friendly because *Rostock* had at once flashed, in Morse characters, the two first letters of the secret British challenge for the day. *Castor*, who had been closing the strangers, replied normally, and was immediately greeted by the two leading strangers—*Hamburg* and *Elbing*—switching their searchlights on and, a moment later, opening fire.[1] As *Castor* was under helm the enemy's searchlight beams first rested on the destroyers *Marne* and *Magic* astern of her. *Marne's* captain (Lieutenant-Commander Hartford) at once rang down his engine room telegraph for 'full speed ahead' but something miraculously went wrong and for a few seconds the destroyer came almost to a stop—the enemy fired furiously but all the salvoes pitched ahead of her. *Castor* then came between *Marne* and the enemy drawing their fire—and searchlights—on to herself. Her action had saved *Marne* but *Castor* came under heavy fire; she replied with her six-inch battery at under 2,000 yards and 'the bursting of the shells . . . was most noticeable'. She swung to port and fired a torpedo; she was holed forward, and had twelve men killed and 23 wounded in this brief minute or two; when *Castor* drew clear *Marne* and *Magic* also fired a torpedo each, and the enemy turned sharply away to avoid them, switching off their searchlights and ceasing fire: one torpedo passed right under *Elbing*, having been set with just too much depth.

Marne and *Magic* would have fired again, but they were being blinded by the flash of *Castor's* guns. The remainder of the flotilla did not fire at all: they were so convinced, in spite of the murderous fire poured in upon *Castor* at point-blank range, 'that a mistake had been made, and that we were being fired on by our own ships'.[2] Nor, for that matter, did the Commodore, having so spiritedly forced the enemy to turn away, lead his flotilla after them in pursuit.

Castor and her destroyers' swift torpedo attack had, by compelling the enemy to turn away, reacted upon Scheer and the main fleet. As soon as he received Boedicker's sighting report, and realised that the clash had taken place little more than six miles from his van, he pulled his fleet round a point to starboard on to south-by-east-$\frac{3}{4}$-east.

[1] Having made the first two letters correctly, just as *Castor* was making the reply, one of the strangers made two wrong letters (T and R).—*Official Despatches*.

[2] *Castor's* report, *Official Despatches*.

Scheer was under the distinct impression that his van cruisers had been attacked; not that they had been the attackers. As he did not wish to be forced continually to the westward, he had altered the fleet's course slightly to remove it from the risk of such attack; the courses of the two fleets were, however, still converging slightly.

Between 10.25 p.m. and 10.30 p.m., von Reuter's Fourth Scouting Group, slightly ahead of Scheer's centre and out to port of it, became aware that further to the eastward of them were dim shipshapes. The night had shut down dark and starless and the sky was completely overcast: there was no moon and there was mist and very little visibility. These 'ship-shapes' were Commodore Goodenough's Second Light-Cruiser Squadron, in line ahead—*Southampton* (flagship) *Dublin*, *Birmingham* and *Nottingham*. It will be recalled that this squadron had gradually worked ahead up the western flank of our battle-fleet and had taken up a position on its starboard quarter, about 4¾ miles to the westward of the block of destroyers astern.

While making for this position, they had seen and heard the crash of gunfire of *Castor's* sharp brush with the enemy and, from further off still, they had noticed a flicker of guns. There was therefore ample evidence that the enemy was around and about somewhere in the darkness and Commodore Goodenough was entirely ready for them when at about 10.20 p.m. five enemy ships in line could be dimly made out some 1,500 yards away on his starboard beam.[1]

The enemy, after a distinct wait—an interval which *Southampton* used to flood her starboard submerged torpedo-tube in readiness for firing—challenged with a string of coloured lights. The reply came from *Dublin*: a single round of six-inch, the flash from which for a split second lit up the whole scene. The enemy were less than 1,000 yards away and *Dublin's* shell could be seen to burst in the side of an enemy ship, giving an officer in *Southampton* 'a nightmare glimpse of her interior'. The enemy's searchlights instantly flashed out from each of the five cruisers, and their guns opened fire simultaneously upon *Southampton* and *Dublin*. The two rear British cruisers, *Birmingham* and *Nottingham*, wisely refrained from switching on their lights and, remaining in darkness except for the flash of their broadsides, were able to pour rapid salvoes at point blank range into the enemy almost without interference.

The fury of the action lasted only a very few minutes. In that short time, *Southampton*, upon whom the enemy's fire had been chiefly

[1] Times differ here. *Southampton* reported this at 10.20 p.m.; *Dublin* at 10.40 p.m.; *Birmingham* at about 10.15 p.m.

concentrated, had three guns and two searchlights put out of action, her wireless destroyed, ten holes in her hull and a big fire burning abaft her funnels as well as smaller cordite fires along her decks; she also had 35 dead and 41 wounded on board. In the midst of the inferno, however, she had managed to fire her starboard submerged tube and the torpedo from it made a direct hit on *Frauenlob*. The German cruiser, already heavily hit and blazing from our gunfire, lurched and staggered—and all her lights went out.

Dublin (Captain Scott) had not suffered quite as heavily as *Southampton*, for she had not had the same concentration of fire upon her. Her charthouse and bridge were however completely smashed, she had eight hits in her hull and all her charts were destroyed; she was on fire between decks and had three killed—including her navigating officer—and 24 wounded.

As *Southampton*'s torpedo hit *Frauenlob*, the enemy squadron suddenly sheered off, switching all their searchlights out; their guns ceased firing. *Southampton* and *Dublin* then turned eight points to port, opening the range, to enable them to get their fires under control; *Nottingham* and *Birmingham* conformed. The fires were soon dealt with, but *Dublin*, chartless, and with her standard compass deranged, now lost touch with her consorts, and steaming on her own was unable to regain contact during the dark hours. Commodore Goodenough, however, held on eastward with the remainder and ultimately sighting the Fifth Battle Squadron, which had dropped more than a mile astern of the rear ships of the other battle squadrons, formed his three ships astern of *Malaya*: he felt that he could still perform good service there by providing protection to the rear of the battle fleet against any future attacks by destroyers or light cruisers.

Turning eastward as they had done, in order to smother their fires, Goodenough's ships had not been able to see the full success of *Southampton*'s torpedo: *Frauenlob*, soon turned right over and sank at about 10.45 p.m., taking with her to the bottom Captain Hoffman, eleven other officers and 307 men. The British squadron's shooting had been effective indeed: *Stettin* had two hits, her steampipes were damaged, and a gun and a searchlight were knocked out; *München* had received five hits and *Hamburg* four—two of them in her port bunkers. Her foremost funnel had been hit, smothering the bridge with flying splinters. She had ten killed and 20 wounded on board.

Commodore Goodenough's first thought now was to apprise his Commander-in-Chief of what had occurred. Unfortunately, his wireless had been shot away, but as soon as he was able he directed

Nottingham to report for him. *Nottingham* finally passed to the Commander-in-Chief: 'Urgent. Have engaged enemy cruisers 10.15 bearing west-south-west (2240)'. But owing to the delays of damaged wireless, this message did not reach *Iron Duke* until 11.38 p.m.

The flash of the guns had been seen all over the fleet, and even in the battle-cruisers miles to the eastward. Jellicoe, however, thought it was most probably a destroyer attack on the rear, and signalled to *Castor* by wireless: 'Urgent. Are you engaging enemy's destroyers? (2243)' To which he received a negative reply at eleven o'clock.[1] In a night engagement, the big ships cannot use their main armament, due to the restricted visibility, and it is therefore impossible to distinguish what class of ship is engaged from the gunfire alone. There was good reason for Jellicoe to make his enquiry in this form and also to assume that the gunflashes were from destroyer attacks astern. At 9.55 p.m. he had received a wireless signal from the Admiralty: 'Three destroyer flotillas have been ordered to attack you during the night (2105)'.[2]

Examining these first two night-attacks; while Goodenough's light cruiser action was quite straightforward there was a sinister feature attaching to the light-cruiser attack upon *Castor* and her destroyers. It will have been noted that *Rostock*, on approaching *Castor*, had correctly made the first two letters of *our* secret challenge. This deserves some comment, for during the hours of darkness this trick was to be used more than once: every time it was used, the result was the same. As soon as our own ships began to answer with the appropriate reply-letters, in Morse, the enemy switched on his searchlights and simultaneously poured in a murderous fire at point-blank range.

The British system of night-challenging at that time was to use one or two letters of the alphabet made by Morse code with a white light; the 'reply' consisted of similar Morsed letters. The letters themselves were secret and changed repeatedly throughout the day, according to a schedule kept in the custody of every British commanding officer. The Germans, for recognition purposes, normally used a system based on the simultaneous switching on of groups of two, three or four horizontal red, green or white lights, which were flicked on and off a particular number of times; any other German

---

[1] *Castor's* signal of reply was made via *Kempenfelt*, since *Castor's* wireless had also been damaged in the engagement.

[2] This signal was a watered down version of Commodore Michelsen's instructions to the German destroyer-flotillas issued soon after eight o'clock, intercepted by our monitoring station, decoded in Room 40 and precis'd by someone else.

warship would answer this with similar groupings of coloured lights. As with us, the nature of the combination of colours was secret. Having no such system of coloured lights, we could not in any way simulate the German recognition signals; the Germans, on the other hand, *could* simulate ours with an ordinary flash lamp—provided that they knew what the correct letters for the day or night were.

At 9.32 p.m., on 31st May, Admiral Sir David Beatty's *Lion*, who some minutes earlier had turned with the battle-cruisers to the south course of the fleet for the night, signalled to her next in line, *Princess Royal*. The Admiralty account says that the signal was made with a flash-lamp; *Castor*, who saw the signal at a distance of seven miles or more, says it was made 'by searchlight',[1] in any case, a brighter light than was necessary for signalling 500 yards. The signal read:

> From S.O. B.C.F. [Vice-Admiral Beatty] to *Princess Royal* [Captain Cowan]—Please give me challenge and reply now in force as they have been lost.

To this request, *Lion*'s signal log contained the comment: '*Challenge and reply passed as requested.*' This log-book annotation is corroborated by the Captain of the destroyer *Manners* (Lieutenant-Commander G. C. Harrison) who saw the reply being made.[2]

Lion was without wireless; but it is a pity that the request was not made earlier, when it could have been made by semaphore; or, failing that, that some discretion had been used in the type of lamp used for the signal.

The signal was read seven miles away in the British line: it was also read by other eyes very much nearer. While Beatty was drawing out south-west to his night station at 9.30 p.m. he had passed unknowingly about four miles south of the German Second Squadron of pre-Dreadnoughts, and about the same distance from the German light-cruiser scouting groups which were both on the eastern side of the fleet; *Minotaur* and her armoured cruisers of the Second Cruiser Squadron had been even closer to the unseen enemy, as they moved south-westward to take their night-station astern of Beatty's battle-cruisers. In both the Second and the Fourth German Scouting Groups and in *Rostock*, the Commodore of flotillas' ship, *Lion*'s flashing signal was seen: it had been made *en clair* and they read it; *Princess Royal*'s reply, also *en clair*, was seen and read. The Germans ships were thus provided with a most valuable piece of Intelligence, which—not unreasonably—they used, and which was to cost valuable lives later.

[1] *Official Despatches.*
[2] *Official Despatches*: *Manners* was astern of *Castor*.

Minotaur's squadron, as has been mentioned, drew close to the German van at about 9.20 p.m., just as a critical manoeuvre was about to be executed: Scheer had decided to station his pre-Dreadnoughts in the rear, and have the night march led by *Westfalen*; the leading pre-Dreadnought, *Schleswig-Holstein* (Captain Bartentrapp), had, indeed, been about to turn to go astern to her new station when a single, steady, bright white light was seen from her bridge, a light which moved south-westwards. In a minute, this was identified as the masthead light of the second or third ship in a line of cruisers—Rear-Admiral Heath's Second Cruiser Squadron—which was seen to be moving across the German van to take station astern of Beatty.[1]

Both Beatty's battle-cruisers, and *Minotaur's* armoured cruisers, were close enough to be brought under heavy fire by the German pre-Dreadnoughts, but neither these, nor the cruisers in the German scouting groups, opened fire, as it was thought undesirable to disclose the presence of the German van at this juncture.

It should be said that throughout the early part of the night numerous tactful signals passed between ships of the fleet, advising each other that lights were being exhibited unnecessarily. The problem of exposed lights may also have had something to do with the next clash between the enemy and our destroyers, our 4th flotilla this time: it seems that the enemy had followed them at a distance for some while. Examining the signals which passed during this time, it appears that this flotilla's blackout was perhaps not quite as complete as captains might have wished and this may have helped their unseen shadowers.[2]

(iii)

Von Koch's flotilla, and Boedicker's Second Scouting Group had returned to report to their Commander-in-Chief their failure to locate and attack the British battle fleet, adding, however, that they had sighted and attacked groups of destroyers. At the moment the latter piece of information was of little significance to Scheer. While his Fourth Scouting Group was engaging Goodenough's squadron, however, at about 10.15 p.m., the key to the problem was placed in his hands, and von Koch's and Boedicker's previously disdained information became of the utmost value.

[1] The following signal is of interest: 9.17 p.m. '*Duke of Edinburgh* to *Shannon*. Your masthead lamp is burning.' This was made by flashlamp.—*Official Despatches.*
[2] A few signals from the *Official Despatches* will suffice: Captain D4 to *Broke*: 'you have lights on fore-bridge and foc'sle' (10.01 p.m.); *Unity* to *Fortune*: 'Switch off stern light' (11.21 p.m.), etc.

At 10.10 p.m. the German directional monitoring and decoding wireless station at Neumünster signalled to Scheer in cipher, for his information: 'Destroyers have taken up position five sea miles astern of enemy's main fleet.' The Neumünster station had in fact intercepted and decoded Jellicoe's 9.15 p.m. wireless message[1] stationing his destroyer flotillas astern of the battle fleet for the night.

Von Koch's and Boedicker's information of their several recent contacts with British destroyers now gained new importance, for it afforded fair indication of the position of Jellicoe's battle fleet— and that was something Scheer particularly wished to avoid. To the German Admiral it now seemed that if he shaped a course direct for Horns Reef, this would lead him astern—unseen and unnoticed—of all British units.

At 10.34 p.m. he therefore ordered *Westfalen* to lead the fleet south-east by east, again adding that this course was to be maintained; he stressed it this time by the use of the word '*durchhalten*'— the course was to be maintained regardless of consequences. It was, Scheer knew, his one chance of reaching the Horns Reef and the Amrum Bank channel safely and by first daylight.

As his fleet turned to the course, his probing destroyers and light cruisers pushed on ahead in their own sectors. Once again it was the luck of von Koch's 7th flotilla to find and locate the British destroyers which could now give Scheer the key to the British fleet's position. After *Castor's* encounter with the enemy at 10.04 p.m., she, with her 11th flotilla had dropped back a little to the northward, with the result that our 4th flotilla was now the nearest to Scheer's advancing van.

As it happened, unfortunately, there was a wide gap between the British 4th flotilla and the next further eastward of it—the 13th flotilla, which also had part of the 9th and 10th with it. This 13th flotilla was about $4\frac{1}{2}$ miles away from the 4th and was also to the northward of it, for it was keeping station on the rear division of the

---

[1] 'Destroyers take station astern of battle fleet, five miles (2115).' This signal is 'logged' as being despatched from *Iron Duke* at 9.27 p.m. The German Official Historian denies the existence of this signal; other authorities suggest that it did not reach Scheer. This is entirely improbable: indeed, the British signal *was* certainly intercepted, decoded and sent to Scheer from Neumünster, and it was also received in his flagship, *Friedrich der Grosse*. Sir Julian Corbett, the British official naval historian says (*Naval Operations*, Volume III, p. 395, 1923 edition): that the signal was passed to Scheer and that he *knew* that the destroyers had been stationed astern of our battle fleet. In the later (1940) edition of that work, however, issued after Sir Julian's death, this statement is modified, presumably to agree with German denials, by the insertion of the following: 'But whether the message ever came to his hand cannot definitely be established.' As the signal certainly reached Scheer's flagship, it is impossible to believe that it was not read and considered by Scheer and his able staff, and the subsequent behaviour of Scheer and his fleet clearly indicates that he was aware of its purport.

First Battle Squadron. This division, with *Marlborough* no longer able to maintain the fleet's speed, was already about 3½ miles astern of station, and the Fifth Battle Squadron instead of being up with the rest of the battle fleet was keeping some two miles off *Marlborough's* starboard beam as a protection for her.

Three of von Koch's destroyers, pressing well south-eastward in advance of the German battle fleet, were sighted by *Unity* (Lieutenant-Commander Lecky) who was at the tail-end of our 4th flotilla. This was at 10.45 p.m., and *Unity* fired on them. The enemy had, however, by then seen what they wanted—destroyers in line; the leader fired a torpedo—which *Unity* avoided—and made off, to report to Scheer what he had discovered.[1] Ten minutes earlier, one of the light cruisers of the enemy's Second Scouting Group had come across to reconnoitre the position and, having seen the same destroyers, had also vanished into the darkness.[2] At the same time *Unity* was attacked, *Contest* also saw destroyers off her starboard quarter, steering eastward, and reported these by wireless. At 10.50 p.m., *Porpoise*—the last but one in the line—reported by wireless 'a German destroyer astern, steering east'. There was thus ample warning that the enemy were in the vicinity, and the destroyers made ready for all contingencies.

From eleven o'clock onwards, the German Second Scouting Group shadowed our flotilla continuously, passing slowly up its starboard side. At about 11.20 p.m., when the four distant cruisers had drawn approximately abreast of the foremost British destroyer, *Tipperary*, their leader swiftly made a challenge, almost simultaneously switching her searchlights on to *Tipperary* and the two or three destroyers next astern of her. The four cruisers then immediately opened a devastating fire on the leading destroyers at a range of barely 1,000 yards. The leading cruiser firing a starshell which lit up the whole of the leading division of the British flotilla.[3]

The enemy appears to have concentrated deliberately upon *Tipperary* and she was hit forward almost at once; her steam-pipes were severed, and her bridge destroyed, killing Captain (D4) and everyone else upon it. The ready-use cartridges along her upper deck were ignited, and a shell exploding in the bunker ignited the fuel. She was brought to an abrupt stop, the flames blazed up from

---

[1] *Official Despatches.*

[2] She had, however, been sighted by *Garland* (Lieutenant-Commander Goff) who reported this to Captain (D4) in *Tipperary*.

[3] The 4th flotilla, in line ahead, consisted of *Tipperary* (Captain D4), *Spitfire, Sparrowhawk, Garland, Contest; Broke* (half-flotilla leader), *Achates, Ambuscade, Ardent, Fortune, Porpoise,* and *Unity.*

her like a funeral pyre, illuminating everything around for a considerable distance. She had however fired both torpedoes before the worst happened, as had *Spitfire* also, astern of her: *Spitfire* had then hauled out of line to port, badly hit, but turned swiftly *westward* across the enemy's bows, to reload—only to find that her torpedo-lifting derrick had been destroyed by gunfire.

Astern of her again, *Broke* hauled out to port in order to fire her after-tube, and then turned south; the remainder of the flotilla followed astern of her, with the exception of the last ship—*Unity*—who lost touch with her flotilla-mates during the turn and headed eastward; she found the nearest flotilla—the 9th—and joined on to that.

Soon after *Broke* was hauling out of line, however, her Captain sighted a new enemy close off the starboard bow: a large two-funnelled ship, with cranes amidships, a description which could only fit a German battleship of the 'Helgoland' or 'Westfalen' class. This large stranger at once challenged with red and green lights, switched on her searchlights and also opened fire. Two other battleships astern of her, who had not previously been seen, also joined in the cannonade. Nevertheless, *Broke* fired another torpedo at the new-comers before turning quickly to port; but as she turned, a shell demolished her lower bridge, disabling and jamming her steering gear so that when he saw another British destroyer (*Sparrowhawk*) close under her port bow, Commander Allen of *Broke* could do nothing to avert collision, for his helm was jammed and his engine-room telegraph had been disabled.

Broke struck *Sparrowhawk* squarely on her starboard side abreast the bridge, plunging her bows deeply in before word could be passed to stop the engines.

Just after this collision, the enemy seemed to cease fire, for their searchlights suddenly went out, leaving only *Tipperary* blazing to illuminate the dark night. In the shifting shadows, *Contest*, coming up fast astern, sheered a few more feet off *Sparrowhawk's* stern for good measure, damaging her own bows in the process. Eventually *Broke* was backed astern and clear, but she and *Sparrowhawk* were in no condition to continue the fight: *Contest* moved on.

Although blinded by enemy searchlights and deluged with a hail of enemy shells, the flotilla had nevertheless managed to fire ten torpedoes before the lights suddenly went out in the enemy ships. What had happened was that the enemy light cruisers—alarmed at the shoal of torpedoes launched by the burning *Tipperary* and her division—had turned sharply away to evade them, only to find themselves so close to the leading ships of the German battle fleet that they could only get clear by passing between the ships in the line. *Frankfurt* and *Pillau* succeeded in getting clear through to the battleships' disengaged sides.

Elbing misjudged the space between the third and fourth battleships (*Rheinland* and *Posen*) through which she wished to pass, and as she turned to pass through, *Posen's* ram plunged deep into her starboard engine-room, promptly flooding the adjacent compartments. As *Elbing* fell clear of *Posen*, it was thought that she could not remain afloat for long.

The blame for this collision could not lie entirely on Captain Madlung of *Elbing*, for once again the leading ships of the battle squadron were recoiling automatically, ships turning together, to the westward away from the British attack. The ships were actually turning as *Elbing* tried to get across; they continued to turn after she had been rammed until they were six points off the course Scheer had ordered and were steering almost south-west by west.

Spitfire (Lieutenant-Commander Trelawney), finding she could not reload her tubes, decided to turn back and offer what help she could to the blazing *Tipperary*. Turning to starboard, her Captain suddenly saw two large 'cruisers', apparently leading a new line of ships, loom up ahead: they were *Westfalen* and *Nassau*, but he had not previously noticed their approach. Searchlights were immediately turned on to this lone destroyer, who unabashed equally promptly opened fire on *Nassau*, knocking out three of her searchlights with his first salvo. *Spitfire* was so near, it seemed, to the German ship that the latter intended to ram her; so Commander Trelawney put his helm hard over and went full speed ahead. The two ships crashed together, almost end on, port side to port side, the German monster dragging closely along the length of *Spitfire's* port side. As she did so, her 11-inch guns roared overhead, but could not be depressed enough to hit their little opponent, although their blast blew *Spitfire's* bridge, searchlight platform and foremast over the side and knocked down the foremost funnel until it rested between the two foremost ventilating cowls 'like the hinging funnel of a penny river steamer'.[1]

When finally Spitfire drew clear, she carried embedded in her fore-part some sixty feet of the battleship *Nassau's* plating, torn out of the German ship's foc'sle—a substantial memento of a remarkable encounter.

It was now 11.40 p.m., barely twenty minutes since the fighting

[1] *Fighting at Jutland.*

had begun. *Garland* had turned back to aid the blazing *Tipperary*—only to be chased off by the enemy but not before she had fired a torpedo at them; *Broke*, *Sparrowhawk* and *Contest* had been locked together but had now drawn clear of each other, the remainder of the flotilla had formed astern of *Achates* (Commander Hutchinson)—*Ambuscade*, *Garland*, *Ardent*, *Fortune* and *Porpoise*—and these six held on southward to pick up their station once more.

The encounter had unquestionably left its mark upon the German battle line: it had imposed a turn of eight points altogether, for the German van had swung back to south-south-west, away from their goal and the road home. Scheer, furious at this diversion which was contrary to his instructions, immediately ordered Captain Redlich of *Westfalen* to get back to his course and again maintain it, regardless of consequence. Redlich hauled round at 11.27 p.m. to south, and at 11.34 to south-east by south, passing close to the mortally wounded *Rostock* as she limped away to the south-westward having been torpedoed either by *Achates* or *Ambuscade*. The encounter had cost the German force two of its light cruisers, for neither *Elbing* nor *Rostock* were to see port again; it had also badly rattled the captains of both *Frankfurt* and *Pillau*, for emerging from the temporary shelter of the disengaged side of the battle line as soon as the destroyers had departed, they hastened at high speed to the east-south-eastward only to find themselves at 11.45 p.m. in the midst of more British destroyers. In their headlong eastward rush, they had run foul of the rear of our 12th flotilla, from which the two cruisers modestly and politely withdrew without firing a single shot, nor standing upon the the order of their going. Their only achievement was to separate *Menace* from *Nonsuch*, and to cause *Nonsuch* to lose her flotilla in the darkness so that she moved off north-eastward in search of them.

Looked at from the other point of view, the brief encounter had cost us *Tipperary*, and *Spitfire*, *Sparrowhawk* and *Broke*: the former irretrievably lost and the other three no longer fighting units. It had also had a much bigger repercussion, not seen at the time: so furious had the enemy gunfire been, including that from their turret guns, that there had been a lot of 'overs' and ricochets, which landed far to the eastward—amongst the destroyers of the 13th, 9th and 10th flotillas. Because of this, *Champion* (Captain Farie) had led his 13th flotilla eastward—without signal—and forced the 9th and 10th flotillas to turn south-east and east as she did so; these in turn had made the 12th flotilla conform. *Champion's* move had therefore removed for the time being the further protection to the eastward of 'the Fighting Fourth Flotilla'. By midnight, *Champion*, with *Obdurate* and *Moresby* in company, was eleven miles north-east of the nearest battleship division (*Marlborough's*), and nine or ten miles north-east of her proper station; the rest of the 13th flotilla were steering south-east on *Marlborough's* port quarter, and the 12th flotilla was twelve miles out of position to the north-eastward. There was therefore little barrier left to the enemy's advance. *Champion's* explanation of this afterwards was:

> About 11.30 p.m. heavy firing was opened on our starboard beam, apparently at some of our destroyers between the 13th flotilla and the enemy. I hauled out to the eastward as I was unable to attack with any of our own flotilla, our own forces being between me and the enemy.[1]

Destroyers of the 13th flotilla, with the exception of *Obdurate* and *Moresby*, lost touch with *Champion* during the night. This was not surprising, for *Champion* had gone on to 25 knots as she headed east without signal.

Thus, despite Jellicoe's prevision the way was now open for a German advance to safety.

The gallant 4th flotilla had not yet finished with the enemy, however: *Achates*, having got six intact units of the flotilla astern of her, now headed southward; at about 12.09 a.m. she sighted what seemed to be a line of ships close on her starboard side. This was again the van of the German battle fleet, which Scheer had ordered back to its south-east-by-east course; it had curved gradually round, to become the target of the 4th flotilla again. *Achates* had no qualms about firing torpedoes: the encounter followed the usual pattern. The enemy challenged with coloured lights, and immediately their leading ships switched searchlights on to the two or three foremost British destroyers and simultaneously opened a devastating, rapid fire upon them. *Fortune* was hit almost at once; she was set on fire, and was obviously sinking. *Porpoise*, astern of her, was hit in the boiler-room, but under cover of the escaping steam and the smoke from burning *Fortune*, managed to haul out and escape to the northward. *Garland* and *Ambuscade* held their ground, fired one torpedo apiece and then, in a hailstorm of shell, sped away eastward; *Achates* followed them. *Ardent* had not been able to fire, but, driven off eastward with the rest, turned back to a southerly course as soon as the searchlights were switched off, hoping to rejoin what was left of the flotilla. The course she selected was unfortunately one which converged once more upon her powerful antagonists.

[1] *Official Despatches.*

Just before midnight, *Ardent* had sighted smoke ahead: it was not the enemy apparently, but a large warship steaming boldly along by herself. Although Lieutenant-Commander Marsden did not know at the time, she must have been the British armoured cruiser *Black Prince* (Captain Bonham), a survivor of Rear-Admiral Arbuthnot's squadron. She had not been seen since the fleet deployed at 6.15 p.m. and what had happened to her in the meantime will never be known; perhaps she had received some damage which had affected her speed. She took some part in Arbuthnot's rush, but 'appeared to come through with little damage'.[1] It is thought that at reduced speed she had tried to rejoin her fleet after deployment; at 8.46 p.m. she had signalled by wireless to the Commander-in-Chief, reporting the existence of a submarine. It would seem that just before midnight, still faithfully following in the Grand Fleet's wake, she was possibly the vessel reported by *Marlborough* as 'the armoured cruiser of the "Warrior" class that has been on our starboard quarter during the first watch'.[2] Just after midnight, she apparently sighted dim ship-shapes to starboard, and thinking no doubt that at last she had come up with her own fleet, she challenged them with the secret challenge for the day, to be greeted instantly with searchlights and a fury of gunfire from *Thüringen*, *Nassau*, *Ostfriesland* and the *Friedrich der Grosse*. *Black Prince's* helm was immediately put hard over, and she sheered sharply away to the north-eastward; but she was already blazing from stem to stern; a furnace raged inside her hull. She held her way through the water for a while, and her flaming course took her near the battered *Spitfire* as the latter began to limp north-westwards, gradually working up to *six* knots. *Spitfire's* crew had collected aft when they saw the fiery apparition loom up out of the black night, missing their stern by feet, it seemed. Her two centre funnels were gone, her voiceless guns were trained out over the starboard beam; she swept past the group of silent watchers gathered on *Spitfire's* after deck with a roar.

The very crackling of her fires could be heard and felt. She was a mass of flames from foremast to mainmast, on deck and between decks. Flames were issuing out of her from every corner. Soon afterwards there came an explosion from the direction in which she had gone.[3]

They had been watching her progress in the German ships too, and they saw the end come at 12.10 a.m. 'For a moment she was

[1] *Valiant's* report, *Official Despatches*.
[2] i.e. from 8 p.m. to midnight. *Official Despatches*.
[3] *Fighting at Jutland*.

outlined in fire; then she vanished totally in an appalling blaze of explosion, like an erupting volcano.'[1]

Ardent was alone now, and her captain was conscious that the duty of holding the western barrier lay upon his little ship entirely. As he held on southward in the course of the fleet, he too saw dim shapes on the starboard side, and the wretched story was repeated again: green and red recognition lights flickering, a dazzle of searchlights, a deluge of well-aimed shells. *Ardent* fired her torpedo, however, and that was the end. Within a minute she had been brought to a dead stop; in another minute, she had been reduced to little more than a heap of scrap-iron. On her foredeck, a petty-officer was heard to urge: 'Give her one more, boys!' to a gun's crew; but they could not— they were lying dead on the deck. The firing ceased, and the searchlights were abruptly switched off; *Ardent* was left to sink in the darkness.

That was the end of the saga of the 4th flotilla—or almost the end. As an organised fighting force it had ceased to exist: *Tipperary* was to sink at about 1.45 a.m.; *Fortune* and *Ardent* had been sunk; *Porpoise*, *Broke*, *Spitfire* and *Contest* were disabled, but able to limp home. *Sparrowhawk* was a hulk, to be sunk after daylight. Between them they had fired thirteen torpedoes: they had torpedoed and disabled *Rostock* and the enemy had to sink her at 3.45 a.m. with explosive scuttling-charges; they had been the cause of *Elbing's* turn-away on to *Posen's* ram, and *Elbing* was also to be sunk by her crew at 2 a.m. The vigour of their attack had forced the enemy van to turn away six points, and then another two; they had thus delayed the High Seas Fleet's escape to safety for a full half hour, and had been responsible for continued confusion, up and down the German line. As Commander von Hase later said:

> We had frequently to stop because the whole line ahead of us was thrown into disorder as a result of the numerous destroyer attacks. In this way, the *Nassau*—originally the second ship of the line—gradually fell into the last place.[2]

What mortal men could do to bar the Germans' road to safety the officers and men of the 4th Flotilla had done: no one could have asked more of them. In the stabbing glare of sudden searchlights, and in the tornado of shell which followed these lights, they had established their own tradition.

Having reduced *Ardent* to a sinking mass of twisted metal and despatched *Black Prince* also to the Haven of Lost Ships the head of the

---

[1] Von Lützow, *Skagerrak*. In *Black Prince* all hands were lost: 37 officers and 825 men.
[2] Von Hase, *Kiel and Jutland*.

German line swung back, at fourteen minutes after midnight, to the east-south-eastward; six minutes later, on Scheer's direct order, it set course south-east-by-south for Horns Reef once more.

Spirits began to rise in the German battleships although there was still a feeling of acute tension—they had, it seemed, a long way to go before they could reach safety. Scheer, however, seems to have felt that the worst dangers had been surmounted: he could estimate that his van was now across the rear of the British battle fleet which must be nine or ten miles to the southward of him[1] and also that—on the basis of the intercepted message stationing the destroyers five miles astern of this battle fleet—he must now be several miles to the northward of these flotillas too and should thus be able to continue his journey to Horns Reef unmolested.

Scheer had, of course, no means of knowing the reaction which *Champion's* precipitate turn to the eastward without signal at 11.35 p.m. had had on the eastern flotillas of the British destroyer screen; indeed, but for the odd repercussions of this sudden turn, he would have been free of further interference. As it happened Commander Goldsmith in *Lydiard* was leading two units of the 9th and 10th (Harwich) flotillas in line ahead when *Champion* made her abrupt turn across his bows: the 9th, 10th, 12th, and 13th flotillas—stationed more or less astern of the port wing column of the battle fleet—formed the eastern bloc of the destroyer barrier. Goldsmith's units[2] were forced by *Champion's* sudden turn to follow *Lydiard* round to the south-eastward to avoid collision, and increasing to 20 knots Goldsmith held on in that direction for almost half an hour. During the early part of this course there had been a number of 'overs' dropping in and around the rear of his line and he had also seen the enemy's ships—unidentifiable at the distance of three miles and more—as they had been occasionally silhouetted against searchlight beams. In Commander Goldsmith's mind, as he steered south-eastward, an idea was taking shape—to cut across ahead of this enemy, whatever it was, and get round to the other side of his line and attack from there. It was an admirable plan, typical for a destroyer commander brought up, as it were, on the offensive doctrines with which Rear-Admiral Tyrwhitt had imbued his Harwich Force. He saw the

---

[1] He received some confirmation as to the battle fleet's position about this time in a report from *Seydlitz* of sighting 4 battleships at 12.05 a.m., and *Seydlitz*, he could assume, was well on her way southwards by that time.

[2] These were the older slower Harwich destroyers: they carried less fuel than the modern destroyers. *Moorsom* of the 10th flotilla had originally been with them but had been hit aft during the afternoon's battle-cruiser action; having lost a lot of oil fuel in consequence she was ordered back to Rosyth by Commander Goldsmith at 9.57, where she arrived next day very short of fuel.

searchlights go out to the westward and the sudden cessation of the firing which, unknown to him, had marked the end of *Ardent* and *Black Prince*; then, at 12.11 p.m., Goldsmith led his line round on to a south-west course which he hoped would cut ahead of the enemy line. Quite unknown to Goldsmith in the darkness the line of destroyers astern of him was now appreciably longer than he could have anticipated. 'I discovered [next morning] what the haze had hitherto hidden from me—that I had a long line of stragglers astern of my division.'[1] Some five minutes before he turned to the south-eastward his division had been joined by *Unity* who had earlier lost contact with her own 4th flotilla and now tailed in astern of the 9th and 10th. She had barely taken her place, when the eastward swing of *Champion* and her 13th flotilla brought the rear destroyers of that flotilla so close that in the darkness they missed *Champion's* lead and followed *Nerissa* into station astern of *Unity* at the tail end of Goldsmith's division. As Goldsmith increased the speed of his following to 30 knots, therefore, he had thirteen destroyers in all under his command; a formidable force.[2]

Commander Goldsmith had rightly assumed that the course and speed of his force would take it across the path of the enemy line: he could not know, however, that Scheer had ordered his van battleships to steer south-east-by-south at 12.20 a.m. and his fleet was now converging swiftly upon the advancing line of destroyers and almost at right angles to it. As *Lydiard* sped on south-westward Commander Goldsmith saw nothing in the hazy blackness around him to indicate that the leading German battleship *Westfalen* was only a few cables' lengths to starboard and *Lydiard* and the next eight destroyers astern of her were across the German van in darkness and safety, entirely unaware of the enemy's immediate proximity. The next two in line were also across in safety when they noticed bow waves and large ship-shapes looming up over their starboard quarter. *Petard*, the last but one in the line, then suddenly saw barely 600 yards distant before her starboard beam a large ship loom up out of the darkness and, judging by the gleam of the bow wave, heading at speed directly at her. Instantly *Petard's* helm went over and she turned sharply to port, then swinging round in a wide arc to starboard to pass ahead of the strangers. As her helm went over, how-

---

[1] *Official Despatches.*

[2] These were, in their order in the line, *Lydiard* (Comdr. Goldsmith), *Liberty, Landrail, Laurel* (all of the 9th flotilla), *Morris* (10th), *Unity* (4th), *Nerissa* (13th), *Termagent* (10th), *Nicator, Pelican, Petard* (all of 13th) and *Turbulent* (10th). *Termagent* and *Turbulent*, although actually belonging to the Harwich 10th flotilla, had been attached temporarily to the 13th which accounts for their joining the tail of the line in *Nerissa's* wake.

ever, the Germans saw her, showed their coloured recognition lights and at the same moment switched on their searchlights. For a moment the beams touched *Pelican's* stern as she hurried away south-westward; then they swung back on to *Petard*. Fire was immediately opened upon her at less than point-blank range, but she was turning very fast across the German ship's bows and she escaped with only 6 hits—3 of them, however, causing considerable damage and casualties. It was *Petard's* tragedy that at this moment when at point-blank torpedo range of the enemy she should have no torpedoes left to fire—they had all been used up, to very good purpose, during the afternoon's battle-cruiser engagement. It was a great pity for, as Lieutenant-Commander Thomson said afterwards, the enemy were 'sitting ducks'. In his post-battle report he expressed this more formally: 'if only *Petard* had had some torpedoes left I am certain a successful attack could easily have been made'. Lieutenant-Commander Thomson, therefore, hauled well out round the enemy battleships bows before resuming his station at the tail of Goldsmith's line. *Petard* had been hit in her No. 2 stokehold, an oil fuel lead had been severed and the escaping oil, ignited by the explosion, had brilliantly lit up the ship for a minute until her engineers had cut off the supply. During this brief illumination the enemy's first salvo had hit the destroyer aft wiping out the entire crew of her after 4-inch gun, wrecking the after-cabins, and killing the ship's young surgeon. The latter was an especial tragedy as it was in these brief moments that *Petard* suffered her casualties—an officer and five men wounded and two officers and seven men killed.[1]

As *Petard* swung clear across the path of the advancing German line their searchlights left her and trained on to *Turbulent*, the last in the destroyer line. Whereas *Petard* had *just* managed to swing clear, for *Turbulent* this was impossible and as the searchlights picked her up in their beams she came under the concentrated fire at point-blank range of the four leading German battleships. Salvo after salvo burst in and upon her; her bridge was destroyed, her decks were torn to shreds, her boilers blown in. Blazing from stem to stern, and with no living hand now at her helm to guide her, she swung in to starboard towards *Westfalen*—to be caught on the battleship's massive ram and tossed aside like driftwood. 'A ripple of fire seemed to run the whole length of her' then she just disappeared as if lifted clean out of the water[2]: the enemy searchlights went out as suddenly

---

[1] *Nicator*, ahead of her in the line, took her own surgeon across to give expert care to the wounded at daylight.
[2] *Fighting at Jutland* (*Nicator's* narrative).

as they had been switched on and the enemy ships swept on their way in the blackness. *Turbulent* took with her to the bottom her captain, Lieutenant-Commander Stuart, four other officers and 85 men.

Commander Goldsmith in *Lydiard* had, meanwhile, continued his south-westerly course quite unaware of the grim tragedy that had been enacted at the tail of his line a mile and a quarter astern of him —indeed, he did not even know the tail was there. There were, however, those who *could* have enlightened him: *Pelican* must for an instant have known the tension which came when the groping enemy searchlight beam touched her stern—and then moved on; *Nicator* saw 'three or four big ships[1], obviously Germans, silhouetted for a moment' against the beams of the searchlights they had trained on to *Petard*; *Petard* was in no doubt as to the true character of the enemy and had recognised them at once as German battleships; 'looking at her [the leading enemy ship] closely there could be no doubt at all what she was, as at the angle we sighted her at, we could clearly see large crane-derricks, and only German ships have these fittings. At the same moment the German battleships switched on recognition lights'.[2] There was thus no doubt at the rear of the destroyer line that they had encountered 'big ships', obviously German and that these were 'battleships'; *Petard*, moreover, had recognised the leader, by the crane amidships, as one of the 'Westfalen' class steering south-east. Here was indeed vital information to pass forward to Commander Goldsmith and, on power-wireless, to the Commander-in-Chief: Commander Goldsmith, one may be sure, would have ensured that this information, if passed to him, went on at once to *Iron Duke*. Yet despite the obvious importance of her discovery, *Petard* did nothing about it: one of *Nicator's* officers somewhat naïvely commented afterwards[3] 'it somehow did not strike us that this was the German Fleet breaking through the line, unluckily at the weakest point': it is pertinent here, perhaps, to wonder what else he thought it could be.

The road ahead of Scheer was now clear; there were no more flotillas to bar his path for *Champion's* swerve to the eastward had forced the 12th and 13th flotillas miles to the northward of their

---

[1] *Fighting at Jutland* (*Nicator's* narrative).
[2] *Fighting at Jutland* (*Petard's* narrative).
[3] Commander Goldsmith's destroyers eventually closed *Castor* (Commodore F) and at 5.36 the destroyers of the 9th and 10th flotillas were sent off to Rosyth to re-fuel; the destroyers of the 13th flotilla were sent to join up with the battle-cruisers, *Unity* remained with *Castor*.

appointed station. The massed destroyer barrier had failed in its purpose: it had been overwhelmed by the superior night-fighting equipment and technique of their enemies.

Throughout all the intermittent firing which had been taking place well in its rear the British battle fleet had held steadily to its south course at 17 knots; nothing had been brought to the notice of the Commander-in-Chief that could have given him any reason to alter this night course. When he had altered the course of the fleet to south for the night at 9.01 p.m. he had done so on the basis of his own estimate, formed from reasonable evidence, that the German Fleet was then some 8 or 9 miles to the north-westward of him and that by turning south he was remaining between the enemy and their bases. Towards 10 o'clock he was able to confirm this original opinion for a belated signal arrived from *Lion* reporting the enemy as bearing north-by-west and steering west-south-west at 9.00 p.m. Beatty had also given his position but this Jellicoe discarded when he found that it almost coincided with that of the *King George V*. Previously, he had *assumed* a position for *Lion* but this time Jellicoe considered that he had a much more accurate basis for at 9.05 Vice-Admiral Jerram in *King George V* had signalled to him 'our battle-cruisers in sight bearing west-north-west and steering south-west'. As at the time that *Lion* was thus reputedly in sight from *King George V* the latter was also in sight from *Iron Duke* Jellicoe believed that at last he had a relative position upon which to work a position free of all geographical errors of reckoning.

The Commander-in-Chief had no means of knowing that Jerram's wireless signal was but part of his battle with Captain Crooke of *Caroline* who had insisted that these ships were hostile. When *Caroline* and *Royalist* had then launched their torpedo attack on these ships they had been 'welcomed' by heavy gunfire—yet Jerram did nothing afterwards to correct this mischievous wireless signal to Jellicoe. The ships that Jerram had seen were *not* 'our battle-cruisers' but, as Crooke had told him, were German battleships—and in his heart Jerram must have known it.

Jellicoe was, however, unaware of this and blending *Lion's* enemy report—crediting the enemy as being north-by-west distant ten miles as they had been at 8.40 p.m.—with *King George V's* position for *Lion*—west-north-west distant about six miles—it was possible to get what Jellicoe considered a firm position for the enemy battle cruisers or at least the van of the enemy battle fleet: this now appeared to have been about fifteen miles north-west of *Iron Duke* at nine o'clock. This 'reckoning' put the enemy rather further northward and westward than his previous estimate, but this was so much to the good—and, moreover, they were reported to be steering further to the westward still. If anything this tended to confirm Jellicoe's views as to the correctness of his night course and his dispositions.

Around eleven o'clock (by the time it had been deciphered in *Iron Duke*) the Commander-in-Chief received a wireless message from the Admiralty giving the position of the rear ship of the German line at 9.00 p.m. and reporting its course as 'southerly'. This message was obviously the result of a directional bearing combined with an intercepted signal and when plotted it placed the rear of Scheer's fleet about 10 miles ahead and south-west of *Iron Duke* at 9.00 p.m. As Jellicoe was quite certain that at that time the enemy was to the north-westward of him he discarded this Admiralty signal in favour of the position based on the visual observation of *Lion*. In point of fact the Admiralty's message was based on a signal intercepted from *Regensburg*, at the tail of the German line—and *Regensburg's* own position was some 13 miles in error at the time.

At about 11.30 p.m. (again after deciphering) Jellicoe received another signal from the Admiralty; this had been despatched at 10.41 p.m. and read:

> German Battle Fleet ordered home at 9.14 p.m. Battle cruisers in rear. Course SSE¾E. Speed 16 knots.

This message, which seemed to convey so much information, in effect did very little beyond stating that the German Fleet was homeward bound. Before any use could be made of the course given, moreover, Jellicoe would want to know when the enemy fleet began to steer it and when they changed to another: without such information the course as signalled gave little clue as to which swept channel the enemy proposed to use.

To help Jellicoe clear up the situation a signal came in at 11.30 p.m. from Captain Duff of the light cruiser *Birmingham*—who, it will be recalled, had turned eastward with the Second Light-Cruiser Squadron after their sharp action with enemy cruisers at about 10.30 p.m. *Birmingham* had turned to port when she had sighted the Fifth Battle Squadron and had, thereafter, lost touch with her squadron. Her signal was of considerable interest:

> Urgent. Priority. Battle-cruisers unknown number probably hostile in sight north-east. Course south.

She added her position at 11.30 p.m. but this could not be reconciled with that of the Second Light-Cruiser Squadron and seemed to be too far to the north; Jellicoe did not pay much attention to this position. Actually *Birmingham* had sighted *Seydlitz* and *Moltke*, but to the north-westward, though their course at the time *had* been south to conform with the German van as it recoiled from the fury of the 4th flotilla's attack. The course factor was important for it suggested that the enemy was not steering east-south-east as the Admiralty signal had indicated. Of the two signals, that of *Birmingham* was a visual sighting report, whereas the Admiralty's was based on direction-finding; Jellicoe preferred to rely on the former, which suggested that the enemy was following *behind* his battle fleet which was thus still between the Germans and their bases.

Eight minutes after *Birmingham's* signal Jellicoe received a signal from Commodore Goodenough of *Southampton* via *Nottingham* (the Commodore's wireless had been put out of action):

> Have engaged enemy cruisers 10.15 p.m. bearing west-south-west.

Southampton's reports throughout the day had almost invariably been reliable and Jellicoe accepted this one as confirmation that the enemy was indeed making a more westerly approach to his home bases and the British fleet was still well between him and home.

It must be realised at this stage that these were entirely justifiable inferences based on the best information available and that beyond this there was no positive indication either as to the enemy's position or his intention as to destination. Nor could Jellicoe draw any conclusions from the various engagements which had taken place astern of the battle fleet since 10.00 p.m.; these had been seen by almost every ship in the fleet and their impact had been consistent. For instance, *Bellerophon* (Captain E. F. Bruen) noted 'during the first watch there was quite a lot of firing going on to the north-east . . . there was further firing astern and for the first hour or so of the middle watch [midnight till 4 a.m.] there was intermittent firing on the port quarter. Otherwise the night passed without incident.' *Lion* (Captain Chatfield) commented 'no exciting incident occurred with the exception of many indications that other portions of the fleet were not having such a peaceful time as we were'. That ship after ship noticed that the firing which commenced around 10.00 p.m. over the starboard quarter of the fleet, by midnight was taking place astern and after that was on the port quarter, made little difference: it suggested that a series of destroyer attacks had been aimed at the rear of the battle fleet and had been beaten off by our own destroyers. The Admiralty had signalled at 9.55 p.m. to warn Jellicoe to expect just this during the night. Jellicoe himself attributed the intermittent actions to destroyer engagements, his flag captain has recorded that he considered they were attempts of enemy destroyers and cruisers to break through the screen of our own destroyers to attack the battle fleet from the rear. There was nothing to suggest anything else, for the flash of a 4-inch or a 4.1-inch gun is the same whether mounted in a destroyer or a light cruiser, and a 6-inch or a 5.9-inch gun has the same flash and sound whether mounted on a cruiser or in a battleship's secondary battery.

Unfortunately, not one solitary report reached the Commander-in-Chief to cause him to change his opinion that these engagements were anything other than destroyer actions; not the slightest hint reached him that German battleships were involved—and by 12.40 a.m. on June 1st they had broken through. As the minutes ticked steadily by after that Jellicoe's chances of stopping the enemy as he had planned to do before they could reach their home bases were slipping away; by 1.30 a.m. they were, to all intents and purposes, gone beyond recall.

The responsibility for this should be laid squarely where it belongs; the truth has been buried far too long. In the first place the Admiralty must accept the full responsibility for the consequences of not passing on to its Commander-in-Chief *all* the material information at its disposal; they began early in the night to *edit* their Intelligence reports for Jellicoe's consumption. The 10.41 Admiralty message informing him that the German Fleet had been ordered home was, in point of fact, a hash-up of *three* signals made by Scheer, intercepted by our monitoring service and decoded in Room 40 at the Admiralty. At 9.14 Scheer had issued his general sailing orders to his fleet; at 9.29 p.m. he had signalled its formation—line ahead in the order of 1st, 3rd, and 2nd battle squadrons, with the battle cruisers in the rear; at 9.46 he had made a slight adjustment to the general course to be steered at 16 knots. All this had been run together as the 10.41 signal.

The Admiralty had also decoded at 10.10 p.m. another signal which Scheer had made at 9.06 asking the shore base to provide Zeppelin reconnaissance for him *at Horns Reef at daylight on 1st June.* This was a positive indication in so many words of Scheer's definite intention to proceed home via the Horns Reef—yet this vital signal was held back at the Admiralty and was not sent to Jellicoe at all. Its arrival in *Iron Duke* would have resolved all Jellicoe's doubts and difficulties: that it should have been withheld was almost criminally negligent.

Unfortunately, this was not the full extent of the Admiralty's failure: between 11.15 p.m. on 31st May and 1.30 a.m. on 1st June, no less than seven other important German signals were intercepted, decoded by the staff of Room 40 and passed by them to the Admiralty's Operations Division. There they were placed on file: the series of signals was passed on neither entire nor edited to Admiral Jellicoe.

It is necessary to realise just how important these seven intercepted messages were: the first was a general course signal made by Admiral Scheer to his fleet at 10.32 p.m., duly deciphered in the Admiralty by 11.15 p.m.: 'Main fleet course south-east-by-south'. The second signal was of much greater importance, however: it was from Commodore Michelsen, the German Chief of Flotillas, and was addressed to all destroyer flotillas: 'Be assembled with our own main body at 4 a.m. [2 a.m. GMT[1]] at Horns Reef, or shape course round Skaw [of Denmark]'. This signal, also deciphered in Room 40 by 11.15 p.m., revealed in unequivocal terms the fact that Scheer's High Seas Fleet and its destroyers were to rendezvous off Horns Reef at 2 a.m. on the morrow, 1st June.[2] Had it been sent at once to Jellicoe, it is very certain that there would also have been an uninvited 'guest' at the meeting-place: the British Grand Fleet.

In the third signal, Scheer had given at 11.06 p.m. a reference position and course to the several units of his fleet: 'C.-in-C. to High Seas Fleet: main body at 1.00 a.m. [11 p.m. GMT on 31st May] is in latitude 56°15′ North, Longitude 5°42′ East. Course SE$\frac{3}{4}$S'. This had been deciphered in the Admiralty and 'passed to Operations' by 11.50 p.m. The next two signals intercepted, and deciphered by midnight and 12.05 a.m. on 1st June respectively, were the two course-alterations which an angry Scheer had ordered his fleet to follow when he noticed them recoiling from the attacks of our 4th flotilla at 11.30 p.m.: 'Resume course SE by S' and 'The course ordered is SE$\frac{3}{4}$S'. Early on 1st June, at forty-three minutes past midnight, Scheer had signalled his fleet's position to the stricken *Lützow*; within forty minutes, this signal had been intercepted and decoded: 'Our main body's position at 2.30 a.m. [00.30 GMT] Latitude 55°57′ North, Longitude 6°15′ East.'[3] Twenty minutes

---

[1] German time was two hours in advance of Greenwich Mean Time.

[2] In decoding this message, the staff of Room 40 omitted the phrase 'with our own main body' in the draft passed to the Operations Division; but the all-important location, 'off Horns Reef', was in the text of this draft.

[3] During the First World War, the German Navy used a confidential chart upon which a grid of small numbered squares was superimposed, to express geographical positions in signals: the squares were irregular in size, but usually 5–7 miles a side. To define a position within such a square, a further code consisting of Greek letters was used; positions were expressed by the square-number, followed by the Greek letter. The positions quoted in these signals have been converted accordingly.

later, at 1.03 a.m., Scheer made the last signal, to Rear-Admiral Boedicker, in command of what remained of the Second Scouting Group: 'Head of our own main fleet at 3 a.m. [1 a.m. GMT] in Latitude 55°50' North, Longitude 6°25' East.' This signal was deciphered by 1.25 a.m.

Had this series of signals been passed on at once to *Iron Duke*, and been plotted as they arrived on Jellicoe's chart, it would have revealed to him beyond doubt that Scheer was heading direct for the seaward end of the Amrum Bank swept channel via Horns Reef; they would have provided positive information of his progress towards his goal. By 1.00 a.m. on 1st June, Jellicoe could have called upon Beatty and his battle-cruisers to follow him and, ordering his destroyers to join him, turned eastward with his battle fleet at 20 knots; he could have been ready and waiting, in line of battle, between the entrance to the swept channel and Scheer's rendezvous off Horns Reef. It would by then have been light enough for the British gunlayers to have seen Scheer's battered and somewhat dis-organised fleet; there would have been seventeen long hours of day-light in which to finish the business in hand. Once more the date would have been a great naval occasion—another 'glorious First of June'.

It was not to be: none of these vital signals was passed on to the Commander-in-Chief. He was left to manage as best he could with what information he could derive from other sources; and much of this, as will be seen, was to be denied to him. For this fateful neglect, the Admiralty's Operations Division was absolutely res-ponsible. The civilian decoders had played their part magnificently, as had our wireless monitoring service. The onus for the blunder lay with Rear-Admiral Jackson and his naval operations staff.

Various seemingly plausible explanations have been advanced to account for the failure: it has been suggested that the chief of staff had left the Admiralty's Operations Room to snatch some much-needed sleep; that in his absence no other officer could be allowed access to Room 40 and its secrets; and that while he was away the Operations Division was left in the charge of an officer with no experience of German operations signals. It has been suggested that this officer recognised the significance neither of the series of signals as such nor of the signal asking for aerial reconnaissance in particular. Another explanation[1] advanced was that the Admiralty had 'lost' its fleet in the darkness and 'did not know where to find it';

[1] Cf. D. T. Moore and M. Waller, *Cloak and Dagger*.

but the Operations Division knew well enough where to find the fleet at 11.48 a.m. when they wished to tell Jellicoe that enemy submarines were putting to sea, and to give him the position of the *Lützow*, which was then sinking; it knew how to find him at 3.12 a.m., to give him the position of the stricken light cruiser *Elbing*. These tit-bits of information were of complete insignificance in comparison with the series of High Seas Fleet movement-signals the Admiralty had failed to pass on. The reason most probably underlying this monumental Admiralty failure can be sought in the attitude of the then Director of Operations, Rear-Admiral Jackson, towards his civilian colleagues; but whatever the cause, the Admiralty was at great pains afterwards to cover up this sorry episode and conceal their responsibility for the outcome of the battle: Sir Julian Corbett, the official naval historian, was not allowed to refer to the existence of these intercepted signals; nor was any mention made of them in the Admiralty's own *Narrative* of the battle (1920), nor in their draft of the Harper Record (1919). The needs of 'security' were invoked to justify these omissions.[1]

(iv)

Admiral Jellicoe's most pressing problem during the early hours of the night was to forecast Scheer's movements and intentions: had the Admiralty passed on to him, unedited, all the information at their disposal, this would of course have provided the immediate solution; but they had not. Almost the same answer could have been obtained had the British Commander-in-Chief been able correctly to divine the portent of the intermittent gunfire astern of his battle fleet and the travel of the outbursts of gun-flashes from the north-westward through north to the north-eastward. Had he been able to do this, he would have gained much the same picture as from the series of signals withheld from him: that of the German fleet moving steadily across his rear and in the direction of Horns Reef.

The sequence of 'fires in the night' between 10 o'clock on 31st May and 1 a.m. on the morning of 1st June could be considered in three distinct phases: there were the probings of Scheer's destroyers as they sought for the whereabouts of our battle fleet; these mostly affected the 11th and 4th flotillas, and when the enemy destroyers were sighted they were reported to the flotilla-leader. In some cases

[1] It was not until the revised edition of Corbett's *Naval Operations* Volume III appeared at the end of 1939 that the signals' existence was admitted in an Appendix. By that time, however, the British people had worries more immediate than 23-year-old Governmental peccadilloes.

these reports were passed on to the Commander-in-Chief.[1] The second phase opened with the light cruisers of Boedicker's Second Scouting Group attacking *Castor* and her 11th flotilla: *Castor* reported this engagement to the Commander-in-Chief at 10.50 p.m., which was as soon as she could, for the signal had to be passed through *Kempenfelt* since the other's wireless had been put out of action. *Castor* reported: 'Have been engaged by enemy cruisers'.[2] From Jellicoe's viewpoint there was nothing untoward in such cruiser intervention either on this occasion or later, in the action which *Southampton* reported (via *Nottingham*) at 10.40 p.m. as having taken place between the Second Light-Cruiser Squadron and the German Fourth Scouting Group (Commodore von Reuter) twenty-five minutes earlier: 'Have engaged enemy cruisers bearing wsw'. Light cruisers could be expected to be operating in support of destroyers, and at night this did not necessarily mean that they would have heavier support near at hand.

Up to about 11.15 p.m., the various engagements astern had been consistently reported to Jellicoe; there was nothing about them that was incompatible with the Admiralty's 9.55 p.m. warning to him to expect such attacks during the night.

With the 11.20 p.m. attack on *Tipperary* and the 4th flotilla, however, the character of these distant engagements began to change: although the engagement had opened with Boedicker's three remaining light cruisers suddenly deluging *Tipperary* with their gunfire, some of the destroyers in rear of her seemed to think they were being fired on by friends—until a wandering enemy searchlight-beam suddenly lit up for a moment the rear of the enemy's line, and showed what was unmistakeably a battleship—a battleship of the 'Helgoland' class. In that instant those destroyers realised that they were in the presence of the German battle fleet. *Tipperary* was blazing from stem to stern and lighting up the whole scene, and it must have been clear to *Broke's* captain, Commander Allen, that the command of the flotilla had now devolved upon him; yet in the few minutes that remained before his own ship was heavily hit, Allen did not report what he had seen; nor did any other destroyer.

As the flotilla continued to press its attack, other destroyers realised that they had found the van of the enemy battle fleet—

---

[1] For instance, at 11.00 p.m. *Contest* reported to Captain Wintour (D4) that he had sighted a German destroyer steering south-east; Captain (D4) does not seem to have done anything about this, but *Canada* picked this signal up and relayed it at 10.30 p.m. by flash-lamp to the Commander-in-Chief. *Garland* had also reported sighting a 'Graudenz' class cruiser.

[2] *Castor* did not give her position in this signal, but it could be deduced with tolerable accuracy.

Garland, Ambuscade and *Achates*[1] in particular—yet none of their commanding officers seemed to realise the imperative necessity of informing their Commander-in-Chief, or some senior officer, that the enemy fleet was steering eastward across the British rear.

Three-quarters of an hour later, the leading German battleships were sighted and recognised by *Nicator* and *Petard* as, following in Commander Goldsmith's wake, they cut closely across *Westfalen's* bows at 12.36 a.m. The German van was now clearly past the rear of the British battle fleet, yet neither *Petard* nor *Nicator* reported what they had seen either to their Commander-in-Chief or to their divisional leader. For want of any information to the contrary, these outbursts of gunfire on the fleet's *port* quarter remained only destroyer-actions in Admiral Jellicoe's appreciation of the situation. If it is difficult to understand why so many destroyer-captains failed to realise the importance of passing on this vital information, it should be remembered nevertheless that destroyers were small craft, that their personnel were not exceptionally numerous and that their wireless installations were neither robust nor armoured; their officers were moreover fighting their ships under conditions of great tension and at high speed, momentarily expecting to be bathed in the fierce glare of enemy searchlights and subjected to overwhelming enemy gunfire.

For the destroyers who failed there was thus some excuse; but for the other ships in the fleet who clearly saw the enemy battleships, yet failed to make any report at the time, there could be none: *battleships* certainly suffered none of the disabilities and distractions of the gallant destroyers.

After ten o'clock that night, *Marlborough* had found it increasingly difficult to maintain the 17–knot speed of the fleet and, with *Revenge, Superb* and *Agincourt* astern of her, had gradually dropped further and further astern of the division's appointed station; the three battleships of Evan-Thomas' Fifth Battle Squadron—*Barham, Valiant* and *Malaya*—keeping station on *Marlborough's* division had also dropped back until they were on her starboard quarter and some three miles to the westward of her. In consequence, the rear ship *Malaya* was barely two miles away when the first furious enemy onslaught was made on *Tipperary's* 4th flotilla between 11.20 and 11.40 p.m. and she thus had a grandstand view of what happened. *Malaya's* captain, reporting after the battle, wrote:

[1] *Achates*, it should be noted, did not hesitate in her captain's post-battle report to comment on the lack of prior information given to the destroyers, presumably by his C.-in-C. Not unnaturally he did not mention his own failure to report the presence of enemy battleships.

Three points abaft the starboard beam [we] observed what appeared to be an attack by our destroyers on some enemy big ships steering the same way as ours . . . . The leading ship of the enemy which was seen in the flash of an explosion, had two masts, two funnels and a conspicuous crane (apparently 'Westfalen'-class).

Captain The Hon. A. D. E. H. Boyle was quite right: she *was Westfalen*, and she was leading the van of the German High Seas Fleet across the British rear. At the time, *Malaya's* guns were loaded; her turrets were trained upon the leading enemy battleship; and the gunnery officer asked permission to open fire. Captain Boyle refused permission. Nor did he make any sighting report, either to his own squadron admiral in *Barham*—half a mile ahead of him—or direct to the Commander-in-Chief. He may have assumed that what he could see, *Barham* could also see; but the latter ship's report noted only 'constant attacks by enemy torpedo craft' and identified no individual ships.

The battleship *Valiant* (Captain M. Woollcombe) on the other hand, lying between *Barham* and *Malaya*, reported after the battle:

At 10.39 observed heavy firing on starboard quarter. . . . This appeared to be a night attack by one of our light cruisers and four destroyers on a column of enemy ships. . . . [At 11.35 p.m.] observed heavy night action on starboard quarter. From the evidence we surmised that there appeared to be on this occasion two German cruisers with at least two funnels and a crane amidships apparently steering to the eastward at high speed.

The only class of German warship which fitted this description was the 'Westfalen' class battleship: if the British officers concerned did not realise this after two years of war, with copies of *Jane's Fighting Ships* and other reference sources available on board, it can only be much regretted. The amount of detail in the reports by these two battleships leaves no room for doubt that the van of the German battle fleet had been seen and identified as it moved eastwards on its homeward journey; yet no immediate enemy-sighting report was made from either ship. The battleships had available every known means of communication, both wireless and visual; they were commanded by officers of seniority and, presumably, experience. The two ships were onlookers undisturbed save for the occasional 'short' splashes near *Malaya* caused by our destroyers' four-inch shells.

After the war, Admiral Jellicoe asserted that had the Admiralty given him the essential information about the requested aircraft reconnaissance over Horns Reef, he would have altered course in that direction during the night; there can be no doubt that had the officers who sighted and recognised the German battleships reported what they had seen, Jellicoe would also on their information have taken the fleet eastward in time to greet Scheer with the daylight of 1st June.

For the sake of completeness, other instances of the failure of individual captains to report or act deserve mention, if only for the somewhat grim humour of the circumstances. It has already been described how after Scheer's second 'battle-turn-away' at 7.20 p.m. the battle-cruisers of his First Scouting Group were no longer effective fighting units: they had received further punishment, moreover, in their brief twilight encounter with Sir David Beatty's force at 8.21 p.m. After turning to the westward out of this action, they were directed by Scheer to take their station at the rear of the German line for the night-march homeward: *Lützow*, heavily down by the head and no longer able to manoeuvre, was at the same time sent to make her own way home under an escort of destroyers who had already fired most of their torpedoes.

Vice-Admiral Hipper, who had been seeking a new flagship since about 7 p.m., had been about to board *Moltke* at 8.20 p.m. when Beatty's ships had suddenly opened fire and *Moltke* had been obliged to move on; the destroyer *G-39* with Hipper still aboard her had to be left astern. Owing to the subsequent westerly movement of the German squadrons and their re-grouping for the night-march, it had been 9.50 p.m. before Hipper was at last able to board *Moltke* and hoist his flag as Vice-Admiral commanding the First Scouting Group. Just prior to this, *Seydlitz* reported to Scheer that she would be unable to maintain the fleet speed of 16 knots owing to the risk to her forward bulkheads; she was given permission to proceed independently to her base via the Amrum Bank swept channel.

Hipper had been obliged to hoist his flag in a ship whose wireless was out of action—though her fighting efficiency was otherwise less impaired than that of her squadron-mates. He was thus unaware of Scheer's wirelessed orders to the battle-cruisers to take station at the rear of the battle line and, signalling his squadron to follow him, set off up the eastern flank of the German battle fleet to take up his traditional post in the van; of his three remaining battle-cruisers, *Seydlitz* alone seemed to be following *Moltke* into the gathering dusk, but she was actually carrying out Scheer's order to proceed home independently. For a while the two battle-cruisers were thus apparently in company and steering east-south-eastward, the course of the fleet.

At about 10 o'clock, and for some time afterwards, the two ships could see gun-flashes not far to the eastward of them—*Castor*'s action with the German Second Scouting Group—and this discouraged them from turning in that direction. Later, they found themselves on the disengaged side of von Reuter's Fourth Scouting Group as it stalked Goodenough's squadron in the darkness. The two battle-cruisers seem then to have decided that they would haul more to the south-eastward: this entailed passing close ahead of *Stettin* who was leading the Fourth Scouting Group, and caused some confusion; it also forced von Reuter's squadron closer to Goodenough's cruisers, who promptly closed in and engaged them fiercely. As the guns of the Second Light-Cruiser Squadron opened up, both battle-cruisers turned back to a more southerly course, and they were again beginning to edge eastwards when Boedicker's three light cruisers engaged our 4th flotilla and set *Tipperary* ablaze. As the German cruisers recoiled from the fury of the British destroyers, they forced the German van to swing back to the westward in sympathy and the two battle-cruisers found themselves alone and heading south. It was on this course later that *Birmingham* had her fleeting glimpse of them, and reported this to Jellicoe.

It seems that soon afterwards the two battle-cruisers lost touch with each other and with Scheer's van: *Moltke* went on to 18 knots and, rightly divining that Scheer intended to make for Horns Reef, decided to proceed independently and meet his Commander-in-Chief there. Turning to the south-eastward, however, he almost at once sighted on his port bow a battleship with a cruiser following astern of her; uncertain that these were not part of the German fleet, Captain von Karpf 'made' his secret red and green recognition lights for the night. He received no instant reply, and realised that he had accidentally blundered into the British battle fleet; he sheered off westward into the darkness, trusting that he had not been seen.

He had, however, most certainly been seen—first by the light cruiser *Boadicea*, which was keeping station 500 yards astern of the battleship *Thunderer*, the rear ship of Vice-Admiral Jerram's Second Battle Squadron: *Boadicea* had seen the stranger approaching abaft her starboard beam, her signal yeoman of the watch noting in the signal log 'sighted enemy cruiser showing four red and four green lights horizontal three times'. *Boadicea*'s captain reported afterwards:

> A large ship was seen approaching about two points abaft the starboard beam at high speed. She challenged . . . when under helm and turning away. Thirty seconds was the time estimated during which the ship was in sight. Directions were given for firing the starboard torpedo, but the time of the enemy being in sight did not permit of this being done.

Boadicea also reported what he had seen to *Thunderer*, close ahead of her: 'Enemy ships on starboard beam'. *Thunderer* (Captain Fergusson) had however seen the same apparition and her captain reported afterwards that 'fire was not opened as it was considered inadvisable to show up our battle fleet unless obvious attack was intended'.[1] The German battle-cruiser had indeed had a lucky escape.

As von Karpf drew clear, he cruised on southward for a few minutes, and then again turned eastward, only to find that Jerram's battle squadron was again ahead of him. Once more he turned back into the darkness. He tried yet once more to get across to the southeastward, but with the same result. On neither of these last two 'visits' was his near approach noted, although von Karpf saw the British ships clearly a mile away. Then Hipper stepped in and ordered von Karpf to steer south at his best speed: at about 12.40 a.m., when the admiral calculated he must be clear of the British van, he gradually hauled round to the south-eastward, cutting across the British line of advance five miles ahead of the flagships at about 1.30 a.m. He then steered direct for a position off the entrance to the Amrum Bank swept channel, and turned back to meet Scheer.

Moltke and her redoubtable admiral had thrice tempted Providence under the muzzles of the eighty 13.5-inch guns of the Second Battle Squadron; and three times they had escaped.

Their adventures had however been by no means as intriguing as those of *Seydlitz*: having lost touch with *Moltke* and being no longer able to steam at more than twelve or thirteen knots, she had turned south-eastwards for home on her own and passed astern of *Boadicea* and the British battle fleet unseen. About 11.25 p.m., noticing that a vigorous destroyer-action was developing on her port beam, she hauled round a little to starboard—catching a distant glimpse of Goodenough's cruisers soon afterwards, and passing astern of the Fifth Battle Squadron without seeing it or being seen. Suddenly, at about 11:50 p.m., still steering south-south-eastwards at 13 knots, *Seydlitz* noticed a line of big ships coming up fast towards her from the northward: down below, her stokers were doing their best to hold a head of steam, ready for any emergency, and in consequence masses of black smoke were pouring from her funnels. As Captain von Egidy looked at the oncoming strangers he was not sure that he could get his water-logged ship across their bows unseen. As it happened, his smoke had already been seen by the leader of the column, *Marlborough*. Von Egidy unhesitatingly turned his ship right round and called upon his engine-room for a burst of top speed; a man of

[1] *Official Despatches.*

infinite courage and resolution, he had decided to run for it down
the side of the oncoming squadron. Travelling on opposite courses
and at *Seydlitz's* best speed, von Egidy had shrewdly calculated that
he could be right down the enemy line and out of sight in two tense
minutes of 'Hail and Farewell': as his engines gave of their best,
he swung his ship on to a course parallel but opposite to that of
Marlborough's division, and started his race down the line.

The first ship—*Marlborough*—was quickly passed.

The second ship, *Revenge*, challenged him with two morsed
letters: Captain von Egidy directed his signalman to reply with the
morse letters *PL*—he could have chosen any other two letters for
that matter. They were of course the wrong letters, but again he
was past without incident. The next ship, *Hercules*, did not appear
to see him at all. The fourth and last ship—*Agincourt*—also seemed
to ignore his existence, as did the light cruiser astern of her. In two
more minutes *Seydlitz* was quite alone in the darkness again; she
turned once more to south-eastward, to make direct for Horns Reef.
Captain von Egidy's desperate chance had paid off, and the British
fleet was now comfortably behind him.

To get the full flavour of the episode it is necessary also to witness
the escape of the *Seydlitz* through British eyes: *Marlborough*, flying
Vice-Admiral Sir Cecil Burney's flag, reported afterwards:

> About midnight smoke was observed ahead of *Marlborough*, which
> crossed from starboard to port and then came down the starboard side.
> It appeared to be a large ship, and was challenged by *Revenge* who was
> answered by two letters though they were not the correct ones. She
> then disappeared.

The latter battleship's captain, Captain Kiddle, was able to corroborate this in his report:

> It was seen that the object was a large ship. She was challenged and
> made the reply *PL* and rapidly disappeared astern. She had the
> appearance of a battle-cruiser and resembled our own. . . . Nothing
> more of interest occurred during the night.

Hercules (Captain Clinton-Baker) either saw nothing or did not
think the matter worthy of comment.

The report of Captain Doughty of *Agincourt*, the last of the
squadron, is particularly illuminating:

> A ship or destroyer [sic] closed *Agincourt* at high speed during the
> night, her track very visible. I did not challenge her so as not to give
> our division's position away. She altered course and steamed away.

Finally, the light cruiser *Fearless*, in station two and a half cables astern of *Agincourt*, was the last British ship to see her that night: her commanding officer, Captain Roper, reported afterwards:

> About midnight GMT a large vessel which appeared to be a German battleship was seen to pass down the starboard side, but as ships ahead did not open fire, and it was considered that she must have been seen, it was thought advisable to take no action.

So the two German battle-cruisers had escaped. Their Captains must have wondered whether they would ever be believed when they recounted the story of it all in after-years. As for the fourteen British ships under whose guns the two ships had passed, no one will question their motives of chivalry and courtesy: there was a subtle touch of the lost age of elegance; it was certainly not war, and one is left wishing that the same delicate restraint from firing had been exercised on behalf of *Black Prince*.

Not one of the British ships which had abetted these two escapes made any report whatsoever to the Commander-in-Chief as to what had been seen: the pill is made even more bitter by our knowledge now that Captain von Egidy, apparently more conscious of his obligations to his Commander-in-Chief than some British captains were, was already reporting to Scheer the position of the four British battleships he had just seen by five minutes past midnight, when he was barely clear of the British line.[1] *Moltke*, having no wireless, was unable to report immediately, but at about 2.00 a.m., falling in with Commander Albrecht of *G-39* again, Admiral Hipper signalled through her to Scheer, reporting the position of the British van. By then, of course, Scheer was bothering no longer, for he was already past the rear of our fleet and heading for home.

The British ships' failure to report the presence of *Seydlitz* and *Moltke* was, indeed, as lamentable as their failure to 'bring to action and engage an enemy then flying', to quote the solemn charge of the historic Articles of War.

(v)

When the van of Scheer's battleships had cut through the tail of Goldsmith's attenuated line of destroyers at 12.36 a.m., it had crossed the rear of the British battle fleet and was to the eastward of its line of advance; it was to the eastward even of *Marlborough's* division, which dropping more and more astern of station had been

[1] He called them 'battle-cruisers' in his report.

barely ten miles away. The German battle fleet had also passed the last of Jellicoe's destroyer barriers, for *Champion's* abrupt turn to the eastward had de-ranged the whole eastern sector of this screen and left the gate wide open for the Germans to pass through.

Admiral Scheer was still not entirely out of danger, however, for the 12th flotilla which had been forced to the north-eastward by *Champion* consisted of some of our most modern 34-knot destroyers, armed with three four-inch guns and mounting four torpedo tubes each; it included two modern and powerful 'flotilla-leaders', *Faulknor* and *Marksman*, and the whole flotilla was commanded by a brilliant and resolute officer, Captain Stirling, as Captain (D12) in *Faulknor*. Since nightfall, Stirling had been keeping station on *Marlborough's* division, and at 11.30 p.m., he was about three and three-quarter miles astern of its rear ship; *Faulknor* was leading the flotilla with the first division of four destroyers on his starboard quarter and the second division, also of four destroyers, on his port. Astern of him, *Marksman* (Captain N. A. Sulivan) led the third division of five destroyers.

When *Champion*, disturbed by the 'overs' falling amongst her 13th flotilla during *Tipperary's* action to the westward of her, and possibly catching a glimpse of ships larger than destroyers silhouetted in the fires or searchlight beams, turned abruptly to the eastward at 11.35 p.m., she had compelled the 12th flotilla to conform; and although the greater part of *Champion's* 13th flotilla lost touch with their leader and tacked on behind Commander Goldsmith's line, *Obdurate* and *Moresby* followed their flotilla-cruiser round.

Faulknor managed to get his first and second divisions round to the eastward, but before *Marksman* with the third division could turn, two enemy light cruisers—*Frankfurt* and *Pillau*, scurrying away from the 4th flotilla's attack—blundered into the tail of his line, cutting in between *Menace* and *Nonsuch*. *Menace* had to put on full helm to turn and avert collision: she recognised the intruders and prepared to give them a torpedo apiece, but they vanished into the darkness before this could be accomplished. *Nonsuch* also had to turn away and increase to full speed to avoid being cut down; when she turned back again, she had lost her flotilla in the darkness and so turned north-eastward on the off-chance of finding them. Failing, she held on to the northward, eventually meeting up with the disabled *Acasta* and towing her home. *Menace* was luckier, and catching sight of her own division she followed *Marksman* round behind the rest of the flotilla.

Faulknor thus brought his whole flotilla round, with the exception of *Nonsuch*, and out of trouble; but *Champion* and her two destroyers were still on his starboard side, and now pressing him further north-eastward. Captain Stirling gave way and headed in that direction, but reduced speed in order to let *Champion* draw ahead. At about 12.15 a.m., he turned his division round to south, the course of the fleet.

His nocturnal adventures had forced Captain Stirling and the 12th flotilla some 25 miles north-eastward of the British battle fleet, and some 20 miles northward of their proper station. At this time also, *Champion*, with *Obdurate* and *Moresby* astern of her, had also turned southwards again, but noticing searchlights and gun-flashes some five miles on the starboard beam at 12.35 a.m.—*Turbulent* being engaged and sunk by the German van—they again turned further to the eastward. Captain Stirling also saw this brief engage-ment to starboard, but continued to steer south; determined to get back into station with as little delay as possible, he increased speed to twenty knots. He was therefore unknowingly closing Scheer's battle fleet again, on a converging course.

Just before 1.40 a.m. *Obedient*, leading the (western) first division of the 12th flotilla, sighted about three-quarters of a mile to starboard and to the south-westward of her, a long line of ships apparently steering east-south-east; not sure whether his flotilla-captain had seen this, Commander Campbell took *Obedient* close alongside *Faulknor*, and by megaphone reported what he had seen. Captain Stirling could also see the line now and ordered *Obedient* to attack with her division. *Obedient* promptly turned inwards, but it was soon apparent that our destroyers had already been seen, for the enemy had turned away together some six points, after challenging with the morsed letter *K*. One of *Obedient's* officers commented laconically: 'This was not the correct challenge for the night, so obviously the ships were German'. Before they had vanished into the mist and darkness, they were indeed clearly identified as German battleships.

Seeing that *Faulknor* was increasing speed, *Obedient* took his division back into station astern of her: *Faulknor* was quite sure that when the coast seemed clear the German ships would resume their fleet course, so he led his whole flotilla ahead at 25 knots on a course parallel to the course he thought the Germans to be steering. By 2.00 a.m. he had reached an admirable position of torpedo-advant-age, and turned sixteen points to starboard, the first division dropping into station astern of their leader as he led round to the attack course:

The enemy were now clearly visible—Dreadnought battleships leading and pre-Dreadnoughts following; a long line of them. Conditions were nearly ideal for an attack, for it was too light for searchlights to be of much use to the enemy big ships and yet with the mist as an added cloak it was sufficiently dark to make the laying of guns on fast-moving targets difficult.[1]

At 2.05 a.m., when about 2,500 yards from the fourth ship of the enemy line, *Faulknor* and *Obedient* fired two torpedoes each and *Onslaught* and *Marvel* four each. *Mindful* could not maintain the speed and found her fire masked by others. *Maenad* and the destroyers of the outer, second division turned to the attack course several minutes after *Faulknor*; *Maenad* fired one torpedo and *Narwhal* two. Just as *Faulknor* fired her torpedoes, however, the German ships opened fire with every gun that would bear, from turret-guns to saluting-guns, while at the same time turning six points to starboard away from the attack.

Captain Stirling could see that one of the torpedoes at least had found its target, for the third ship in the German line—the pre-Dreadnought battleship *Pommern*—had been hit amidships just at the waterline. There appeared

a dull red ball of fire. Quicker than one can imagine it spread fore and aft until reaching the foremast and mainmast it flared upwards in long red tongues of flame, eventually burying the mastheads in a long black cloud of smoke and sparks. Then one saw the ends of the ship come up as though her back was broken.[2]

Pommern vanished in a huge explosion, taking with her her captain, Captain Boelken, seventy other officers and 773 men.

As the German ships drew westward, several enemy light cruisers came out from their rear and also poured a heavy fire into the British destroyers who managed to withdraw with little damage, however, by dodging between the salvoes. *Onslaught* at the tail end of the line was by far the worst hit, a salvo striking her bridge, destroying charthouse and charts and killing both her captain and first-lieutenant. *Marksman*, who had been leading the third division of the flotilla on a course still further west than that of the second division, found her destroyers coming under heavy gun-fire even before they reached the turning point. Instead of turning after the others, therefore, she held on to the south-eastward; and a quarter of an hour later she joined up with *Champion*. *Maenad's* offensive spirit seems to have been unappeased by the one torpedo she had fired, for she

[1] *Fighting at Jutland.* [2] Ibid.

then turned sharply to starboard, out of line, and held on through south and south-west until she again sighted the enemy battleships. At 2.28 p.m. she gave them another two torpedoes for good measure, and then turned away to the south-eastward, where a few minutes later she met up with *Champion*.

Altogether, it had been an outstanding attack, admirably executed, which had shown that the British flotillas not only could deliver a full-scale attack but knew that it was their duty to do so when any opportunity offered. The 12th flotilla's attack was also outstanding by reason of Captain Stirling's swift realisation that the presence of enemy battleships must be reported to the Commander-in-Chief at once: at 1.52 a.m. he had twice signalled on 'power' wireless: 'Urgent. Priority. Enemy battleships in sight. My position 10 miles astern of First Battle Squadron.' It was a model enemy-sighting report, for it defined the 'target', and gave the reporting ship's position in relative, not geographical terms. Sixteen minutes later, Captain Stirling had again signalled Jellicoe by wireless: 'Urgent. Am attacking'. Finally, when he had seen the enemy battleships turn away from his attack, Captain Stirling had signalled at 12.12 a.m., 'Urgent. Course of enemy is ssw'.

It is particularly unfortunate that these determined efforts by Stirling to apprise Jellicoe of the presence of German battleships should have been in vain: the first signal was incompletely logged in *Faulknor*; although made twice on power it was unanswered and not taken in by any ship in the fleet, as a subsequent close examination of ships' logs was able to reveal. The second signal, at 2.08 a.m., was received by no ship at all; the third signal, also made twice on power, was picked up and logged only by *Marksman* a couple of miles away. No other ship received the signal. At the time, the ether was full of general radio traffic, but this alone is insufficient explanation; heavy jamming by the German ships seems a more likely reason, although jamming was not specially reported at the time. A possible reason may have been that *Faulknor's* wireless was out of adjustment. Whatever the cause, the fact remained that the only reports of enemy battleships that were actually transmitted to Jellicoe that night had failed to reach him. Had Captain Stirling's 1.52 a.m. signal reached him, and had he turned at once and steered to the eastward at twenty knots, he might have caught Scheer at about 3.30 a.m. at a range of some ten thousand yards. (Beatty's force could not have advanced in time to scout for the British battle fleet, however, and such a turn would probably have been an unprofitable undertaking.) As it was, Admiral Jellicoe had lost his last chance of striking at the fleeing Admiral Scheer before he vanished down his swept channels towards Germany.

(vi)

Mention has already been made of *Marksman* and *Maenad* joining up with *Champion* just to the south-east of the scene of the 12th flotilla's magnificent effort. When she had swung eastward so abruptly she had lost touch with her 13th flotilla with the exception of the destroyers *Obdurate* and *Moresby*; as *Achates* began her attack on the German van, *Champion* and these two destroyers steered north-eastward for almost a quarter of an hour before turning back at 12.05 a.m. to the south course of the fleet. By two o'clock *Champion* was 28 miles from *Iron Duke* and 18 miles from *Marlborough*: to all intents and purposes she was 'off the board'.

Just before 2.10 a.m., however, she noticed flashes five miles away on the starboard beam and in the growing early light turned westward five minutes later towards the gunfire.

The German battleships were just swinging back into line ahead and their course and that of *Champion* were converging. As the latter in turn altered course to the southward, *Marksman*, in the growing morning light, could dimly see a long line of ships three or four miles away to the south-westward. Not wishing to make a mistake about them, Captain Sulivan signalled *Champion* asking what they were: he received the answer: 'Germans, I think'. Beyond expressing this thought, Captain Farie of *Champion* seems to have done nothing more about the strange ships; at 2.34 a.m. he turned to the eastward, putting the alleged enemy more or less astern of him.

As the light cruiser turned east, however, *Moresby*—halfway down the line—got a clear glimpse through the mists of four pre-Dread-nought battleships, about four thousands yards to the westward and steering to the south-east at speed. Her captain, Lieutenant-Commander Alison, 'considered action imperative' and hoisted 'Compass Pendant: West' to draw attention to that direction; he then hauled sharply out of line to port and, turning in a wide circle, closed the enemy battleships to 2,500 yards. At 2:37 a.m. he fired a torpedo before withdrawing eastward to rejoin the others. His torpedo scored a hit on the German destroyer *V-4*; his approach through the mist must have passed unnoticed by the Germans, for they believed that *V-4* had struck a mine.

Champion turned northwards and steered to rejoin the British battle fleet; she had missed one last golden chance of delivering a powerful torpedo attack on the unsuspecting enemy. On this unfortunate episode Vice-Admiral Beatty commented in his Despatch:

> Strange vessels were sighted by *Champion* and *Obdurate* . . . and it is much to be regretted that *Champion* did not take steps to identify them. If, as is probable, they were the enemy, an excellent opportunity was missed for an attack in the early morning light. More important still, a portion of the enemy might have been definitely located.[1]

Since well before midnight, an almost impenetrable veil of 'unawareness' had thus enveloped the British fleet: its warp was the abysmal failure of the Admiralty to pass on to the Commander-in-Chief *all* the material information in its possession; its wooft, the absence of reports from the commanding officers of those British ships which had seen and identified enemy units.

Admiral Scheer had been more fortunate: throughout the night and early morning, he had been kept continuously supplied with enemy-reports from his destroyers and cruisers alike. Even the anxiety-stricken *Seydlitz* and *Moltke* had contributed to this jigsaw picture of the situation. His Admiralty had co-operated by furnishing him with every scrap of information that had come its way. Despite the failure of Scheer's request for aerial reconnaissance to reach its destination, Captain Strasser of the shore staff had anticipated the admiral's wishes and six Zeppelins had taken off between 8.45 p.m. and 1.00 a.m.; these thoroughly reconnoitred the area to the westward, and also the area between the coast and Scheer's line of advance, and they had already been able to warn Scheer of a possible screen of hostile submarines to the west of the Vyl and Horns Reef lightships.

Nor had Scheer been bothered by inhibitions as to whether ships sighted would be friend or foe; *all* were 'foes', and to that extent his Third Battle Squadron had at one time fired a few rounds into an unidentified German destroyer-flotilla. Such ships as had been disabled and were a liability to the plan of withdrawal had been left to fend for themselves: *Lützow*, *Elbing*, *Seydlitz* and *Rostock*, for example. Throughout the 'night-march' he had accepted the destroyer-attacks as they came: whenever his van had faltered or appeared to recoil from the fury of a British attack, there had been his harsh unswerving purpose, expressed in his order: '*Durchhalten!*'— 'Maintain your course for the night, regardless of consequences.'

At 3.09 a.m. it would be sunrise. This implied that it would be almost full daylight by 2.30 a.m., and that from two o'clock onwards

[1] Vice-Admiral Beatty's Despatch, in *Official Despatches*.

the light would be improving steadily: but even with full daylight it was obvious that the morning's visibility might be marred by mist. Jellicoe's original intention had been to turn eastward with his fleet at daylight and to make towards Horns Reef, but it seems that at about 1.45 a.m. he now realised that he might not be able to do this. With the exception of the Fourth Light-Cruiser Squadron, just off the bows of *King George V*, he had no other cruisers in company as far as he could ascertain. His destroyers would moreover be well scattered after their night-engagements, and none knew better than he the risk of advancing without destroyer protection into hostile waters that were likely to be patrolled by enemy submarines.[1]

As the light now improved, there were no destroyers in sight; and to cloud the situation still further, Jellicoe learned now for the first time that *Marlborough* had been obliged to drop astern during the night—how far he did not yet know. Looking astern in the improving light, *Colossus* could see no sign of *Marlborough's* division and reported to the Commander-in-Chief that the four battleships of this division were no longer in visual touch.

As the moment of decision drew near, therefore, Admiral Jellicoe was almost without scouting cruisers or destroyers, and now it appeared he might be without four battleships, should he suddenly encounter Scheer. In the circumstances, Jellicoe considered that his best move now would be to turn north to meet them, since he still believed the enemy to be to the *northward*; he would collect his scattered destroyers and cruisers on the way.

At 2.15 a.m. *Iron Duke* therefore signalled by lamp to all the fleet's units:

> At 2.30 a.m. Second Battle Squadron alter course to starboard [i.e. westabout] to North. Fourth Battle Squadron will follow round. Battle fleet will form single line ahead in 5th organisation. (0200).

Seven minutes later he signalled by wireless to the Senior Officers of all cruiser and battle-cruiser squadrons and to the captains of all destroyer-flotillas, giving his reference position at 2.30 a.m.: 'Priority. Altering course to north. Conform and close. (0212).'

Twelve miles to the westward of *Iron Duke*, Vice-Admiral Beatty received the order to turn northwards and close his Commander-in-Chief. He still firmly believed the enemy to be to the *westward*—a belief that had been strengthened by the mutilated signal at 11.30 p.m. from *Birmingham*. Beatty had intended asking Jellicoe's permis-

[1] 'There are great difficulties in concentrating detached flotillas . . . prior to battle.'— *Grand Fleet.*

sion to sweep to the south-westward for the enemy at daylight, but
on receipt of the orders to 'conform and close' he 'proceeded accordingly'.[1] Just after 2.30 a.m., the battle-cruisers, armoured cruisers
and light cruiser squadrons under Beatty's orders also turned
northward, later altering eastward to close the battle fleet. By 2.54
a.m. the British fleet was once more in line of battle—steering
north at 17 knots—with the three 'Queen Elizabeths' of the Fifth
Battle Squadron two miles ahead. As Jellicoe wrote in his despatch:

> I deemed it advisable to disregard the danger from submarines due to
> a long line of ships and to form line of battle at once in case of meeting
> the enemy before I had been able to get in touch with my cruisers and
> destroyers.

In the battle fleet, officers and men welcomed the change of course
and the improving light, and as full readiness for action was resumed
there was everywhere the conviction that the enemy would soon be
sighted and battle re-joined. In the cruisers and battle-cruisers there
were the same buoyant hopes that a finite decision was now within
reach. But at that moment Scheer's van was some thirty-three miles
to the eastward of *Iron Duke* and only just over twelve miles from the
Horns Reef lightship. The two fleets were drawing further apart
with every minute that passed. Another hour and a half's steaming
would take the German battle fleet to the entrance to the Amrum
Bank swept channel.

[1] *Official Despatches.*

10

The Glorious First of June

WITH the British battle fleet steering north and in single line of battle once more, the belief hardened that the enemy would be quickly found and brought to action: one of *Neptune's* officers, stationed aloft, commented 'the visibility was quite good and gave promise of a better day; we had plenty of ammunition and felt that, given the chance, we could make short work of what remained of the enemy. . . . The guns had been left loaded all night and were as ready as we were to start again.' There were, however, still no destroyers in sight.

Within a very few minutes, Jellicoe's wisdom in not turning immediately towards Horns Reef and the Bight until he had at least some destroyers to form an anti-submarine screen was confirmed: at about three o'clock on 1st June, a message reached him from the Admiralty, belatedly warning him that 'enemy submarines' were putting to sea from German ports. It also informed him that 'a damaged enemy ship, probably *Lützow*, was in Latitude 56°26' North, Longitude 5°41' East at midnight'.[1] Jellicoe at once signalled to Vice-Admiral Jerram leading the line in *King George V* to keep a lookout for a damaged battle-cruiser believed to be ahead, and he also repeated the signal to Beatty.

At about 3.20 a.m. the unmistakeable sounds of gunfire were heard to the west-south-westward; some minutes later there was the added thunder of heavy guns. But their target was not the German fleet: it was a solitary Zeppelin, *L-11*, which had been briefly shadowing Beatty's force until it had come within range of the guns of Napier's Third Light-Cruiser Squadron and then of the battle-cruisers themselves. *Indomitable* and *Tiger*, putting extreme elevation on their turret guns, 'unloaded them at her'. Rear-Admiral Napier

---

[1] The time of origin of this message was 1.48 a.m., by which time *Lützow* had been sunk; Beatty also received this signal, via *New Zealand*, at 4.10 a.m. The latter vessel was keeping wireless watch on that wavelength, and repeated Admiralty messages to *Lion*.

reported this to Jellicoe, and on the principle that the Zeppelin might be scouting for a German fleet nearby, he turned his battle fleet at 3.42 a.m. towards the sound of guns in the west. Ten minutes later the same Zeppelin appeared off his port beam, now quite obviously watching the battle fleet's movements. The battleships at once opened fire with their turret guns and such anti-aircraft guns as would bear. A midshipman in the control top of *Neptune* described how 'the airship lifted its nose disdainfully to the morning breeze and disappeared to the south-westward, and a signal was received ordering us not to waste ammunition. Not until the Zeppelin was out of sight did I realise the full significance of this early morning visit. It meant that the Germans now knew exactly where we were. . . .'

The same thought was also passing through other minds, including that of the Commander-in-Chief; though not all might have been yet prepared to agree with the prediction with which the midshipman concluded his observation, that '. . . we should not see the High Seas Fleet *that* day'.

Admiral Beatty, still inclining north-north-eastwards to rejoin the flag, remained convinced that the enemy fleet was still somewhere to the westward, and possibly making for home via the Ems or Heligoland-West swept channels; at 3.50 a.m. he signalled Jellicoe begging him to allow his force to sweep south-westward to locate the enemy. The latter was certain that the enemy could not be to the south-westward and he refused his colleague's request. Beatty therefore continued to close the flag as directed, but he spread his light cruisers out in a wide arc of search to westward, while still instructing them to maintain visual touch with each other. He also signalled his force: 'We hope today to cut off and annihilate the whole German fleet. Every man must do his utmost'—a somewhat ambitious exhortation.

At about 4.15 a.m., however, Admiral Jellicoe was reading the Admiralty signal which was finally to destroy all hope of such good fortune: at 2.30 a.m., the main German fleet had been located only just over fifteen miles from the Horns Reef light vessel, and only 24 miles from the entrance to the Amrum Bank swept channel, or about one-and-a-half-hour's steaming at its reported speed of sixteen knots. So by 4.15 the enemy was most probably already within the fringe of protecting minefields.

For the British Commander-in-Chief, this was the bitter moment of truth.

As Admiral Jellicoe turned away from the chart table, outwardly as impassive as at any time during the testing day and night, there were lines of weariness and disappointment on the weatherworn face. He made no comment, but he signalled to Beatty: 'Enemy fleet has returned to harbour. Try to locate *Lützow*.'

The grim tidings ran through the fleet like wildfire. That the Grand Fleet had been left commanding the seas as completely as before, that British, Allied and Empire sea-communications were as secure as ever, that the Allied 'blockade' would continue to strangle the economic life of the enemy Powers—all these considerations paled before the personal sense of disappointment now felt keenly by every officer and man in the Grand Fleet.

(ii)

There was still much to be done: the seas through which the fleets had fought must be searched for survivors; there were damaged enemy ships to be located; there were our own disabled ships to be shepherded safely back to British ports.

Soon after *Moresby's* gallant solitary attack upon the German van, Admiral Scheer had reached a point some ten miles westward of Horns Reef lightship. The German admiral now felt that he could ease his fleet speed considerably, to allow his stragglers to catch up with him. By 3.30 a.m. he knew that *Lützow* had been abandoned and sunk; by that time too *Seydlitz* had been located, ten miles away to the north-eastward, and moving slowly southward. *Moltke*, with Hipper aboard, was closing the main German fleet from the southward, ready to take Hipper's traditional stand at the head of the line.

At 3.38 a.m. Scheer signalled his fleet to reform for the last stage of their journey home. The remains of the First Scouting Group were stationed ahead; then the First Battle Squadron; then the pre-Dreadnoughts and the Third Battle Squadron with the battle-cruisers *Derfflinger* and *Von der Tann*, and what remained of Boedicker's light cruisers bringing up the rear. *Moltke* would lead the way in, and in view of a Zeppelin report at about midnight referring to the presence of hostile submarines west of the Vyl lightship, destroyers were spread ahead and on the bows as an anti-submarine screen. He set course direct for the Amrum Bank swept channel and reached the entrance to it soon after four o'clock.

Between 3.30 a.m. and 4.30 a.m. his fleet passed over the three British submarines which the Admiralty had detached to the area west of the Vyl light-vessel; but the submarines were sitting on the bottom, unaware of the Germans' passage overhead, in obedience to their orders to remain on the bottom until the morning of 2nd June.

Even then there was another hurdle to be surmounted, of which Scheer was in ignorance: the new minefield laid by *Abdiel* that morning.[1] As it happened, Scheer's fleet was advancing on a course which passed eastward and clear of this field; but in doing so it only led towards a similar line of mines which *Abdiel* had laid on the night of 4th May. At 3.20 a.m. there was a loud explosion, and *Ostfriesland* (Rear-Admiral Schmidt's flagship) hauled out of line, damaged below water. At first this was assumed to be the work of British submarines, and for the last time Scheer's harsh signal: '*Durchhalten!*' flickered down the line; the line steadied, *Ostfriesland* still able to steam obeyed the order and took her place once more at the head of her squadron. The homeward journey continued. What confidence there had been was now badly shattered, however, and something near panic set in: ships fired in all directions at fancied submarine-periscopes and *Stettin* complained from her position in the van that her own battleships were firing upon her.

By 6.30 a.m. the whole German fleet was beyond British reach—except perhaps *König*, which, drawing nearly 35 feet of water, grounded on the Amrum Bank shoal itself, and had to wait there until high water at nine o'clock enabled her to float off and continue her journey.

Towards high noon of 1st June, watchers off Wilhelmshaven and the crews lining the decks of the Jade River patrol vessels saw their fleet return: it had paused briefly during the final stage of its journey for each ship to transfer its dead and wounded to a hospital ship which then went discreetly ahead and berthed separately. First into the Schillig Roads came the destroyers. Next came *Moltke*, with Hipper's flag aloft: still a proud ship and outwardly little damaged, but low down in the water, with a thousand tons of salt sea below decks. Then followed the line of battleships, with more than one ploughing deeply in the water and many showing ugly battle-scars; behind them followed the light cruisers, very scarred indeed. There was a gap in the line, and then *Derfflinger* came in—her rear turrets spreadeagled, her guns pointing skyward—battered and almost unrecognisable, awash forward and with 3,500 tons of water in her; *Von der Tann* followed astern; *Seydlitz* was yet to come in.

Captain von Egidy and the crew of *Seydlitz* had had to fight the sea with the same high seamanship and courage with which they had fought their guns. *Seydlitz* soon grounded on Horns Reef, having 5,000 tons of water in her forward compartments and her decks already awash. She floated clear again at high water, to ground

---

[1] She had reported to Jellicoe that the minefield had been laid as ordered at 2.17 a.m.

once more; then, despite the desperate efforts of her crew and of the tugs sent out to her, she was towed slowly into the swept channel only to ground again. Once more they had to wait for high water before she could float off, and begin a slow journey, stern-first, into the entrance to the Jade River. There, drawing 42 feet of water and with the sea lapping the fish painted on her bow *above* the hawsepipes, she grounded once more on the afternoon of 2nd June, before being dry-docked at Wilhelmshaven. A seemingly unsinkable ship had come back, with an indomitable captain and crew.

There were other German ships, also damaged, that were still afloat during Scheer's night-march, and these would never return to the Jade: *Lützow* had done her best, heading wearily southwards; at midnight she was listing heavily, the water was gaining, and her speed had fallen to three or four knots. Soon after 1.40 a.m., her flooded bows had begun to sink steadily deeper in the water as the bulkheads gave way: first the sea had reached her jackstaff; then it had lapped along the foc'sle deck, past her capstans to the foot of the barbette; her captain and commander got the remainder of her crew and all the wounded on the aft deck and called alongside the four destroyers —*G-40*, *G-37*, *G-38* and *G-45*—detached by Scheer as escorts. The wounded were carefully transferred to them, as the battle-cruiser's bows dipped more and more. Presently the lights went out, and with the sea reaching almost to the guns of the foremost turret, her propellers lifted out of the water and the ship came to a stop. It was time to go: nothing further could be done and her crew abandoned her, climbing down into the four destroyers alongside; her commander and then Captain Harder were the last to leave.

Lützow still seemed reluctant to go, so a destroyer despatched her at about 1.45 a.m. with a torpedo as the men crowding the decks of the destroyers cheered. The four destroyers slipped off into the dark with the 1,210 survivors packing their decks; a report was sent on to Scheer that they were on their way.

After a brief skirmish with the cruiser *Champion* in which *G-40* was disabled and had to be taken in tow, all the survivors, protected now by the cruiser *Regensburg* sent out by Scheer on hearing of the interference from *Champion*, reached Wilhelmshaven.

Another victim of the night had been the light cruiser *Elbing*: after the collision with the battleship *Posen* it had been decided to abandon her. Her crew of 477 were put on board a destroyer, which moved off for Wilhelmshaven; but her commanding officer, Captain Madlung, elected to stay on board together with a small scuttling party and a cutter's crew. Captain Madlung felt that there might still be a possibility of saving his ship, and he broke out an emergency-sail and drifted slowly eastwards on the south-west wind.

Soon after one o'clock, however, destroyers were sighted; to prevent *Elbing's* falling into enemy hands, the cutter was brought alongside and the scuttling-party got ready to perform the last office. The charges were set and the officers and scuttling party climbed down into the cutter, which was rowed clear.

They could see an injured British destroyer which seemed to turn in circles, a destroyer without bow or stern—*Sparrowhawk*. Someone was seen swimming in the water and was hauled aboard: he was the doctor from the sunken *Tipperary*. A little later the cutter sighted a raft with men singing: these were from the crew of the *Tipperary*. A flare was burnt to attract attention and the cutter was later picked up by a Dutch trawler. Its crew were landed safely in Holland next day.

Rostock (Captain Feldmann) was the last of the disabled German vessels afloat: hit in her engine room and with two compartments rapidly filling with water, she had hauled out of line; her engines had come to a stop and the lights went out. She called a destroyer of the 3rd flotilla alongside and *Rostock's* crew abandoned her, taking their wounded with them, leaving only the captain and a scuttling party on board. Other destroyers took the injured cruiser in tow with some difficulty and the slow homeward journey began. By 3.10 a.m. she had only made twenty miles of southing when her escorts intercepted a wireless report from Zeppelin *L-11* claiming to have sighted 'twelve English battleships and many light forces' steering north-north-east at high speed—almost directly towards them. To Captain Feldmann it seemed the time had come for *Rostock* to go, before she fell into enemy hands. The charges were set and Feldmann and his party boarded the rescue destroyers. *Rostock* went down at 3.45 a.m., the last to go.

(iii)

Convinced, as he had told Beatty by signal, that the enemy had returned to harbour and was by now well beyond reach, Jellicoe's primary concern was with finding and dealing with any damaged ships they might have left behind; he could not of course know that the last of these—*Rostock*—had already gone to the bottom. According to the Admiralty's message *Lützow* might still be somewhere ahead: he held on to the northward, with his fleet in cruising formation, both to search for this and other enemy ships and to recover his own flotillas.

Soon after five o'clock, the Battle-Cruiser Force was in visual communication, still well to the westward, with *Iron Duke*. It was now that Jellicoe learned for the first time of the loss of *Queen Mary* and *Indefatigable* during the previous afternoon's battle-cruiser engagement. Beatty now swept to the southward, and Jellicoe swept south-eastward; but neither saw anything. Jellicoe turned northward, Beatty north-eastward; but again to no avail. Had they cast their net still further eastward towards Horns Reef, they might then have encountered *Seydlitz*, and despatched her. When the fleet learned later of the struggle that *Seydlitz* had put up against the sea, most officers and men were glad that she had not been hunted down: the general opinion was that she deserved to get home.

Throughout the forenoon, battleships and battle-cruisers quartered those waters over which the fleets had battled; but they found no ships. The seas bore plentiful sign of the bitter fighting of the night. There were lifebelts, patches of oil, drifting spars, doors, lockers, and stray pieces of timber—and there were bodies. These between them told their own tale. At 10.44 a.m. Jellicoe advised the Admiralty, 'Am ascertaining that no disabled ships are left, and am then returning to base.'

By noon, the fleet's course was set for Scapa, and the return journey began. It passed without incident, and the fleet was back in Scapa in the forenoon of 2nd June where it at once commenced refuelling and re-ammunitioning. At 9.45 p.m. that night, Admiral Jellicoe reported to the Admiralty that the British battle fleet was again ready for sea at the customary four hours' notice: the Trident of sea command was still where it had been four days before.

This was perhaps the acid test.

With the Grand Fleet fuelling and making ready again for sea, those warships which had been disabled were still steadily ploughing homeward across the North Sea. *Marlborough* had set off for Rosyth or the Tyne at three o'clock on 1st June, escorted by the light cruiser *Fearless*. At about ten o'clock she sighted two submarines, which promptly dived as she turned away from them; three-quarters of an hour later she was attacked by *U-46*, but the torpedo missed and the battleship carried on her way, to arrive at the Tyne late on 2nd June.

Warspite, detached late on 31st May, had spent the rest of the evening dousing her fires and patching up damage wherever possible. Towards nine o'clock she sighted two destroyers in the half light and signalled to them: 'Take station astern: speed 16 knots'. Unfortunately, these two destroyers were O*nslow* in tow of *Defender*—the 'Cripple and the Paralytic'. As their speed was barely six knots, *Warspite* rapidly disappeared over their port bow. 'We were not 16-knotters', as one of *Onslow's* officers explained afterwards. *Warspite* was heading for the remains of Scheer's U-boat trap off the Firth of Forth and was expecting to be attacked by submarines; it was just as well that she was prepared, for at 9.35 a.m. she was seen by *U-51*, which fired two torpedoes, both of which passed very close to her. *Warspite's* captain increased speed still more; he reported his position and destroyers were sent out to meet him. Just as they appeared, another submarine, *U-63*, was sighted very close to the bow; *Warspite*, under full helm, forced her down so that she could not attack. By 3 p.m. on 1st June *Warspite* was safely above the Forth bridge, at the end of her anxieties.

Warrior (Captain Molteno) was the only other sizeable ship trying to make her way home. Her crew had managed to put out the fires and to plug some of the holes in her hull, but both engine-rooms were partially flooded and in the end, despite the efforts of her engine-room staff, she came to a stop. Captain Molteno requested *Engadine* to take *Warrior* in tow. At slow speed, they struggled on for over one hundred miles across the North Sea, with a falling barometer and rising wind and sea. Finally, *Warrior's* bulkheads began to give way and she settled more deeply in the water. Her captain realised that she could not remain afloat very much longer, and ordered all hands to fall in to abandon ship. The ship's company fell in by divisions, as if it were a normal Sunday morning affair in Spithead; they dressed back against the funnel-casing, for the short seas were now breaking over *Warrior's* bows and weather side. All secret books and confidential papers were destroyed. When *Engadine* came alongside, *Warrior's* wounded were tenderly passed across. One man staggered, slipped and fell between the two ships: Lieutenant Rutland, the same pilot who had gone up to observe the enemy in the afternoon's battle, instantly dived in, but failed to bring the man back alive.[1]

The upper deck was now nearly awash. A hurried rush to the side might have ruined everyone's chance: on the captain's order, the bugler sounded the 'Still'. One of *Engadine's* officers who witnessed the scene has said:

The result was wonderful. Not a single man passed from *Warrior* to *Engadine* after the bugle sounded but every man fell back against the

[1] For this act of gallantry, Rutland received the Albert Medal.

funnel-casing . . . It was a wonderful sight, an inspiring sight, a triumph of organisation, discipline and courage combined. I am not ashamed to say it brought tears to my eyes. Every man in the *Warrior* must feel proud of being one of such a ship's company. When the 'Carry On' was sounded, all then left in *Warrior* hastened to abandon ship . . . finally the officers, and lastly the captain. Three cheers were given for their old ship, as we parted.

Warrior went down some time during that stormy night. *Engadine* arrived off Rosyth at 1.35 a.m. on 2nd June.

With the homing destroyers it is not easy to know where to begin. *Defender*, towing *Onslow*, had continued to steer towards 'somewhere in Scotland' at six knots after *Warspite* left them, in a rising wind and sea. Three times the tow rope parted, and each time *Defender* picked up *Onslow* and continued the westward journey. They intercepted a signal that an enemy flotilla was searching for them. The guns were made ready and ammunition brought up from below; but nothing came of it. Early on Friday morning, 2nd June, tugs came out and towed 'the cripple and the paralytic' safely into Aberdeen.

Acasta had had a grandstand view of the battle fleet during deployment as she lay stopped and disabled between the fleets. She was lucky: at 8.00 a.m. that morning *Nonsuch* came across her and took her in tow, joined later by *Unity* from the 4th flotilla; the three set off in rising weather and also arrived at Aberdeen on 2nd June.

The destroyer *Spitfire* had rammed the German battleship *Nassau*, and now had twenty feet of the battle-ship's forecastle plating embedded as a memento in her mess-decks. The crew had brought the fires under control; the remains of a chart were found and stuck together, and the captain decided to steer westward. On the way, *Spitfire* met a Norwegian ship, which offered to take off the crew; but the captain declined. With a torn chart and a batten from a bookcase as a ruler, the ship was navigated to the Tyne, where she arrived on 2nd June, to be joined by *Garland*, *Porpoise* and a damaged *Contest*. The memento-piece of *Nassau's* forecastle had—not surprisingly—shrunk, for charity begins at home: it shrank still more when friends and others came aboard with hammers, eager for mementoes of the battle.

During the 2.00 a.m. attack on the German line *Onslaught* had been heavily hit almost as soon as the German battleships opened fire. One salvo had destroyed her bridge and killed captain and first lieutenant. Sub-Lieutenant H. W. Kemmis took command and safely navigated her back to Rosyth. The destroyer *Broke* had rammed *Sparrowhawk* amidships during the 4th flotilla's night engagement. Both captains made arrangements to transfer their crews to the safety of the other vessel, but no bulkheads gave way, and *Broke* was able to pull out of *Sparrowhawk*. As she drew away *Contest* came out of the darkness and cut into *Sparrowhawk*'s stern; *Sparrowhawk* was left with neither bow nor stern. The badly damaged *Broke* moved off into the night. The engineer-officer believed he could keep steam for ten knots speed, and course was shaped north-ward. The surgeon had been killed, so the captain tended the 34 wounded as best he could; the forty-two dead were buried with full honours. With the first streak of dawn two German destroyers closed in on them at high speed. *Broke's* only serviceable guns were now aft, so she turned and awaited attack. The enemy closed to 500 yards and opened fire, scoring two hits: *Broke* at once replied, and to their delight the two Germans then made off as fast as they could. During the night the wind increased and the sea rose, and at midnight the foremast rolled over the side. Towards sun-down, however, on 2nd June, the weather eased. But it was not until 5.00 p.m. the next afternoon, 3rd June, that she sighted land. *Broke* was met by destroyers sent out to look for her, and escorted into the Tyne, after a return journey of sixty-five hours all told.

Sparrowhawk's captain, Lieutenant-Commander Hopkins, still had some hope of saving his bow-less and sternless ship, but early that morning, a single German destroyer closed within a hundred yards and then stopped engines. *Sparrowhawk's* crew prepared to sell their wreck dearly: only one gun and one torpedo-tube were work-able, but both were manned and loaded. The German moved off and disappeared into the darkness. At about 3.30 a.m., a German cruiser suddenly loomed up out of the early mist and swirled past them; once more they prepared to reply to any attack. No attack came, and the strange ship was already almost a mile and a half away. She appeared to list sharply to port, and 'settled down forward very slowly, and then gently stood on her head and—sank . . . You can imagine what we felt like.'[1] They had seen the scuttled *Elbing*.

Things were quieter after that, though the men still talked in whispers. Then an officer with binoculars saw a Carley raft full of men paddling erratically towards them; they faintly heard the song, '*It's a long, long way to Tipperary*'. It was sung hoarsely, with cracked lips and almost on one note: but unmistakable nevertheless. It took an hour and a half to get the raft alongside; then they hauled its occupants, survivors of the destroyer *Tipperary*, on board. Three were dead. Out of those who came aboard, seven more soon died. The rest

[1] *The Fighting at Jutland*

seemed 'tremendously pleased to have reached something more substantial than their Carley raft at last'. Soon after 7.00 a.m., the destroyer *Marksman* was sighted coming up fast from the southward. She took everyone possible on board and tried to tow *Sparrowhawk* home, but the towing hawser soon parted and, on orders from Admiral Jellicoe, *Sparrowhawk* was sunk by eighteen rounds of lyddite from *Marksman's* guns.

The firing of these rounds startled another survivor below decks in *Marksman*: this was Lieutenant-Commander Marsden, captain of *Ardent* which had been swiftly sunk soon after midnight; there were only two survivors. The lone destroyer had come under the concentrated fire of four or more German battleships; realising that the ship could not long remain afloat Marsden had done his utmost to get his men clear of the ship, but most of the guns' crews lay dead or dying, and most of the men below had been killed outright. The ship had given a lurch, hurling the captain into the sea. With her tattered ensign still flying the waters had closed over *Ardent*.

Looking around him, the captain could see forty or fifty heads bobbing in the water; there was not much to support anyone, and the ships and fleets had moved on. Commander Marsden said:

> I spoke to many of my men, and saw most of them die one by one. Not a man of them showed any fear of death, and there was not a murmur or complaint or cry for help from a single soul. Their joy was, and they talked about it to the end, that they and the *Ardent* had 'done their bit' as they put it. . . . None of the men appeared to suffer at all: they just seemed to lie back and go to sleep. . . . I woke to find the flotilla-leader *Marksman* close alongside me. I sang out for help and in reply got a welcome reassuring shout: 'You're all right, sir; we are coming!'

Marsden had no recollection of being picked up at all; he had been almost six hours in the cold North Sea, and survived.

What Captain Marsden had to say of *Ardent's* crew might be said of all, on both sides, who did not return after this battle, but took their 'long last trick' down on the Jutland Banks alongside the wreckage of the ships they had manned and fought:

> All hands fought the ship with the utmost gallantry and in a most tenacious and determined manner until she sank beneath them, and then met their death in that composed and happy spirit that I am convinced comes to all those who do their duty to the end. May they rest in peace.[1]

[1] *Fighting at Jutland*. At the time of writing (1966) Captain Marsden is the Chairman of the Shipwrecked Mariners' Society.

Index

253

Index